I N S I D E R ' S
BALI
G U I D E

by Bradley Winterton

Photographed by Nik Wheeler

Contents

MAPS

Bali	8–9
North Bali	150–151
Sanur	157
Denpasar	159
South Bali and Bukit	163
Kuta	169
Central Bali and the Heights	188–189
East Bali	209
Nusa Penida	221

TOP SPOTS ... 11

See Ulu Watu	11
Brave a Bungee	13
Visit a Temple Festival	15
Ride a Camel	16
Watch Dolphins at Play	18
Raft the White Water	20
Climb a Volcano	21
Dare a Dragon	24
Watch Woodcarvers	24
Buy a Painting from a Woman Artist	26

YOUR CHOICE ... 29

The Great Outdoors	29
Sporting Spree	32
The Open Road	38

Backpacking	40
Living It Up	43
Family Fun	46
Cultural Kicks	50
Shop till You Drop	52
Short Breaks	55
Festive Flings	57
Galloping Gourmets	60
Special Interests	62
Taking a Tour	66

VOLCANOES IN THE SEA 69
An Equable Climate 72
A Tropical Landscape 72
From Java Man to Golkar 76
Language 83

BALINESE CULTURE 85
A Village Upbringing 87
Banjar and Subak • The Cult of
Rice • Where Do You Sit? • Naming of
Names • Sex Roles • Birth, Childhood,
Love and Marriage • Tooth Filing
Men and Gods 96
Balinese Hinduism • Hotels for the
Gods • Time Passes • Three Festivals •
A Village Cremation • Magic and
Witchcraft • Heroes and Villains

The Balinese at Play 115
Silver Rain • Dance and Drama •
Shadows in the Dark • The Affrighted
Sun • Cricket Fighting • Bird Orchestras
Art and Crafts 133
Painting • Woodcarving • Masks: The
Other Face • Stonecarving: Portable
Shrines • Weaving: *Endek, Ikat* and *Batik* •
Gold and Silver
Food and Drink: From *Rijsttafel* to *Kretek* 139
Festival Fare • Drinks • Tropical Fruits •
Coconut Palms • Salt in the Wounds •
Betel • *Jamu* • *Kretek*

THE BROAD HIGHWAY 147
North Bali 149
Getting There • Bali's Old Capital:
Singaraja • Lovina's Black Sand
Beaches • Springs and Temples • Pura
Beji's Unheard Melodies •
Sawan's Gongs • Yeh Sanih •
Sembiran: Village with a View
Sanur 155
What to See and Do • Where to Stay •
Where to Eat • Nightlife • Shopping

Bali's Capital: Denpasar   158
    General Information • What to See and
    Do • Where to Stay • Where to Eat •
    Shopping • Getting Around
Nusa Dua and the Bukit   161
    Nusa Dua: Five-Star Luxury • Tanjung
    Benoa • Turtle Island • Jimbaran •
    Temple above the Stone • Surfing Mecca
Kuta: Yellow Sands and Technicolor Sunsets 168
    General Information • An Exotic
    Fairground • A Day in the Sun • The
    Sunset Event • A Meeting of Cultures •
    Lethal Rips • Kuta's History • A Leap
    in the Dark • Where to Stay • Where
    to Eat • Nightlife • Shopping
South Bali: Tanah Lot to Ubud   179
    Tanah Lot • Kedaton's Fruit Bats •
    Mengwi • Sangeh • Taman Burung Ali
    Bird Park • Ubud
Around Central Bali   189
    Tegalalang, Pujung and Sebatu •
    Tirta Empul • Gunung Kawi • The
    Moon of Pejeng • Yeh Pulu • Goa Gajah:
    The Elephant Cave • Bangli
The Heights   195

    Penelokan • Air Panas: Hot Springs •
    The Ascent of Mount Batur • Across
    Lake Batur • Trunyan • Climbing Mount
    Abang • Batur and Kintamani •
    Penulisan • Besakih • The Ascent
    of Mount Agung • Rendang to
    Klungkung • Bedugul
East Bali   205
    Klungkung • Gelgel and Kamasan • The
    Coast Road • Padangbai • Tenganan •
    Candi Dasa • Amlapura (Karangasem) •
    Water Palaces • Amed • Tulamben

OFF THE BEATEN TRACK   219
Nusa Penida and Nusa Lembongan   221
Nusa Penida: A Limestone Island   221
    Sampalan and Excursions • Cross-
    Country
Nusa Lembongan   223
    Jungubatu
West Bali   226
    West Bali National Park • Along the
    Coast • Buffalo Races

THE EARTHLY PARADISE 229
Infinity Everywhere 231
The Hippy Trail 232
The Future 232

TRAVELERS' TIPS 235
Getting There 237
  From the Airport
Travel Documents 237
Customs Allowances 238
Drugs 238
Health 238
Currency and Banking 239
  Rate of Exchange
Getting Away 240
  Departure Tax • Airline Offices
Beyond Bali 240
Getting Around 241
  Car Rental • *Bemo* Culture • Motorbikes
Accommodation 242
Eating Out 243
The Press and Radio 243

Communications 244
  Telephone • Mail
Time 245
What to Wear 245
Bargaining 245
Tipping 246
Water Sports 246
  Water Safety
Church Services 247
Etiquette 247
Sex 247
Language 247
Consulates and Embassies 248
Selected Indonesian Missions Abroad 249
Recommended Reading 250

QUICK REFERENCE A–Z GUIDE 251
To Places and Topics of Interest with
Listed Accommodation, Restaurants and
Useful Telephone Numbers

INSIDER'S BALI GUIDE

S. Pabean

JAVA SEA

Lovina Beach

Banyuwangi   Pulaki

Gilimanuk   Seririt   K

Cecik   Mt Kelatakan   Mt Sangiang

uwedang

Mt Mesehe

BALI STRAIT   Candikesuma   NATIONAL PARK

Negara

Rambutsiwi

Prancak River

CHINA   TAIWAN

BURMA
    LAOS
THAILAND
        VIETNAM
    CAMBODIA

        THE PHILIPPINES

MALAYSIA
    BORNEO
                        PACIFIC OCEAN

INDONESIA

Bali   AUSTRALIA

N

10 km

Pura

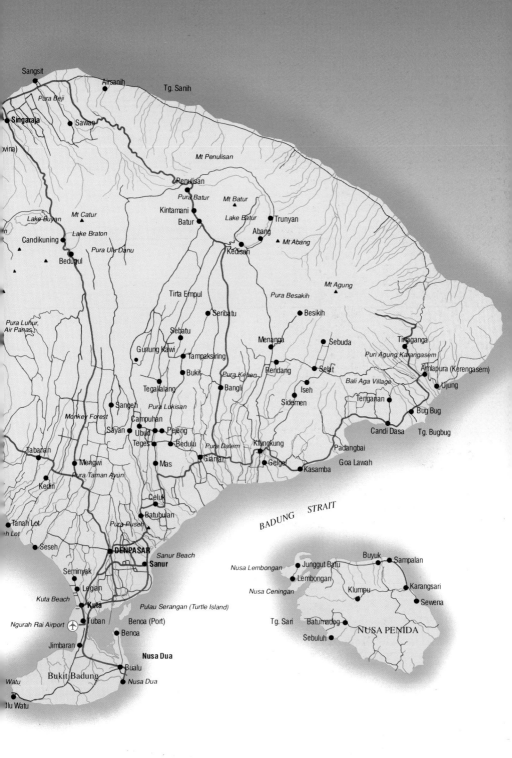

TOP SPOTS

See Ulu Watu

ONE OF THE MIDDLE EAST'S CELEBRATED MONARCHS IS REPUTED ON ARRIVAL IN BALI TO HAVE TOLD HIS DRIVER TO CONTINUE STRAIGHT ON TO ULU WATU TEMPLE. You could do worse than follow his example.

Ulu Watu is a tiny place and as such, representative of Bali, itself a small island. Because it's a temple, going there starts you off on the right foot. But, whether or not you feel the spirit moving there, the Balinese undoubtedly do. In fact it's arguable that they feel religious everywhere and all the time.

Religion is at the heart of Balinese life. The more money they make from tourism, the bigger and better the religious ceremonies they create. These ceremonies and the way in which life revolved around them, were the reason the first foreign visitors came to Bali in the 1930s. You are the successor to these first visitors, in the same way that the modern Balinese are the successors to those temple celebrants 60 and more years ago. So going to a temple early in your visit is both right and apt.

Ulu Watu temple is situated on the tip of a short headland, itself an extension of a larger headland. It juts out into the Indian Ocean like an irregular tooth, and 76 m (250 ft) below it, the ocean rolls in regular and endless waves.

It's one of the six holiest temples of Bali — this is saying something in an island that has hundreds of thousands of temples and shrines. Ulu Watu is perfect

and unspoiled, just as Tanah Lot was before tourists descended on it and someone decided to "develop" it.

One of the many miracles of Ulu Watu is that tourists don't arrive here in their coach loads in quite the same way they do day after day at Tanah Lot. To help prevent Ulu Watu going the sad way of Tanah Lot, go there alone, or as a small group with a driver. That way one of the smaller wonders of the world will be preserved for a little while longer.

You'll have to make a donation (of Rp1,100) and for that will be lent a sarong and strip of cloth for a belt, so that you can enter the little temple appropriately attired. You'll be pestered by the temple's sacred monkeys who will snatch at anything you put down and run up into a tree with it. Chance's are you won't mind: Ulu Watu's position is so wonderful your thoughts will be on things less material than that pair of two-dollar sunglasses. You'll gaze at the sea, admire the carved deities and contemplate the fact that neither they not you will last for ever. Such reflection is understood as liberating in many faiths, and is wholly appropriate in this sublime place.

Ulu Watu has its secular side too. A kilometer (just over half a mile) or so to the north of the temple is the Ulu Watu that is one of the finest surfing locations in the world. It's here that the surfers ride the truly gigantic waves. Unless you are a

One of Bali's six holy temples, Ulu Watu, on arid Bukit Badung, presides over the best surf breaks in Bali.

professional, don't be tempted to join them. Instead, sit and watch. Consider while you do so that you have seen the two faces of Bali, and something approaching the best of both.

Half a day is enough to see everything Ulu Watu has to offer. The easiest way to get to Ulu Watu is by taxi. Negotiate a round-trip fee (US$10 is about right), or if you plan to stay a long time, a one-way fare. You should have no difficulty finding transport back to Kuta, Sanur or Nusa Dua if you leave before 4 PM. Ulu Watu is half an hour's drive from any of these centers.

Brave a Bungee

BUNGEE JUMPING HAS BECOME ONE OF THE MOST POPULAR SPORTS FOR THE INTREPID IN BALI DURING RECENT YEARS.

Every year since 1987 when the New Zealander A.J. Hackett jumped from the Eiffel Tower, this daredevil sport has been attracting new adherents. There are now four bungee jumping sites in Bali, and none of them with the obstacles Hackett must have encountered on his pioneering Paris leap. For whereas the activity used to be confined to scaling and then launching off from urban monuments, today this is a sport that is carefully organized and accords to international safety regulations.

Nowadays you jump down into empty and obstacle-free air from specially constructed towers, usually with a swimming pool underneath you. The harness (round your ankles) and the elasticized rope itself are claimed to be 100 percent reliable, and the pool exists not in case of mishaps but to give you the added pleasure of a quick dip in the water at the end of your initial descent. If that's what you opt for, the rope will be lengthened accordingly. There are three thicknesses of cord, and one will be chosen to fit your weight.

You will be offered a video at the end with a history of bungee jumping, ending with recorded interviews with you, before and after your leap.

The Hackett outfit, **A.J. Hackett Bungee** (0361-730666 FAX 0361-730466 is right next to the shore at Legian's Blue Ocean Beach, at the end of Jalan Enam-Enam (Jalan "Double Two").

On Saturday nights, believe it or not, you can disco then jump, then disco again. This particular bungee jumping site shares a compound with Bali's nicest dancing space. Only the swimming pool separates the dance floor from the bungee tower, and rows of nightlife aficionados sit along the pool wall, beers in hand, and cheer the jumpers as they come hurtling down through the warm Balinese night air.

Every day at sunset there is a lucky draw at the bar. The prize? What else but a free bungee jump?

The other bungee jumping centers in Bali are **Bali Bungee Co.** (/FAX 0361-752658 slightly inland at Kuta, the nearby **Adrenalin Park** (0361-757845 FAX 0361-757844 and **Bungee-in-Bali** (0361-758362 where you leap in front of a waterfall. Free T-shirts, photos of your jump and transport to and from your hotel are included by this last operator.

Adrenalin Park has additional attractions. As well as a climbing wall, there is the terror-inspiring Bali Slingshot. Here you are harnessed, alone or in twos,

For those whose idea of fun is an adrenaline-kick from fear, bungee jumping OPPOSITE and the catapult slingshot ABOVE provide the means.

inside a padded open-air capsule which is then catapulted into the air. A video camera records your facial distortions as the thing swivels round and is propelled up and down several times by the diminishing thrusts of its elastic cords.

"Absolute adrenaline!" they claim, and who could doubt them? They also claim their tower at 50 m (164 ft) is Bali's highest.

Heart, spine and eye doctors have found that bungee jumping causes no abnormal abdominal stress to a healthy body. You certainly wouldn't think it did when you see them coming down at that blue poolside, with Acid House music pumping away in the background.

Visit a Temple Festival

"THE WITCH AT BATUBULAN IS ONLY AN ILLUSION," said the man in the blue headdress and mauve sarong standing beside me in the temple forecourt. "But here she will be for real."

It was my fifth trip to Bali. I had been off the plane but two hours when the hotel porter told me there was to be a festival that very evening in the next village; I knew I couldn't miss it.

Batubulan is where the famous Balinese Barong Dance is staged every morning for, frequently, a large crowd of tourists. But Balinese dance is sacred in origin, designed to be performed at festivals, known as *odalan*, for the rededication of a temple. At Batubulan they run through their routine for the benefit of visitors. At the temple festivals they do it for the gods. This was what the man in the mauve sarong had meant — at the temples the magic is "for real".

In essence, Balinese dance is all magical. Its purpose is to adjust the balance between good and evil leaning it in favor of the good. The Barong Dance is the most dramatic instance of this purpose. A witch, known as the *rangda*, is opposed by a shaggy dog, the *barong*. All the main actors in this dance are men: the *rangda* herself, the two men who act the *barong* in a single costume like a

British pantomime horse, and the would-be stalwart assistants of the *barong* who try to attack the witch with short swords but are rendered powerless by a magical white cloth she waves at them.

As the man said, it's all for real in a temple festival: The man who plays the witch is expected to be possessed by the spirit of a *leyak*, a real witch, and frequently he indeed does seem to go crazy, running off the stage and out into the paddy fields under the witch's powerful direction. Then the crowd really gets excited. A true witch has become caught up in the sacred drama, just as it is hoped the real gods will come down from their home, the summit of Mount Agung, and sit in the ceremonial chairs left empty for them throughout the festival.

You should do your best to go to a genuine Balinese temple festival. The Badung Tourist Office in Denpasar produces a list of them every month and will fax it to you at your hotel if you give them a ring. I usually just ask the hotel

Dance is arguably the finest flower or Balinese art. OPPOSITE: The Sword *(kris)* Dance demonstrated at a show for tourists. ABOVE: The evil *rangda* from the Barong Dance.

staff where I'm lodging — they always know what's on and where in the neighborhood.

When you go, dress appropriately. You'll need to purchase a sarong, sash and (for men) a simple headdress at any of the shops selling sarongs — if they don't have the headdress, they'll tell you where to find them. I'd suggest you buy your sarong at the first place, as a gesture of gratitude for the information.

If you rent a car for the excursion, the driver will expect to wait for you to bring you back. Nine o'clock in the evening is a good time to arrive — later if you like. These festivals go on until dawn and if you stay till 1 AM or so you'll have seen a great deal.

The *gamelan* orchestra will be playing almost nonstop throughout, and they alone provide a wonderful spectacle. Their dexterity and energy is extraordinary, especially considering they will probably have spent the day selling cheap watches on Kuta Beach, or driving a taxi for 12 hours. Balinese culture is such that everyone learns a part in childhood: playing an instrument, taking part in the *kecak* (monkey-dance), or singing the timeless songs which usually bring these astonishing nights to a close.

Bali *is* its dance, though many a visitors these days leave having seen only a tame version staged for hotel guests. At a temple festival you will see the real thing, with much else besides. Make no mistake, your visit will be a highlight of your trip.

Ride a Camel

A CAMEL? I HEAR YOU ASK. Yes, a camel, a ship of the desert. Hardly what you'd expect in this lush, even steamy climate. But camel "safaris" are now on offer as well as moonlight camel treks.

The rides are based at the state-of-the-art Hotel Nikko on the edge of ultra-

The Sword *(kris)* Dance, usually seen as the culmination of a temple's *odalan* festival; entranced men attempt to wound themselves with sharpened weapons. They never succeed.

fashionable Nusa Dua. They've brought in camels from drier climes, and now you can ride them along Jimbaran Beach by day or night.

You can wear anything except thongs (flip flops), but a hat against the sun is recommended in daytime. If you're interested contact **Bali Camel Safaris** (0361-773377 extension 210.

Nor are camels the only beasts of burden to ride astride. You can also trek Bali by elephant. Twenty minutes north of Ubud, in the wooded Balinese interior, **Wisatareksa Gajah Perdana** (0361-286072, offers you an adventure to remember.

Elephants are not native to Bali, but at least, unlike the camels, they are used to the humidity. There are elephants on Sumatra, for instance, and in climatically similar Burma and Thailand, not to mention India.

This is a peace-inducing experience because the elephants are such calm beasts. When the ride is over you can help wash down the world's largest land mammal — probably the most enjoyable part of the experience.

Then there are horses. In the region north of Tanah Lot temple you can go on a day tour. You'll first be assessed for your riding ability and then allocated an appropriate steed. They have everything from ponies to full-sized horses (though "full-sized" in Bali may not be quite what you're used to back home if you're an experienced rider). Your horseback tour includes rice terraces, bushland and the beach, where you can stop for a swim (so bring your swim suit along). As with the camels, don't wear thongs since they catch in the stirrups.

It's a good way of spending a day. Horses are a traditional means of transport in this part of Bali, and there aren't many other tourists around the area where they take you. You don't need any experience, though operators won't take anyone under 12, and 15 is the suggested minimum age for those entirely new to riding. The guides are expert, and they will even attach your horse to a lead string if you're nervous.

The place to contact for these trips is **Bali Jaran-Jaran Keneka** (0361-751672 FAX 0361-755734 at the Logi Garden Hotel, Legian.

For all these rides — camel, elephant and horseback — the companies will pick you up at your hotel. If you wish to extend the trip, Ubud has no shortage of attractions. A meal at one of its many wonderful restaurants could conveniently be added after the elephant ride. The same applies to hiring horses from Legian. As for the camel rides at Jimbaran, late afternoon, or even one of the moonlight rides would be best, allowing you could eat afterwards at one of the fine open-air barbecue restaurants on Jimbaran Beach.

Watch Dolphins at Play

PEOPLE TELL FABULOUS STORIES ABOUT DOLPHINS. In a small *losmen* in Lovina, I heard tales of how they leap into the air just beside the boat, twisting themselves as they do so, only to dive deep into the

waves and then come up again and repeat the performance.

This won't happen every day. But one thing you can be fairly certain of — if you take a trip out with the fishermen at sunrise off Lovina Beach in North Bali you will see dolphins. Perhaps they'll arch their backs above the ocean as if they are turning somersaults underwater. (Actually they're swimming in a regular up-and-down motion that cuts through the surface.) Sometimes they do seem to be playing and even performing just for you. They leap and twist in the air, and you come back to shore at 8 AM knowing that, even if you do nothing else, your day has already been made.

From start to finish, the experience is beautiful. You are awakened early, and on the water by 6:15 AM. (Lovina is a small place and nowhere you stay will be more than a few minutes from the beach.) The sun has not yet risen, but it's light and the sky is already bright with a golden yellow glow in the east.

The boats, the wooden *prahu* that are seen all over Indonesia, are small and

brilliantly painted in white, red and blue. They can take four or five people, and they're extraordinarily stable. In fact, with their two solid bamboo poles attached by artfully constructed wooden arms on both sides, they must be some of the most stable vessels on earth. You need have no fear when setting out in a prahu for the quarter of a mile or so they need to go to the place where the dolphins play.

There will be a dozen or more such boats out on the average morning, with additional bona fide fishing vessels a little further out to sea. When the dolphins appear, the skippers vie with each other to be first on the scene, revving up their engines and racing for the spot.

Then the lordly sun rises. But already people are absorbed by the dolphins. They are everywhere, in schools of 10 or 20, arching their backs above the element they live in, gray-blue curves above the

Hardly Lawrence of Arabia, more like Takmitsu from Tokyo! Camel rides on Nusa Dua are proving popular with tourists looking for something a bit different.

water that is quietly lapping against the side of the boat.

Altogether you're on the water for two hours. For the last half hour, from around 7:30 AM, the dolphins will have gone, chasing fish out into deeper waters. The fishermen switch off their engines and hand you sweet tea and cold fried bananas. This is the "breakfast included" part of the deal that most advertise.

These trips to see the dolphins play are wonderfully inexpensive. You should be able to secure a trip for about US$7.50 or less. It's such good value, the odds are you will be back the next morning — assuming you don't just turn over when the fisherman knocks on your door. Get up! It's much more rewarding than merely seeing these beautiful creatures gambol their way through your dreams.

You can pay considerably more for a big marine sports company to take you to see dolphins in other locations, especially in southeastern Bali. **Bali Diving Perdana (** 0361-286493, for instance, will take you at the same early hour from your hotel in the area to Sanur, then ship you round to the Ulu Watu area for dolphin sighting. The cliffs are dramatic as a backdrop, but your chances of actually seeing the creatures leaping are no better than in Lovina.

Raft the White Water

"WELL, WE HAD A WONDERFUL TIME. IT WASN'T AS DANGEROUS AS I'D EXPECTED. IN FACT, IT WASN'T DANGEROUS AT ALL. There were half a dozen of us on this inflatable raft and we did go down some rough bits. But nobody fell off, and nobody was ever in any danger of falling off. I suppose if there's a lot of water in the river there might be more chance of a tumble. But then if there's *really* a lot they'll cancel the rafting for the day. What I think is, you'll only experience being fished back out of the water and onto the raft again by the assistants if that's what you're really looking for. In other words, if you jump in."

The lady was a buxom matron from Sydney and, having just come back from a day's rafting on one of the rivers of eastern Bali, she can be assumed to have known what she was talking about.

The Bali rafting companies have burgeoned in recent years and now there are four — perhaps more by the time you read this. Those four all use the rivers of the eastern part of the island as these are both the most suitable and easily accessible from the hotel areas of Nusa Dua, Sanur, Kuta and Legian. They're not far from Candi Dasa either.

You'll be picked up from your hotel at around 7:30 AM if you opt for the morning tour, and you will be back not long after lunch. In fact, to maximize their equipment, the companies give afternoon sessions too; some even have four daily starting times. The rivers you will raft down are rocky in places, just enough to provide the white water experience but nowhere are they truly rough or scary.

It's true there was one accident some years ago when some Hong Kong tourists were drowned. But everyone seems to have learned from that experience, and if there are any complaints they're likely to be that the trips are not as adventurous as people might like. All in all, it's a safe pursuit. Rafters are provided with helmets and given a quick course of instruction on safety procedures. Radio contact with base is maintained at all times, and most of the rafts are imported from Australia or the United Kingdom.

A mark of their confidence is that some companies accept children aged eight and up; with others it's nine or 12. Those familiar with the technicalities, might like to know that the rivers contain grade II to grade IV rapids. Trip length is up to 12 miles.

As you travel down the river you will see waterfalls, giant ferns, vines and creepers growing down to the water's edge, plus the rural inhabitants of inland Bali washing their clothes in the river, bathing their children and watering their animals.

The riverbanks are steep higher up, and you will be asked to carry your equipment down to the water; someone will be there to carry most of it up at the bottom end.

You should take a change of clothes with you. Waterproof bags for cameras are provided.

As with many of these adventure sports in Bali, the inspiration is from Australia and New Zealand. In almost all cases there are Australasians on hand masterminding the operation.

Companies that cater for this sport are: **Bali Safari Rafting** (0361-221315 FAX 0361-221316, **Ayung River Rafting** (0361-238759 FAX 0361-224236, **Raging Thunder Adventures** (0361-758822 FAX 0361-758814, **Sobek** (0361-287059 FAX 0361-289448, **Bali International Rafting** (0361-757052 FAX 0361-752956, and **Bakas Levi Rafting** (0361-289379. Trips cost around US$60 per person.

Climb a Volcano

BALI HAS TWO VOLCANOES, AGUNG AND BATUR, THAT HAVE ERUPTED THIS CENTURY — you can see the steam rising from them

when you reach the crater, and some intrepid adventurers have even scrambled down into Batur and boiled an egg in the hot mud and sulfurous water to be found in the lower depths.

Mount (Gunung) Agung at 2,743 m (9,000 ft) is a stiff proposition. The round trip takes two days, though some very tough customers have managed it in one. Either way it's no easy matter. The surface is crumbly, and footsteps tend, in places, to go two steps forward and then gently slither at least one pace back. Nights on the top are cold, but it's the blazing sun during the day that makes climbing Mount Agung such heavy going (see THE ASCENT OF MOUNT AGUNG, page 202).

Mount Batur, Bali's other active volcano is another story. Though the top is over 1,600 m (5,500 ft) above sea-level, it's an easy, short ascent. This is because Batur rises from within the crater (or caldera) of a much older and bigger volcano. Climbing begins at a point that's already some 900 m (3,000 ft)

Rafting, one of Bali's newer sports, is at its best towards the end of the monsoon rains, late March, when the River Ayung is at its fullest.

up the route. Three hours will usually see you up and down Mount Batur (see THE ASCENT OF MOUNT BATUR, page 196).

Many go up Batur to see the sunrise. Whether you stay at the foot of Batur at Air Panas or up on the crater ridge at Penelokan (a 15-minute drive from Air Panas), you will be awakened early indeed — at around 3 AM — and given breakfast before you start out. Despite the uncivilized hour, it's the best time of day for walking and climbing, before the heat of the sun is grows intense. When at around 4:30 AM you start to ascend you'll in all likelihood be in the best of moods. The cocks will be crowing, the air will be fresh, and before long, as the first light shows on the eastern horizon, you'll hear the birds begin to cry out below you, and the crater ridge will be in sight.

Your guide will lead you along the ridge to where there's a *warung* selling refreshments and, after a most welcome cup or two of coffee, you'll settle down to watch the sun rise at around 6:30 AM — give or take 15 minutes, depending on the time of year.

Then down again, and when you reach the shores of Lake Batur something wonderful awaits you: a dip at the spot where the hot waters flow into the lake. The accumulated sweat will disappear in a moment, and your tired muscles will respond, as muscles invariably do, to the warmth and to the water.

Then it's back to the hotel for, no doubt, another breakfast and then perhaps bed to make up on that lost sleep.

Anyone in Air Panas, (which means "warm water") will tell you how to find a guide to go up Batur. You don't need one in the daylight, but if you're going up in the early hours to see the sunrise, you will definitely need one.

If you stay in Penelokan at the Lakeview Hotel (the only viable accommodation there) the hotel will arrange everything for you. They'll

Sacred Mt. Agung at 2,743 m (9,000 ft) tempts climbers, but it is far from an easy ascent. It is essential to hire knowledgeable guides to ensure a safe trip.

charge you US$30 (with a minimum of four people needed to run the trip). Down in Air Panas — at Under the Volcano Homestay, for instance — you can arrange the trip for much less outlay.

Dare a Dragon

THERE WAS A TIME WHEN THE KOMODO DRAGONS COULD ONLY BE SEEN ON THE ISLAND OF KOMODO. These giant monitor lizards hid out in this remote Indonesian island situated between Sumbawa and Flores. Now Jurassic Park is here, alive and well on the island of Bali.

The monitor lizard of Komodo, a kind of land crocodile, is a remnant of prehistoric times and a close relation of the dinosaurs. Three meters long and weighing up to 70 kg (150 lbs), these extraordinary carnivorous creatures can be seen at Bali's Indonesia Jaya Reptile and Crocodile Park. There are only 5,000 left in the world, and eight specimens are on show here.

These creatures are believed to be the inspiration for the Chinese dragon — with a little imagination their long yellowish-red tongues look like fire. You would need to use your imaginative powers, because they can be quite dangerous, eating whole goats or deer for dinner after sawing them up with their barbaric and forceful teeth. They are the fiercest lizards on earth, just as the Chinese dragons were emblems of ferocity and power.

The **Indonesia Jaya Reptile and Crocodile Park** (0361-243686, is at Banjar Binoong, Desa Werdi Bhuwana, Kec Mengwi, Badung, Denpasar Utara. It's open from 9 AM to 6 PM, with shows (mainly wrestling with crocodiles) at 10:30 AM and 3 PM.

If this is not enough for you, complete the day with a visit to an especially fine bird park. The **Taman Burung Bali Bird Park** (0361-299353 at Singapadu, between Denpasar and Gianyar, is a wonderful place for both study and relaxation.

There are king birds of paradise, black palm cockatoos, blue and yellow macaws, and many more exotic tropical bird species, all housed in beautiful garden surroundings.

With over 1,000 birds and 250 different species, this is a major collection as well as a wonderful place to visit. The park also has Komodo dragons.

Food and drink are available at the park, and it's only a 30-minute drive from Kuta and Legian or Nusa Dua — less than that from Sanur.

Watch Woodcarvers

MAS IS THE CENTER FOR WOODCARVING IN BALI. Today the main road from Denpasar, which runs through the village on its way to Ubud, is lined with large, affluent-looking galleries selling Balinese carved objects. Every visitor, it is assumed, will want to take at least one specimen home as a souvenir.

But which one to choose? As the imposing façades succeed each other in solemn line the choice appears impossible. So why not steel your courage and head for the best?

Ida Bagus Njana, born in 1912, was the most celebrated Balinese woodcarver of his time. Today, his Njana Tilem Gallery, is where the world's richest art collectors go when they want to acquire a Balinese woodcarving.

Of course, the prices are high. But a visit to the gallery is a marvelous insight into upper caste (Brahman) Balinese life, and you are not obliged to buy anything. Alternatively, you could splash out and buy a small piece, either from one of the two masters, or from one of their numerous apprentices whose work is also on display.

Balinese woodcarving originated as art for the temples, just as Balinese dancing and drama originated as constituent elements of Balinese religious festivals. When the first foreign visitors came to study art and life in Bali, they sought both to copy and influence Balinese artistic styles. Woodcarving in Bali then began to become more international, meaning that it slowly

began to evolve from the traditional patterns into new forms. The Balinese artist was encouraged, in other words, to express his own individual creative personality, and as a result individual styles were born.

Ida Bagus Njana was the greatest of these individuals. His work sold in galleries in New York and Amsterdam. He evolved a style that was semi-abstract, thus following the style fashionable in international art circles at the time. He was a genius of sorts and the extraordinary products of his chisels can still be seen in the gallery, as can the products of his talented son.

These are the carvings that became sought out by the connoisseurs, both

during his lifetime and after.

Today the gallery is both a kind o f museum for the work of this exceptionally talented family and a showroom where visitors can buy the products of father and son, or members of their school.

Just as Rembrandt and other celebrated painters employed apprentices to work first on the less specialized parts of a portrait before the master, himself, filled in the face and hands of his distinguished subject, so too these woodcarvers instructed followers with

A tradition of exquisite woodcarving, made famous by Bali's mastercarver Ida Bagus Tilem, is the best reason to stop at Mas, on the way to Ubud.

whom they worked together in their workshop. When you hear about an Ida Bagus Tilem school of woodcarving, this is what it means.

Go along to their gallery in Mas, and witness the marvels on display. Enjoy too the beautiful compound which contains fine specimens of Balinese architecture — the milieu of talented artists who in time acquired worldly success.

If you find yourself so imbued with the creative atmosphere, so overcome by an experience which can include watching carvers at work, then perhaps you will delve deep into your pocket and come away with a thing of beauty.

Buy a Painting from a Woman Artist

BALINESE PAINTING AND TEMPLE DANCES WERE THE TWO MAIN REASONS THE FIRST FOREIGN VISITORS ARRIVED ON THE ISLAND IN THE 1930s. Being for the most part artists themselves, these early visitors settled in the inland village of Ubud and founded an artists' cooperative of sorts, an organization that would help local painters to market their astonishing products in Europe. It was called the Pita Maha.

For 50 years, though women were prominent and indeed famous in the world of Balinese dance, they were never accepted as painters. This was on account of traditional divisions in gender roles — women could harvest the rice or dance, but it was men who painted, just as it was men who went fishing or became priests in the temple.

Western influence has begun to change that, however. Foreign artists continue to come to Bali, in particular to Ubud, to paint and to benefit from t he relaxed lifestyle. Some of these artists are women, and they have began to ask where the Balinese women artists are.

Today there's a gallery especially devoted to the work of Bali's women painters. It's called the **Seniwati Gallery** (0361-975485, is at Jalan Sriwedari N°2B, Ubud, and it's run by its cofounder, British-born Mary Northmore.

Buying paintings in Bali has become a highly specialized activity. Some of its male artists, Ida Bagus Made, for example, have become world-famous, and their work now sells for sums in the region of US$30,000 in London and New York.

Women artists haven't yet reached that level of celebrity, so if you aren't an art expert but fancy the idea of taking home an original Balinese painting, give the Seniwati Gallery a try.

This gallery is currently the only place in Bali where women painters can exhibit. As a result, you'll see all the paintings by women Balinese artists that are anywhere currently on offer. But do note that the gallery accepts almost any art by a Balinese woman. You'll have to use your judgment.

You might pick up a masterpiece. Since all Bali's women artists exhibit here. If there's a future Picasso among them, this is where her work will be hanging. Internationally, collectors' attitudes to women painters are no different from their to attitudes to men, however the Balinese may look down their noses at female painters. One day a Balinese woman painter is going to hit the big time. If you've gotten there first and acquired one of her early masterpieces, you could find yourself sitting on a small fortune.

It's an idea. If you do follow this advice, and you do turn up trumps, make sure you tell the newspaper reporters knocking at your door in which guidebook you read this advice!

Perhaps more than any other art, Bali is known for its painting. What started out as a craft for village and temple festivals has, with the help of some foreign artists who made their home on the island, become a veritable industry. Culture-vultures will seek out the museums in Ubud which show the evolution of true Balinese painting.

YOUR CHOICE

The Great Outdoors

Bali has a great advantage in its wide variety of terrain. There are beaches and offshore diving locations, areas of low-lying paddy fields, the little-populated dry region to the west, the coastal strip in the north, and finally volcanic landscapes of the center of the island. All of these provide different opportunities for the outdoors enthusiast.

HIKING

To begin at the highest point, you can crown your stay in Bali — if you're fit enough — with an ascent of its highest mountain, the volcano Mount Agung (Gunung Agung).

This is a two-day trip and is done from either Besakih or the upland village of Sebudi. Neither starting point favors the length of time needed for the ascent. You'll definitely need a guide, and you can find one easily in either place by asking around (saying "Gunung Agung jalan-jalan," meaning "Mount Agung on foot," will convey your intention perfectly).

Stout footwear is essential. The present writer can testify to the damage done to the feet by attempting the ascent in sneakers — the half-walk, half-slither mode of descent, which is the only one possible in places, wreaks havoc on the toes and renders progress painstakingly slow.

Far easier is the climb up Mount Batur (see CLIMB A VOLCANO in TOP SPOTS, page 21, and THE ASCENT OF MOUNT BATUR in THE BROAD HIGHWAY, page 196).

The central region of the island offers volcanic panoramas of every kind. On a clear day, from the crater rim at Penelokan or Kintamani you can get stupendous views of Mount Batur quietly steaming, and from just round the rim, you can see Agung, resplendent in its loftiness, not far away to the east. While on the rim, incidentally, you can easily climb to the modest, extinct volcanic summit of Mount Abang.

OPPOSITE: Worth the effort of an early rise in cool conditions: the sunrise seen from Lake Batur. ABOVE: Bougainvillea flourishes everywhere in Bali.

PARKS AND RESERVES

As for national parks: Bali has one — though it could be argued that the entire island ought to be declared a national park.

The west of the island is the place to go. Menjangan Island and the neighboring coast have been included in West Bali National Park (see below) on account of the incomparable coral and tropical fish to be found beneath the waters there. You're not allowed to stay on the island itself, but accommodation is available on the mainland within easy reach of the diving and snorkeling locations.

The **West Bali National Park** (Bali Barat National Park) has its headquarters at **Cekik** near Gilimanuk. This quiet place is where the now tragically extinct Balinese tiger was last seen. It's a good place to get away from the tourist jamboree in Kuta and elsewhere (it sometimes seems as though this encompasses almost all of Bali) andtake a solitary walk. The park covers over 750 sq km (290 sq miles), though much of this area is out of bounds to the public. The authorities at the National Park headquarters will suggest routes and tell you what you should take along with you.

Camping isn't popular in Bali — it's simply too hot and humid for it to be much pleasure. In any case, the small *losmen* are affordable and friendly, and staying in them absolves you of the need to carry camping equipment.

Also because of the heat, hiking is demanding. The place to do it is up in the hills where it's cooler, often quite much cooler, with rain showers common in the middle of the day. There's a trail, for example, that branches off from the road that runs along the island's north coast and ends at the Bali Aga village of Trunyan. Watch out for a sign not far from Air Sanih that points to a "hiking trail to Trunyan," four hours away (or so they claim). It will be a steep ascent, but the air grows cooler as you climb. Don't try setting out on this trail in the late afternoon without a good and reliable torch (flashlight). There may be no moon to light the way, or it may be clouded

over in these mountainous parts. There certainly won't be any street lights.

Nature is everywhere on this precious isle. There are few more dramatic experiences on Bali than the moment at first light during your ascent of Mount Agung (an ascent which often starts at 2 AM), when a single bird shrieks out, flying along an invisible contour line near you, alerting others to the arrival of the new day. Then all the birds begin their ecstatic dawn chorus, both above and below, and within minutes the sun itself appears, casting the volcano's shadow onto the plain below, a huge and symmetrical triangle.

Flowers proliferate on Bali, both native ones and species introduced by the island's many appreciative visitors. A reference for beginners can be found in Margaret and Fred Eiseman's *Flowers of Bali*, and a wide range can be seen at the **Botanical Gardens** at Bedugul (see under THE BROAD HIGHWAY, page 205).

OPPOSITE: Remote (by Bali standards), the West Bali National Park is a haven for bird life and flora. Its drier conditions are conducive to a different range of species than the rest of the island. ABOVE: Hiking around Danau Tamblingan, in north-central Bali. Guides recommended!

Butterflies, difficult to study at close quarters in the wild, can be seen far more easily during a visit to the **Bali Butterfly Park** (0361-814282 FAX 0361-814281. It's on Jalan Batukaru, Sandan Wanasari Tabanan.

BEACH AND SURF

Sun, sea and sand are central to most people's visit to Bali, and the magnificent surfing beach extending from Kuta through to Legian and Seminyak is the center for it all. Professional wave riders have their own special places — notably the world famous surfing locations at Ulu Watu and Padang-Padang. But ordinary mortals, and many good surfers besides, will be found at Kuta and Legian beaches waiting for that perfect wave. You can join them, but you should be aware that there are dangers. The surf can be huge, and the currents can, in places, present a fatal dangers. People die surfing at Kuta and Legian every year, despite the beach watch mounted by the Badung Surf Rescue. Do be careful.

Try out the waves first on a boogie board. These small, rectangular boards are easy to use — you can probably master them in a morning — and can be rented by the hour everywhere along the beach. The usual rental rate is around US$5 per hour, less once you become a regular. Catch the waves at a depth suitable to you. Stay between the red and yellow flags and you'll be fine — these are the safe places, and the designated areas watched over by the Surf Rescue. (If you do get into trouble, hold your arm high in the air —this is the sign the rescue workers look out.) The technique for boogie boarding is to catch the wave just in front of where it's foaming towards you, hold your board so that your chin is about a quarter of the way down from the top, and the bottom edge somewhere in the middle of your belly, and off you go! The first wave you catch properly is a wonderful experience and will probably have you wading back out to catch another. The salt water that will undoubtedly be pouring from your nose will, I'll guarantee, not deter you for an instant.

Sporting Spree

DIVING

Diving is one of the major specialist pursuits in Bali, and there are several places where seasoned practitioners take the plunge with enthusiasm. Indonesia's waters provide some of the least known diving locations in the world, and although Bali's sites are well-dived these days, their splendor is none the less grand.

You've never dived before? The diving companies on Bali will all undertake to teach you if you can spare the time and the money.

A fine authority on these waters is *Kal Muller's Diving Indonesia*, subtitled optimistically, *A Guide to the World's Greatest Diving*. With over 300 pages, it's a comprehensive and professional survey of diving in Balinese waters (the author has had over 20 years of diving experience), and all the guide companies specializing in water sports have copies lying around their offices.

Bali's top diving locations are as follows: **Tulamben** and **Amed** on the northeast corner of the island, **Menjangan Island** (Nusa Menjangan)

LEFT: Masks on sale for snorkeling. RIGHT: On the north coast, Pemuteran is a fine stepping-off point for diving or snorkeling on the nearby reef.

in the northwest, **Nusa Lembongan** (Lembongan Island) and its neighbor **Nusa Penida**, and places off **Candi Dasa** in East Bali.

Tulamben is notable, at least in part, because there's nothing else to do there except dive the wreck and snorkel. The beach consists of round surf-polished stones derived from Bali's highest volcano, Mount Agung, which towers above Tulamben from the far side of the road. The row of little beach hotels that line the coast for a few hundred meters are all devoted to the cult of diving. When I was last there, I spotted one of the most famous of Indonesia's divers getting out of a Suzuki Jimny, heading straight for the water and the famous wreck that makes diving here so intriguing.

The wreck is so celebrated that nowadays there are divers' maps of it. Built in the United States in 1915 as a cargo steamship, the vessel is 120 m (400 ft) long and named (typically) the *Liberty*. She was torpedoed on January 11, 1942 by a Japanese submarine 15 km (nine miles) off Lombok while carrying a cargo of raw rubber and railway parts. She was then towed to Bali by United States destroyers but was leaking badly.

The crew was eventually evacuated and the *Liberty* was beached at Tulamben.

Over the next 20 years she was stripped of valuables. Then in 1963 Mount Agung erupted with accompanying earthquakes. The sea received streams of molten lava, and the remains of the *Liberty* slid down into deeper and deeper water, the hull cracking in several places.

But it wasn't too deep for divers and even snorkelers to explore. Some of the superstructure lies a mere two meters under the surface (about seven feet), and much of the rest at around five meters (16 ft). There's nothing marine life loves so much as a wreck. Sponges, eels, anemone, gorgonian fans, coral gardens and some 400 species of brilliantly colored tropical fish now inhabit this wreck. It has become the most popular dive site in Bali, with over a hundred divers visiting it on peak days.

Ironically, the person who is most likely to help you at Tulamben is a Japanese woman, Emiko Shibuya. Her company, **Dive Paradise Island** (0363-41052 has offices at the Paradise Beach Bungalows.

Menjangan Island is 30 minutes from the mainland and suitable for diving in all seasons. It is considered by many to be the most beautiful diving location in Bali, and is now part of West Bali National Park. Various sites near Nusa Penida's somber cliffs offer spectacular dives, with steep drop-offs and the chance to see large creatures such as the Napoleon wrasse and giant clams.

It must be emphasized that diving is a sport that requires training. Beginners are strongly advised to take a course with one of the major diving companies on Bali before attempting any of these sites on their own, or even with local experts.

If you don't have the courage or simply the interest to take up diving on your Bali vacation, there's always **snorkeling** to give you a glimpse of the underwater wonders. Most hotels will help you arrange this — the Bali Hai day-tours to Nusa Lembongan, for instance, provide the equipment plus a good lunch afterwards. Instruction takes a couple of minutes, and then you can be off on your own in areas they will point out to you as the best for underwater life.

Or you can go to Lovina in North Bali and go snorkeling with the fishermen. It's the simplest thing in the world to arrange — you will be asked all the evening by half the locals you meet whether you'd like to go out to see dolphins or whether you'd like to go snorkeling. They'll provide the equipment in the twinkling of an eye, and it will cost you a fraction of what the tour companies charge.

For diving proper, however, you do need the reassurance provided by professionals. The biggest diving company in Bali is **Baruna** (0361-753820 FAX 0361-753809. They will give you full instruction and take you on your first dives in the safe waters along the coral reef off Sanur and Nusa Dua.

Other companies are **Citra Bali Dive Center** (0361-286788 FAX 0361-424324, **Bali Pesona Bahari** (/FAX 0361-287872 (formerly Bali Marine Sports), **Indonesian Cactus Divers** (9361-462063

FAX 0361-462164, **Mega Dive** (0361-288192, **Bali Diving Perdana** (0361-286493 FAX 0361-288871 and **Bali Club Diver** (/FAX 0361-462078.

GOLF
Bali has four golf courses. The **Bali Golf and Country Club** (0361-771791 FAX 0361-771797 at Nusa Dua is an 18-hole, par-72 course is of championship standard and has already hosted several major competitions. Designed by Robin Nelson and Rodney Wright, it offers a special golfing experience with multiple tees to ensure playability for both professionals and novices.

The course has two parts. The first features waterfalls, creeks and canyons with small stone walls lining the sides of fairways and tees in the style of Balinese rice paddies. The second half runs through a mature coconut grove, with palms of up to 30 m (100 ft) tall. Fairways dominate here. Then for the last two holes you are by the sea. The 17th hole is played into the wind (usually), out towards the sea over sand dunes; the final hole sees you coming back from the sea's edge to a green beside a six-and-a-half-hectare (16-acre) lake.

You can rent clubs and shoes at the club house, and electric golf carts stocked with cold drinks help you endure the rigors of the climate. Even so, it's best to book a time as early in the day as possible, or failing that in the latter part of the afternoon, any time after 3 PM. Multilingual caddies see that you find your way round the course.

In the Balinese style clubhouse afterwards, you can eat an Indonesian meal, take a dip in the swimming pool, or knock back a few well-deserved drinks at the bar.

At a somewhat cooler elevation stands the **Bali Handara Kosaido Country Club** (0361-22646 FAX 0361-287358 at Bedugul, on the main cross-island road from Denpasar to Singaraja and Lovina Beach.

Here the 18-hole course was designed by Peter Thompson and Michael Wolferidge & Associates, and is also a

championship-standard course. Apart from the altitude, a great advantage here is that you can also stay at the country club overlooking the lake. There's a karaoke bar, a traditional Japanese bath, while the place is also geared for business conferences, making it a great place to combine business with leisure. The complex has been voted one of the 50 best golf clubs in the world.

Back at sea level, there's the congenial nine-hole golf club at the **Hotel Grand Bali Beach (** 0361-288511 FAX 0361-287917 at Sanur. You can see it on your right as you enter the hotel grounds along the drive from the main entrance, or walk round to it if you arrive at the hotel from the beach.

Finally, there's the brand new 18-hole championship course at Tanah Lot, the **Bali Nirvana Resort (** 0361-815900 FAX 815901. This is Bali's newest course and overlooks the famous island temple of Tanah Lot.

PARASAILING

For parasailing go to Tanjung Benoa where **Lingga Sempurna (** 0361-771457, provides all the equipment. This is also the place for **jet skiing** and **snorkeling**. You can parasail at Bedugul, too. Contact the Bali Handara Kosaido Country Club (see GOLF, above) for details.

ABOVE: Bali Handara Kosaido Country Club, voted among the 50 most beautiful golf courses worldwide. OVERLEAF: Parasailing is popular on Sanur, Tanjung Benoa, and even in Bedugul.

MORE DIVERSIONS

For **fishing**, again try the **Lingga Sempurna** (above) or ring the **Bali Diving Perdana** and **Marine Sport** (0361-286493 FAX 0361-288871.

For **horse, elephant** or **camel riding**, see RIDE A CAMEL in TOP SPOTS, page 16.

For **white water rafting** — very big in Bali — see RAFT THE WHITE WATER, also in TOP SPOTS, page 20.

For **kayaking** on Lake Tamblingan, contact the rafting company **Sobek** (0361-287059.

Finally, how about **go-kart racing**? You can do it in central Kuta at **Bali Road Runner Go-Karts** (0361-758459 around a 400-m (440-yd) outdoor track.

The Open Road

There aren't many roads on Bali, and as a result some of the major ones in the southeast get crowded. But west and north, things are still relatively peaceful.

The route visitors are most likely to experience is the one running over the island from **Denpasar** to **Singaraja**. This is the most practical way of getting from the tourist centers in the southeast to the

quieter north coast and the popular, small beachside places at Lovina.

The road rises soon after Denpasar and then enters a flat upland hollow. This is a quiet part of Bali, though many of its visitors are well-heeled on account of the Bali Handara Kosaido Country Club, standing sedately beside the lake with its 18-hole golf course.

Parasailors and kayakers do little to break the silence of the area but they do present a surprising addition to what looks at first sight like a scene of primordial serenity. The parasailors float into view against a brilliant blue sky like apparitions from outer space, or pilots descending in utter silence from some distant and now forgotten aerial crisis.

The road soon enough begins to descend, and if there are clouds and mist here it won't be unusual. Nor will it bode ill for the weather on the north coast, half an hour's drive further on. The north of Bali is one of the driest parts on the island, and the sun will in all likelihood have been blazing down all day while you were glowering at the raindrops splashing on your car's windshield.

Once in Singaraja it's only another 10 minutes to **Lovina** and that long-awaited seafood dinner, then an early night in preparation for dolphin watching early the next morning.

The road that runs right along the coast of North Bali makes fine driving. You can stop, if you like, to see the various sights along the way — the intricately carved temple at Sangsit, the slightly desolate beach location and natural pool at Air Sanih, both to the east of Singaraja, or the monkeys at Pulaki and the hot spring pools (these are wonderful) at Banjar. Both of these latter places are west of the former Balinese capital.

If you continue east you will pass the fabulous diving location of Tulamben with its famous wreck, nowadays home to innumerable marine species. A mere 10 minutes farther on there is the road that leads off on your left for Amed, Bali's newest and still little-known beachside development.

If you want, you can attempt the drive all the way round this piece of coast, from **Amed** to the ruined floating temple at **Ujung**. There are rough parts where pot holes will all but bar your way; the

state of the road changes from season to season and according to whether or not it has been repaired recently. Usually it is passable and the views of the coastline below are beautiful.

Carry straight on, however, avoiding the Amed turn off, and you'll soon be in **Amlapura**, and not much further on, you'll reach **Candi Dasa**.

If you opt to drive the other way, west from Singaraja, you'll be surprised how quickly you're in **Gilimanuk**, located at the extreme end of the island and the place where the ferries leave for the short trip to Java. From there you have no alternative but to turn round and set off along the busy south coast road for **Tabanan**, and then the populous southeast again.

One of the most popular routes for visitors who have rented cars is up to **Kintamani** via **Bangli**. This takes you to the volcanic area centered on **Lake Batur**, and you then have the choice of following the crater road west towards **Penulisan**, or east to Besakih.

OPPOSITE: With its ingenious irrigation system, Bali is able to produce three rice harvests annually. ABOVE: Anything goes when it comes to transport.

Both ways are attractive. If you take the eastern option, you can descend the long country road that eventually leads to **Besakih**, Bali's preeminent temple.

This is a fine route with memorable views of **Mount Agung** on your left as you descend.

From Besakih there is another scenic road — this one running from the Mother Temple down to **Klungkung**. It's the road taken by almost all Balinese when approaching their temple for grand celebrations, and it goes nowhere else after Besakih. How could it? Besakih is the center of the Balinese spiritual world.

Another attractive country road — which is surprisingly quiet considering how close it is to the heavily-populated and tourist-frequented part of southeastern Bali — is the road that runs from the great temple of Taman Ayun at **Mengwi** to the Monkey Forest at **Sangeh**. It's a cross-country route and not at all popular — perfect, in other words, for the motorcyclist, as in fact are all these country roads of the island.

But what many motorcyclists like to do is explore the *really* quiet roads of upland Bali. You can do this only by following your nose. One way of getting started would be to take the road that runs upwards into the mountains from the North Bali coast road between **Sangsit** and **Kubutambahan**. You pass through the villages of Jagaraga and Sawan (where the gongs are made for the Balinese *gamelan* orchestras), and from Sawan onwards it's remote country where you're on your own.

There's no need to arrange stopovers on these inland Balinese trips, unless you particularly want to. At a mere 150 km by 80 km (90 miles by 50 miles) the island's too small for that. You can, in fact, go to and from anywhere in Bali within the inside of a day's journey.

Because Bali is so compact there are maps of it reproduced on every hand. The free advertising magazine, the *Bali Echo*, for example, always has one as its center double-page spread.

Backpacking

Bali has long been a premier backpacker's destination. It still is, but these days more and more of what were once favorite backpacker haunts are being "developed" and turned into high-price destinations for affluent visitors.

Ubud is a prime example of this trend. Ten years ago humble *losmen* were everywhere. How different things are today. Now there are coffeeshops galore offering cappuccinos at US$2 (a day's pay for the staff who serve you) and hotels where rates of US$200 are not at all uncommon (one of them charges in excess of US$450 for its cheapest bungalow).

There are still backpackers' places in Ubud, but they don't rule the roost and set the tone in the way they used to, and in the way they still do in other less frequented islands of the archipelago.

The same is true of Kuta, that former backpacker's resort par excellence. A huge new luxury hotel is being built

where Jalan Pantai meets the shore, right in the very heartland of former backpacker territory. Kuta Square is already a glossy, high-priced reality, as is the Matahari department store.

The result has been that the backpackers have retreated to other necks of the wood. North Bali is still a good deal for anyone on a tight, or tightish, budget. So is Air Panas, beside the crater lake under the shadow of mounts Batur and Abang, despite the opening of a smart new hotel there.

You can still stay in one of the nicest, quietest and most private places in all Bali, the Homestay Balakiran, right in the heart of the former royal palace at Amlapura (Karangasem), for just US$5 or so, the current price for budget accommodation on the island.

There are still places to be found, either with the help of this book or under your own steam, but they're not the dominant styles of accommodation they were in the 1970s, and even the early 1980s. Bali tourism has become very big business, and as usual it's at the expense

of the budget traveler and backpacker plus, of course, the locals who are as often as not deprived of their own entrepreneurial opportunities when the international companies arrive.

Fortunately, budget transport is still available all over Bali. The celebrated (though frequently maligned) *bemo* minibus is still going strong. For instance, a *bemo* will take you from Denpasar to Singaraja and Lovina Beach for less than US$2 — a trip of two hours. Not bad value even if, like this writer, you have to sit on a pile of telephone directories in lieu of a seat.

On short trips along the beach road, such as those between Jalan Pantai and Legian, you'll find US$.30 will suffice. Usually the *kernet* (the boy who touts for passengers and takes your fare) will take more if you offer a larger amount or if you make it obvious you don't know the right fare. But if you get into the habit of offering US$.30, and looking confident, even nonchalant, it's

A trip on the crater lake, near Mount Batur.

probable he'll only ask for more if the fare truly is more — such as on the route from Kuta to Denpasar where it's around US$.50.

There's nowhere better to learn about the best — and cheapest — places to stay than in the places that other backpackers frequent. At a restaurant in Kalibukbuk village in Lovina, a beachside drinks stall in Padangbai, or at a simple *losmen* on Nusa Lembongan (all these, incidentally, are backpacking citadels), you are bound to get the best advice there is on where to stay. At Kuta and Legian, there are still plenty of cheap places left, as indeed there still are in upmarket Ubud. They're there because the Balinese owners want to run them, and because they will never be able to compete with the big companies, their own or the international ones, in the upper price brackets.

Ask around in Seminyak or along Monkey Forest Road in Ubud, and you won't be disappointed. The welcome will be as warm as it ever was, the tips the owner will offer you as useful and well-informed as ever — far better, probably, than you'd get in places charging 20 times as much.

Remember, too, that temple festivals are free. You will be welcome there as long as you turn up wearing a sarong and sash, and especially if the men wear a little white headdress, available for only a few thousand rupiahs at any sarong stall that's catering to the Balinese rather than to the tourists. People will compliment you on your good manners. The Balinese, like thoughtful people everywhere, have never believed these celebrations are the exclusive property of the rich and famous.

Living It Up

Bali is, today, an enormously powerful magnet for the affluent vacationer. There's everything here anyone could possibly want, barring ski slopes and nightly performances of Italian opera. It has become a wonderful playground for those with the means to enjoy it to the full, and every year hundreds of thousands of such visitors fly in, from other parts of Indonesia and all points of the globe, expecting nothing less.

That said, it should be noted that all such temples to tourism are in the southeast of the island. Sanur, Nusa Dua, Ubud and Seminyak are the fashionable places in Bali.

Sanur is where many expatriates live, and there are numerous fine hotels and restaurants in this area. The beach is tame compared to Kuta's, but safe. Several hotels have night clubs, and all of them have restaurants which are delighted to welcome the well-heeled diner.

Nusa Dua is a specially-built tourist enclave containing only five-star hotels. These too have their restaurants and nightlife, but the distance to Kuta or Legian is shorter — a mere 15 minute-drive — and so the glittering lights of this brasher resort area exert that much more of an attraction.

The long beach favored by surfers that extends from the airport (misleadingly called Denpasar Airport) through Tuban, Kuta, Legian, Seminyak and beyond is the center of both brashness and high society. You couldn't get much more brash than some of the nightlife places closest to Bemo Corner, but you can't get much more exclusive, either, than restaurants such as Seminyak's beautifully situated **La Lucciola** or hotels with Old World elegance such as the nearby **Oberoi** or the new all-suite hotel further along the beach from the Oberoi, called simply, **The Legian**. It's because of the youthful, sometimes rowdy, crowd that gathers along Kuta's streets that the area's nightlife has a vibrancy that draws people to it from Sanur and Nusa Dua alike. Legian's **Double Six** is the finest discotheque on the island, and **Goa 2001** one of the nicest places to unwind and get into the mood before going there.

There are problems. There have been muggings in the narrow *gangs* (lanes) leading to houses where some expatriates live in the Seminyak area, and snatching

Sanur is known for its tranquil luxury.

handbags is becoming more common along the Kuta end of Jalan Legian, the main thoroughfare.

Even so, the lure of the area is all but irresistible. The beach is wonderful, the nightlife is compulsively attractive, the restaurants — **Café Luna**, **Poppies**, the **Swiss Restaurant**, **Kafe Warisan** — are as often as not excellent. The little boutiques that are springing up all over Seminyak represent the most chic, up-to-date shopping in all Bali.

Even so, there isn't anywhere more exclusive in Bali or beyond, than the famous Aman resorts, of which Bali now has three. They are the **Amanusa,** atop a hill overlooking the golf course at Nusa Dua; the **Amandari** just outside Ubud with its walled bungalows many of which hide private swimming pools, and **Amankila** with its stunning clifftop location outside Candi Dasa. Nothing is overlooked here. They even have a helicopter to ferry you from one to the other without having to set foot in the ordinary world that separates them. You won't get in, or out, for less than US$460 a night, but you'll want for nothing.

These, then, are arguably the top hotels. The Legian and Oberoi are firm favorites on the Legian–Seminyak side of the island while, down on Jimbaran Beach where the sand meets the rock of Bukit, is the **Four Seasons** hotel. Individual plunge pools, huge villas and wide open views of the sea make this a memorable place to relax, while just a short walk away in the center of Jimbaran Beach, itself, is the newly renovated beach hotel of **Pansea Puri Bali**. On Nusa Dua there is a choice of six hotels but the original **Nusa Dua Beach Hotel**, with its gorgeous gardens, manage to be both smart and informal at the same time. Further afield on Bukit you'll find **Bali Cliff** which is, as its name implies, on a cliff. And what views! On Sanur, head for one of the oldest hotels, still run by its family of owners. **Tandjung Sari** has hosted many a famous celebrity (though it would be indiscreet to mention more than Mick and Jerry, David…) and is renowned for

its sophisticated seclusion. Then, you just have to see **Bali Hyatt**, another hotel where tropical gardens are given a special touch. The hotel is, as it always has been, one of the best on the island.

But the list grows by the hour. There are exclusive resorts and garden hotels in and around Ubud such as the small **Kupu Kupu Barong** and the larger **Ibah Villas**, **Pita Maha** and the new **Four Seasons** in Sayan, not perhaps equal to the Amandari but wonderful, luxurious places nevertheless. The Aman resorts have a sibling in the **Chedi**, a hotel that manages to offer much of the Aman class, at a slightly more affordable price. It's definitely the place for a weekend with a loved one.

The latest new hotel, is Le Meridien, by Tanah Lot, a golf and spa hotel that promises to bring new dimensions to both hostelry and the once quiet temple at Tanah Lot. Increasingly, and on all sides, there are secret little resorts, constructed and maintained with exceptional imagination and devotion,

OPPOSITE: A latecomer to tourism, the lovely beach at Jimbaran, seen from the Inter-Continental Hotel. ABOVE: Watching the sun set at Kuta is an institution.

with perhaps only 10 or 12 private, flower filled bungalows, tucked away in such a manner as, it seems, to give you all the more pleasure in seeking them out. The reality is that they can all be booked via agents in Tokyo, London, Sydney and New York.

Whether you are looking for accommodation, food or nightlife of the best possible kind, you're going to find it in Bali. The **Lotus Cafés** (in Ubud, Candi Dasa and elsewhere) are delightful places to indulge your palate. What better place to dine than around a lotus pond? **Poppies**, too, in Kuta offers such rare pleasures. The large hotels all have their smart restaurants, of course, and if you want to eat in elegant style a beachside meal at Four Seasons, the Bali Hyatt, Sanur or Tandjung Sari will certainly dig into your wallet, but it will leave you with wonderful memories. Health food lovers should head for **Café Batu Jimbar** in Sanur, where delicious dishes are prepared with organically grown produce from the cafés own market garden high in the mountains. With its stunning views across the beach and sea, **La Lucciola**, in Seminyak is a great place for sunsets, sundowners and dinner. Or indeed a long lunch if you want to spend a couple of hours off the beach. Recently opened, the **Olé Olé** in Nusa Dua's Galeria, offers exceptionally good Spanish cuisine.

In fact, you'll stumble upon good restaurants in Ubud, Legian and Sanur in abundance. Enjoy it all while you can. Prices are rising steadily, but for now you can enjoy the high life in Bali for perhaps a third less (sometimes even less) than what you would pay a few thousand miles closer to home.

Family Fun

There are so many things for children to do in Bali, it's likely they'll never want to leave this kids' paradise.

The only real drawback for vacationing with children in Bali is the hot and often humid climate. Make sure they dress appropriately for the heat.

They should be kitted out in hats, shorts and the flimsiest T-shirt or shirt you can find. Cotton is best — it's far cooler than anything else and doesn't irritate the skin the way synthetic fibers do. Loose-fitting shirts allow breezes in, cooling the skin and drying perspiration.

The **beach**, of course, is the prime spot for the family. Here again, you must be mindful of the sun, especially during the hours between 11 AM and 3 PM. Apply plenty of protective sunscreen, cover their shoulders, as that's where they're most likely to burn, and top them off with a floppy hat which protects the neck as well as the head.

To all this, add frequent dips in the sea — they won't need much persuading on that count. On Kuta, Legian and Seminyak beaches swimming and wading should *always* be in the company of an adult — the waves can be very big, and there are dangerous currents in some places. Adults and children alike should swim only between the red and yellow flags — this is the area designated as safe from dangerous currents, as well as the section watched over by the lifeguards.

At Sanur and Nusa Dua the beaches are safe. A coral reef protects the shore line from waves, and the lagoon inside slopes gently towards the reef. Indeed, there may not be much water around at low tide, but then the kids can explore the rock pools, along with numerous locals who are there foraging for the booty of the sea.

WATER FUN
Waterbom (0361-755676 FAX 0361-753517, is at Jalan Kartika Plaza, Kuta, is perfect for kids. The park features a set of pools, slowly moving artificial rivers and water slides integrated in a beautiful garden setting. For the entrance fee you can stay all day and use all the facilities — except restaurants — free of charge (though there is a small charge for the use of lockers).

TOP: You are rarely alone for long in Kuta. Sometimes a blessing, sometimes not! BOTTOM: Waterbom is one of the newer attractions aimed at family fun.

Some of the big slides are quite fast and on these children should be accompanied. The attendants know their jobs, however, and will require that children comply with the park's rules and safety regulations.

There's a special supervised children's park where kids can play while you take a rest. This part is particularly well-supervised and safe, and the kids can play to their hearts' content.

In fact, Waterbom is more suited to children than to adults. The biggest slides are tame for adults. Also ideal for children, is the river where you float slowly along with the water's movement in big rubber dinghies — they can meander along for hours on end, shaded from the sun by overhanging bushes and trees, trailing their hands in the warm tropical water.

You can be fairly certain that if you go once the kids won't let you leave Bali without taking them there again.

Entrance is US$12 for adults and US$6 for children; children under five get in free. Kids under 12 must be accompanied by an adult. Hours are 9 AM to 6 PM.

WILDLIFE
The celebrated Komodo dragon (actually a giant monitor lizard) can be seen at two places — the **Indonesia Jaya Crocodile and Reptile Park** and the **Taman Burung Bali Bird Park** (see DARE A DRAGON in TOP SPOTS, page 24).

On the whole, the bird park is the best place to see the dragons, though there's no reason why you shouldn't visit both it and the reptile park. The bird park, in addition to the fascinating lizards, has 250 exotic species of birds and a lovely garden to relax in. The reptile park, on the other hand, has snakes and crocodiles which may make it popular with older kids.

Then there's dolphin watching. From Lovina in North Bali you can take the children out to see these beautiful creatures frolic at dawn (just about the time young children may be waking up and asking you to take them out anyway). It will cost you very little and

it's an experience both you and they will not forget. For more details, see WATCH DOLPHINS AT PLAY in TOP SPOTS, page 18.

Children are fascinated by **monkeys**, and there are many places to see them in Bali — **Sangeh Monkey Forest** is the most famous, but it's overcrowded for most of the day. Better to go to one of the quieter locations. If you're in North Bali, don't miss taking the kids to the **Monkey Temple** at Pulaki. Here a tribe of the creatures virtually bring what little traffic there is to a halt as they scramble across the road competing for the fruit thrown down for them from passing vehicles. These monkeys are considered sacred, and the fruit given them is in the nature of a temple offering.

Then there are monkeys at **Ulu Watu temple** (refer to SEE ULU WATU in TOP SPOTS, page 11 and TEMPLE ABOVE THE STONE in THE BROAD HIGHWAY, page 167), naughty ones these who will steal anything you happen to put down, even if you only leave it for a moment.

A special experience is to be had at the small monkey forest at **Kedaton** (see SOUTH BALI: TANAH LOT TO UBUD in THE BROAD HIGHWAY, page 182). Here there are only a relatively small number of monkeys, though their numbers are likely to grow if they see you have peanuts or bananas.

Also at Kedaton you can see the awesome giant fruit bats hanging in the treetops like torn strips of black plastic.

CLUB MEDITÉRRANÉE
Anyone coming to Bali with children should consider booking into the **Club Meditérranée**. Much has been written about the advantages and disadvantages of Club Med vacations; but, if you have children to consider, the advantages decisively outweigh the disadvantages.

Club Med operates a Kid's Club in which all except the youngest children are taken off your hands for the daylight hours. They form a tribe with the other kids and, under the supervision of

Pura Pulaki, Pemuteran, West Bali. Every village, however small, has its village temple.

friendly and young group leaders, they dress up, have their faces painted, learn songs, swim and engage in all the games the imagination can devise. It's paradise for children and for their parents. Both have the vacation of their dreams.

No one else organizes this kind of holiday quite like Club Med. Children often spend their vacations longing to make friends and yet never quite getting it off the ground. Here the combination of kids from all over the world, new friendships, shared experiences, doing things geared especially for them and leaving parents free to relax as they wish, is an unbeatable combination.

Cultural Kicks

As a friend once remarked to me, dance is the key to Balinese social behavior. However much money the Balinese make from tourism, it's their festivals, with all the rituals and dance, they care about most. This is where much of the profits go.

In Bali, religion and culture are inseparable. Taken as a whole, it is what binds people together in a humane and life-enhancing way. Although it is capable of changing with the times, its underlying premises are fixed, expressing an attitude to the universe and enacting that expression in colorful rituals that ordinary people can both understand and participate in.

Despite its airport and gas stations, Bali is a living example of a world where the collective good still benefits the individual, a world which is coherent, hierarchic, ornate and sustaining.

When you go to see a Kecak Dance, as you must, it is important to be aware what it is you're seeing. The men chant unaccompanied, joyfully playing their parts. They are at one; it's their being, their life. They know that the tourists they serve in the daytime earn 30 times more than they do, but they have something few of their onlookers can claim — a society that gives their lives meaning.

The place to see Balinese dance and theater — and they are essentially one and the same — at their best is **Ubud**. You can see the authentic artical in context at a temple festival, where the dances are being performed, as they were intended, for the benefit of the gods. But in Ubud, though the dances are being put on for your benefit, at least they are being done well, for connoisseurs and not for a mass audience.

The following schedule for dance performances in and around Ubud may have changed by the time you arrive in Bali, but it's unlikely. In essential form it hasn't changed in many years. Most performances start at 7:30 PM and tickets are generally priced around US$3.50.

Monday, there is a performance of the Legong Dance, preceded by other dances, at the **Ubud Palace**. At the same time, in nearby **Bona Village**, there is a Kecak and Trance Dance, while at **Ubud's Jaba Pura Padang Kerta, Padang Tegal Kelod**, there are Barong and Kris dances.

Tuesday, see the Mahabharata Dance at **Teges Village**, three kilometers (two miles) from Ubud, the Ramayana Ballet in Ubud Palace, and several other dances elsewhere.

Wednesday, see the Wayang Kulit, the shadow puppet plays, at **Oka Kartini,** the Legong and Barong dances at Ubud Palace, and a repeat of Monday's Kecak Dance in the same location as on Monday.

Thursday, it's the turn of the Gabor Dance at Ubud Palace and the Calonarang Dance at the village of **Mewang**, nine kilometers away (transport from Ubud is provided for these out-of-town shows).

Friday, see another Barong Dance performed by a different troupe at the Ubud Palace, a Legong Dance at **Peliatan Village** (two kilometers or just over a mile from Ubud) and a Kecak and Trance Dance at the **Pura Dalem**.

Saturday, there is another Legong program at Ubud Palace from a different troupe plus a Calonarang Dance (as on Thursday).

Tourists can buy souvenir *rangda* masks to take home.

Sunday, see the Kecak Dance repeated as for Monday, another Kecak in Ubud itself.

The full list can be obtained from the **Ubud Tourist Information Office** on Jalan Raya, Ubud. They don't have much else, but this list is useful, indeed vital. They also sell tickets.

Even on Kuta Beach you can't escape Bali's distinctive culture. Processions arrive at unexpected moments, and whether you're playing football or sunning yourself, it won't make the slightest difference to the celebrants.

There are museums in Bali, of course, but museums are a poor reflection of what Balinese culture is about. It's no wonder, nor does it perhaps matter much, that many of them appear neglected. When a people are living their culture in the way the Balinese are, they don't need museums. It's only when cultures have died that museums spring up as a testimony to what has been lost.

Shop till You Drop

There's a world of shopping in Bali, but take it easy, and don't let the low prices and high quality go to your head.

First, there are the giant shopping plazas that are now a feature of Indonesia and Bali. **Bali Shopping World** and **Plaza Bali** are both on Jalan Bypass, Ngurah Rai, near the airport.

On a more manageable scale, there is **Matahari**, the department store on Kuta Square (not to be confused with the other, smaller Matahari on Jalan Legian). Here, in the Kuta Square Matahari, Indonesian and foreign goods are sold at very much metropolitan prices, though the air-conditioned and compact nature of the place make it convenient.

Kuta Square itself is the big new addition to Bali's shopping scene. It's lined with shops that are certain to appeal to the visitor, even though for an hour or so he may think he's back in Perth or Singapore. This is where the typical single story boutique-style shops of Legian and Seminyak give way to a

three-story shopping street, with broad pavements and bright street lights.

By and large, prices here are fixed, unlike those in other parts of Bali, but you might get a discount if you buy more than one item. The important thing here is to ask.

Casual and **fashion clothes** are on offer at Jack Nicklaus (for sportswear), Sweet Poison and Rascals (specializing in women's swimwear, plus local products such as sarongs and batik fabrics).

More formal styles can be seen, as you would expect, at Nina Ricci, Polo Ralph Lauren, Dolce and Gabbana. For casual wear there's Benneton and Perahu, Hammer, Milo and many more. For **surfing gear** check out Billabong and Dreamland.

As you'll by now realize, Kuta Square is mostly for fashionable international labels, possibly somewhat cheaper than you'd find them at home. If it's **locally produced items of clothing** you're after, take a deep breath and head for the so-called Arts and Crafts Market at the end of Jalan Bakungsari, close to Matahari and facing the beach.

Bargaining is the name of the game at the Arts and Crafts Market. Everything will be offered to you at a much higher price than the retailer is prepared to accept. Bargain hard, but not too hard (see BARGAINING in TRAVELERS' TIPS, page 245).

Sarongs, T-shirts and shorts are the staples of this market. You'll be tempted to go into some stalls simply to get out of the sun — don't fell obligated to buy. Many of the same goods can be seen in stall after stall, such as the infamous T-shirt that begins "No, I don't want a *** bemo," and carries on in a similar fashion down the list of Bali's much-touted attractions.

Over in **Nusa Dua** things are a great deal more sophisticated, and a great deal more expensive. The place to look here is

Balinese life is by no means all temple ritual — TOP: A vendor of non traditional masks in Denpasar. BOTTOM: Massage at Kuta Beach. Note the numbered sun hats. All masseurs must obtain a license. Half an hour's massage costs under US$1.

the shopping complex called **Galeria**. It includes a supermarket, Tragia, and a department store, Galeri Keris. It's a good place to search for a host of presents in one air-conditioned, hassle-free environment. You'll find perfumes, woodcarvings, cafés and banks. But don't expect bargains.

Sanur is notable for its quiet, exclusive shops along Jalan Danau Tamblingan where you can buy, notably, antiques and reproductions. These are often hard to distinguish, and to the Balinese mind not worth distinguishing. If something's well made they tend to think it doesn't matter much how new or old it is.

Also in Sanur are exclusive fashions, including leather, but not much in the way of mass-produced trinkets. See SANUR in THE BROAD HIGHWAY, page 155, for specific recommendations.

Ubud is the place to go for **paintings**, but it's a specialized market these days. See ART AND CRAFTS in BALINESE CULTURE, page 133, under UBUD in THE BROAD HIGHWAY, page 185, and BUY A PAINTING FROM A WOMAN ARTIST in TOP SPOTS, page 26, for advice.

The best approach to buying art is simply to choose something that pleases you. **Club Med** has an excellent selection in an area of the hotel where local retailers sell their wares. Access to Club Med for nonguests is now available in lunchtime and dinnertime packages. See under NUSA DUA AND THE BUKIT in THE BROAD HIGHWAY, page 161, for details.

Mas is the place to buy **woodcarvings**, and **Celuk** is the spot for **silverware**, with the neighboring village of **Singapadu** offering considerably lower prices for similar, sometimes identical, products.

If you enjoy looking in **boutiques** and **intimate accessory shops**, the place to go is the burgeoning center of **Seminyak** where there are numerous small shops of high quality catering for the discerning buyer. Picture frames made to order, highly original wrought-iron candlesticks, handmade clothing — all these things are to be found along the road called for much of its length Jalan Legian, but

which changes its name several times as it turns and turns again on its way out into the paddy fields of Canggu, in the direction of the landmark Oberoi Hotel.

Short Breaks

If I had to steel myself to accept just a short trip to Bali, this is what I would do in three days, and in five.

THREE DAY STAY
With only **three days** there, I'd spend the first on the beach at Legian, staying at the Legian Beach Hotel with its access directly onto the sand. The surf on the beach is incomparable, and part of the very essence of Bali. You certainly don't need to be a professional surfer to enjoy these often huge waves, and between periods of frolicking in them you can sit on a sun chair under a large white umbrella and watch the brilliant action.

I'd take lunch at one of the little beach stalls located just a short walk west, perhaps the one called Tivoli which is especially attentive to hygiene. Later, after admiring the incomparable sunset, I'd dine at the modest but always

OPPOSITE: At almost all tourist spots in Bali visitors will encounter entrepreneurs such as this woman selling fabric at Lake Batur. Though ubiquitous, these vendors are honest and usually offer good value. ABOVE: Masks make fun and inexpensive mementos of a Balinese visit.

excellent French Restaurant at Topi Kopi, a kilometer or so away. I'd then spend the evening at Goa 2001 and afterwards at whichever discotheque was open that night, hoping it would be Double Six, but happily settling, if need be, for the nearby Gado Gado (they open on alternate evenings).

The second day I'd go up to Ubud. Lunch at Café Lotus would be followed by a few hours wandering along the paths that crisscross the quiet countryside nearby, in preparation for dinner at a hotel (Kupu Kupu Barong if I could afford it). Then I'd go to a dance or *wayang kulit* shadow puppet performance. These are staged every night, either in Ubud itself or nearby.

On my last day I'd get driven out to Ulu Watu to see the cliff top temple, come back into the Kuta, Legian and Seminyak area for some shopping, and then repeat the first night's clubbing — there's probably nowhere to equal the scene anywhere in the world.

FIVE DAY STAY

With **five days** at my disposal I'd add a trip to Lovina, North Bali. I'd stay at the humblest of *losmen*, probably the Pulestis with its large fan-cooled rooms and little swimming pool, and have dinner after I arrived at the friendly and comfortable Sea Breeze restaurant overlooking the beach. I'd then get an early night in preparation for a 6 AM start in order to go out with the fishermen to see the dolphins and the sunrise.

After breakfast, perhaps at the Warung Kopi, I'd arrange transport and drive west to say hello to the monkeys at Pulaki Monkey Temple on the road to Gilimanuk. Then I'd turn back towards Lovina and take the side road up to the hot springs at Banjar. There I'd lie for an hour in the soothing waters before taking lunch at the modest poolside restaurant.

I'd then drive up to Kintamani and check in at the Lakeview Hotel at Penelokan and admire the view of Mount Batur and Lake Batur beneath it. After dinner at the hotel, and another early night, I'd awaken at 3 AM in order

to climb Mount Batur, with a guide arranged by the Lakeview, for another incomparable Balinese sunrise.

IN THE LAP OF ABSOLUTE LUXURY

Alternatively, with absolutely no spending limit, the following possibilities present themselves.

Ubud's **Amandari** or **Kupu Kupu Barong** provides a wonderful introduction to inland Bali. After one night at either of these you could take an hour's taxi ride to Nusa Dua and check in at the **Amanusa**. (If you've stayed at Amandari in Ubud, the company will, of course, transport you to their other themselves in the style to which you will be no doubt quickly be becoming accustomed).

The third day the Aman resorts people would whisk you, perhaps by helicopter, to their Amankila cliff top retreat above Candi Dasa.

This would be a trip featuring the most exquisite food, the finest wines, spacious accommodation which manages to be luxurious yet, at the same time, full of delightful local elements, plus Balinese dance in the evenings in Ubud, golf at Nusa Dua, and sea bathing at both Nusa Dua and Candi Dasa.

If five days are available add two nights at Legian's **Oberoi Hotel**. The beach here is greatly superior to those at Nusa Dua and Candi Dasa. You have to watch out for dangerous currents a short way to the left or right of the hotel, but there is a Surf Rescue watch at the Oberoi so you should be all right there.

The Oberoi's accommodation is in individual rooms set singly (or in pairs) in a beachfront garden. There is a coffee shop in sight of the surf, plus extensive room-service. All the restaurants and fashionable boutiques of Seminyak and Legian are within a few minutes' drive.

Festive Flings

Bali is a nonstop festival. On almost every day of the year there's a temple somewhere celebrating its *odalan* (the anniversary festival when the temple is rededicated). Only on a few days deemed especially inauspicious is there nothing on.

You can go to any of these festivals without an invitation — see VISIT A TEMPLE FESTIVAL in TOP SPOTS, page 15, for details of how to arrange it.

Sometimes it's the day for the big one. It's not possible to list dates for these major festivals here because they're fixed, like the Christian celebration of Easter, according to a changing calendar. In the case of Bali it's both the lunar calendar and a 210-day cycle. Ask the Badung Government Tourist Office in Denpasar for the dates of Galungan and Kuningan (which follows ten days after Galungan). Unlike the *odalan* festivals celebrated at just one temple, these are big island-wide occasions. Galungan has been described — inaccurately — as the Balinese

OPPOSITE: Each day the Balinese make offerings of food and fruit to appease the gods. They can often be seen, late afternoon, carrying these to temple. BELOW: The colorful Malasti ceremony, Pantai Purnama, near Sukawati. OVERLEAF: Building a paper and bamboo funeral tower.

Christmas. But it's certainly a time for many traditions to be aired, giant *barong* masked figures to be paraded through the streets, the fluttering *penjors*, bamboo banners, to be erected outside each home and long and elaborate dance dramas to be performed. It is a time to visit family and friends, to share a feast together and to visit the recently cleaned temples.

Kuningan is quieter, a purification day related to the holy spring of Tirta Empul at Tampaksiring.

Nyepi is the **Balinese New Year's Day**. Many visitors are caught unawares by this holiday. It's a day when no one is allowed out of their hotels. That's right, you have to stay inside your hotel or its garden all day on this one day of the year, falling at the end of March or early April. No one is allowed on the beach, and you could get into serious trouble if you try to go there. The hotels apologize, caught half way between their desire not to upset visitors and their reverence for Balinese tradition. Fires are forbidden, power supplies are switched off in town (though the bigger hotels have their own generators, and shaded lights within their compounds are in practice tolerated).

The idea behind Nyepi is to deceive the evil spirits into believing the island is uninhabited. The showing of any light on the night of Nyepi (though not the eve) can result in stones being thrown through offending windows. Though flights continue to operate, and cars, with special permits, are allowed on the streets to take tourists to and from the airport, all other forms of transport are forbidden. Even on the day after Nyepi many shops remain closed, though beach life more or less gets back into full swing.

If you don't want to run into Nyepi on your holiday, ascertain the exact date from your travel agent and plan accordingly. It can be a major cause of annoyance and of complaints from visitors, especially if they're in Bali for only a few days.

On the other hand, the night before Nyepi is a great and wonderful festival. Giant images, known as *oggi-oggi*, are paraded through the streets, each section

(or *banjar*) of a town competing in the size and imaginativeness of its constructions. They are carried down the streets on bamboo platforms held aloft by 20 or so young men, and in Denpasar the display is particularly marvelous. The parade was banned in 1997, ostensibly on the grounds that there had been disturbances the previous year, but more likely because of the national elections that were then pending. This spectacular event should be back in its usual place and time in future.

Galloping Gourmets

There's nearly everything on earth for gourmets in Bali. It's astonishing how cuisines from places as far from Bali as Mexico and China, Korea and Italy, can all be found here, often with a choice of competing venues. Vegetarians will find plenty of dishes in most of the local restaurants which correspond to their requirements.

Balinese food itself is not among the world's great cuisines. This is reflected in the fact that, although you can find some traditional dishes, most restaurants and cafés serve Indonesian specialities, foreign cuisines or, more interestingly, cuisines where East and West marry in a novel synthesis of flavor.

For Indonesian food there's nowhere better than the beach restaurants at Jimbaran at dinner time; we had a fine meal at Ramayana, and the others are likely to be just as good. Try **Lagoona** at the Bali Hilton in Nusa Dua, the **Tandjung Sari** in Sanur, or else the **Ikan Restaurant** in the Sheraton. Other places to enjoy Indonesian fare are the **Melati Restaurant** at the Kartika Plaza hotel in Kuta and the nearby **Ratna Satay Terrace** on the roof of the Bali Hai Holiday Inn.

Aromas of Bali on Kuta's Jalan Legian is the famous vegetarian place, with its exotic dishes and quiet garden setting. On Sanur, **Café Batu Jimbar** specializes in healthy dishes as the owner operates his own organic vegetable garden up on the road to Pupuan.

Remember the old favorites where just about anything can be found. Top of the list are **Poppies**, in Poppies' Lane, Kuta, and **Made's Warung**, with its original location on Jalan Pantai in central Kuta, and its new incarnation three kilometers (two miles) west in Seminyak.

Japanese food is popular in Bali on account of the large numbers of Japanese visitors who holiday there. There's the **Benkay Japanese Restaurant** at the Hotel Nikko, the **Genji** at the Bali Hilton, the **Hamabe** at the Sheraton and the **Inagiku** at the Grand Hyatt — all in or very close to Nusa Dua.

For sushi there are the four restaurants run by the **Ryoshi** chain, one situated on Jalan Raya Seminyak in Legian, near Goa

2001; and there's more sushi at **Goa 2001** itself, late night from 10 PM until 2 PM. Don't be put off by the crowds standing round drinking beers; the sushi bar is at the back — just walk on through.

Top class Cantonese and Szechuan specialties can be eaten at the elegant **Telaga Naga** (281234, extension 8080, run by the Bali Hyatt in separate premises in central Sanur. The situation is delightful enough in itself, a traditional Chinese garden with little arched bridges and red paper lanterns. At the Grand Hyatt in Nusa Dua (note that there are two Hyatt hotels in Bali) you can eat classic Cantonese dishes at

Balinese rice cakes (*jaja*) presented in banana leaves.

the **Mei Yan** restaurant, including anything from diced abalone to Peking duck.

When it comes to **Italian** food you're spoiled for choice, whether you're in Legian, Seminyak, Sanur or Ubud. Café Luna on Jalan Legian is one of the best — fashionable but serving large portions — while La Lucciola on the beach is elegant (and solidly booked not only for its Italian-Australian cuisine but for its sunsets which are out of this world). At Ubud there's the fine **Lotus Café** with its homemade pasta; they have restaurants in several other places including Candi Dasa. In Nusa Dua the Grand Hyatt has its **Salsa Verde** and the Sheraton its **La Trattoria**. In Sanur there's the beachside **La Taverna Italian Restaurant**, and the excellent **Mamma Lucia** on the main street. For Italian-Californian cuisine try **La Cascata** at the Grand Mirage hotel in Tanjung Benoa.

Mexican food is on offer in several places. There's the long-established **TJ's** in Poppies' Lane in Kuta, **Poco Loco** on Jalan Padma Utara, also in Kuta, with another branch in Nusa Dua on Jalan Pantai Mengiat.

Opposite this, you'll find **Spanish** food and tapas at **Pica Pica**. At Galeria in Nusa Dua, the **Olé Olé (** 771886 has built a reputation for itself with its Spanish and Mediterranean cuisine. Also there is **On the Rocks**, a new restaurant where you eat meats, poultry and fish, Pacific islands style, cooked on hot rocks. The desserts are "to die for." Another top notch restaurant is the **Kafe Warisan**, in Jalan Raya Kerobokan, which has recently reopened with a talented French chef and has already earned a reputation for itself.

First-class **Korean** food is available too, though at only one place on the island — **Chong Gi-Wa** on Jalan Bypass in Sanur.

In addition to the world of dining, Bali has at least one food product on offer that you might want to sample or take home with you. **Balinese coffee**, or *kopi bali,* as the locals call it, has a distinctive flavor — different from Brazilian, Kenyan or

Colombian coffees. A couple of packs will remind you of your stay when you get home, or do nicely as presents for some of your favorite coffee-loving friends. This is not the grainy, black coffee served for breakfast everywhere from Gilimanuk to Ulu Watu, but the export quality product that the Balinese coffee growing industry has been perfecting over the years. You can find fine Balinese coffee at any supermarket. Look for the Butterfly Globe Brand of Bali Gourmet Coffee. Or visit the special showroom and taste a good coffee in Denpasar at Jalan Gajah Mada 80. Look for the "Bhineka Jaya" sign.

Special Interests

The origins of tattooing were in the East, but this art form was popularized throughout the world largely by sailors.

Although you'll find tattooists in practically every country, it's not surprising that many enthusiasts look to the East in search of magnificent designs and skilled craftsmanship, as well as for prices a great deal lower than they would have to pay at home.

62   YOUR CHOICE

Bali's tattoo artists do a vigorous trade from people seeking to have traditional Asian skills writ large all over their bodies. You can take holiday mementos of various kinds home with you; none is more vivid than a tattoo.

When the world's first tattooing convention was held in Vienna in the early 1990s, with a poster featuring a tattooed Mozart, Bali's tattooists were not forgotten. They may work in small premises often on equally small side streets, but the result of their labors travels with its recipients, and their work is seen worldwide.

Whether enthusiasts choose Bali for the inexpensive price of its tattoos or their high artistic quality, there are several artists' establishments to choose from. **Alit's Tattoo** (0361-483527 just outside Denpasar (at Jalan Imam Bonjol N°198) is famous — his needle rattles and jumps as the traffic roars past his windows. **Made Bugik's Demon Art Tattoo,** on Jalan Double Six, does a fine job, too, with thousands of designs to choose from. Agung Wah ("Tonto") has his place, called **Tattoo Body Art Design** on Jalan Benesan in Kuta, the side street that runs towards the sea almost

opposite the Matahari cinemas on Jalan Legian.

PRETTY AS A PICTURE

If you don't want a design on your body, maybe you'd like your body as part of a design.

There are a couple of companies that specialize in the ingenious concept of postcards bearing a photograph of the customer wearing Indonesian traditional costume. Your friends back home may expect to see snapshots of you on the beach or postcards saying "wish you were here," but it's likely they'll be surprised to receive a picture postcard bearing a photo of you smiling out at them in the garb of a traditional chief from Kalimantan, a Javanese bride or a Balinese prince.

Sari Artistik Foto (/FAX 0361-758882, Kuta Center, Block III, Shop N°E7, will arrange it. You go there for an hour or so one day, and three or four days later they will have produced old-fashioned-looking sepia photos, individually hand-colored and then printed. You can also order a large framed version to hang on your livingroom wall.

Quicker, and cheaper, are the color photos of you in similar dress arranged by **Diamond Photo Studio and Photo Supply** (0361-426903, at Jalan Thamrin N°5, Denpasar, and also on Kuta Square.

LETTING OFF STEAM

Lastly, let's hope you can sublimate your fighting instincts rather than stimulate them by engaging in simulated war games. **Bali Splat Mas** (0361-289073, Jalan Danau Tamblingan N°118, Sanur, allows you to fire paint balls at your friends in one of a series of "jungle skirmishes" where the aim is to capture the enemy's flag. Safety supervision is by Australian and Indonesian referees.

As an extension to its already internationally acclaimed artistic repertoire, the island has gained a reputation for its fine and innovative tattooing. OPPOSITE and ABOVE: Two fine examples of this art, seen along the east coast. OVERLEAF: Lilies and flowering trees adorn the shores of a "floating" temple.

Taking a Tour

There's an intensely competitive world of tours in, around and beyond Bali. Everyone seems to be in on the game of taking you somewhere and showing you what to do. And, because so many of the key Bali attractions are to do with the sea, most of the tours are by water.

You can, for example, go on various tours organized by **Bali Hai** (0361-701888 FAX 0361-701777, which leave from Benoa Harbor. Two of them will take you to Lembongan Island for the day. Their Beach Club Cruise Family Package includes snorkeling, buffet lunch on the beach, special children's program, optional SCUBA diving (recommended) or glass-bottom boat trips (not recommended on account of the poor condition of the coral reef in the area) and fun rides on banana boats — long inflated sausages you sit astride in a line and hope for the best. Or you can opt for all of these activities in a single package, called the Lembongan Island Reef Cruise.

Bali Hai also offers the Sunset Dinner Cruise (two and a half hours) where the entertainment is one of the most amusing around — an all-Indonesian drag show.

Quicksilver Tours (0361-771997 FAX 0361-771967 will take you over to Nusa Penida, the large, mostly barren limestone island east of Benoa and Sanur. Departures for this are from Tanjung Benoa (not to be confused with Benoa Harbor where most of the other tours leave from and a 20-minute drive away on the other side of the bay).

Quicksilver's deal is similar to Bali Hai's, with a semi-submersible coral-viewing submarine, optional snorkeling or SCUBA diving, and trips onto the island.

Touring also to Nusa Lembongan, **Lembongan Express** MOBILE (0811-393387 or (0361-724545 is a locally-run operation that gives you the off shore experience at about half the price of the others. Using a traditional 20-m (65-ft) outrigger, they also offer an overnight option on the

island. "Secure jobs for locals and protect our environment!" they say. You could certainly give them a try, though the smaller size of their vessel may upset some people in the often heavy swell of the Badung Strait that separates Nusa Lembongan from Bali.

The organization known as **Waka Louka** (0361-484085 FAX 0361-484767 runs several tours. One of them is again to Lembongan Island, but in this case its by sailing ship. The 23-m (75-ft) catamaran sails from Benoa Harbor, and, in addition to all the facilities offered by the other Lembongan cruises, you have the option of staying at the small but upmarket Waka Nusa Resort on the island (see under NUSA LEMBONGAN in OFF THE BEATEN TRACK, page 226, for details).

Other sailing experiences are to Lembongan are offered by **Rasa Yacht Charters** (0361-288756, with 30-m (100-ft) vessels taking eight and 12 people, and **Island Explorer Cruises** (0361-289856 FAX 0361-289837 in an 18-m (60-ft) sailing yacht, the *Island Explorer*, which heads off in the same direction (Penida and Lembongan), as does their motor cruiser. *Sojourn* (0361-287450 FAX 0361-287125 also takes you in the same general direction in red-sailed splendor.

Note that all of these cruises have to negotiate the swell prone Badung Strait.

Trips inland are also organized by Waka Louka (above). They will drive you up to their Rainforest Camp in a Land Rover and show you hot springs, rice terraces, a traditional farmhouse and generally get you into the feel of upland Bali, as well as giving you a smart lunch.

For other Bali land tours, try **Satriavi Tours** (0361-287074 or **Tunas Indonesia** (0361-288581 FAX 0361-288727. For trips from Bali to the other Indonesian islands, see BEYOND BALI in TRAVELERS' TIPS, page 240.

Everywhere you travel in Bali, you'll hear the sound of water. Each village has a water engineer whose job it is to ensure the smooth flow of water from one rice terrace to another. In managing the water so efficiently, the villagers are able to cultivate three crops a year using simple, traditional methods of plowing, planting and harvesting.

Volcanoes in the Sea

MOST GEOGRAPHERS believe that Australia is slowly but unstoppably moving northward. It's nothing to worry about — reliable estimates put the speed of this movement at approximately equal to that of the growth of a human fingernail. Nevertheless, the immense area of ocean floor surrounding the Australian landmass has, over the millennia, edged up against the sea bed extending south from mainland Asia, and, where they have made contact, been forced downwards and underneath it. Consequently, the edge of what the geologists call the Australian Plate

To be accurate, not all the islands of this immense country, which straddles the equator for 5,500 km (3,400 miles) and spreads itself over three time zones, are volcanic in origin. Bali is, though. Virtually the entire island is made up of what volcanoes past and present have pushed above the waters of the Indian Ocean. Bali is its volcanoes. Two of them, Agung and Batur, have erupted this century, Batur twice. Yet despite this, Bali, like its neighbor Java, teems with people. The reason is simple: No soil is as fertile as that produced by volcanic ash; with a constant

now lies under the edge of the Asian one, and, as it nudges its way northward, it is forced deeper and deeper into the molten magma of the earth's inner mantle.

Owing to the phenomenal heat in the earth's depths, these slowly descending rocks have melted. In addition, movement on such a scale has caused unimaginable pressure to build up underground. Consequently this newly molten material has taken advantage of weaknesses in the earth's crust to burst through and surge upwards. The result has been, strung out along a line marking the meeting point of two continents, a chain of volcanoes, and subsequently of islands. These islands were for long known as the East Indies and are now called Indonesia.

supply of water for irrigation guaranteed year-round by the water retaining volcanic uplands and craters, the island is a rice grower's paradise.

With over 170 million people, Indonesia is the fifth most populous country on earth, after China, India, Russia and the United States. Two and a half million live on Bali. This may not seem excessive for an island 150 km (90 miles) by 80 km (50 miles), but when you consider that the mountainous interior is thinly populated, that the inland

OPPOSITE: Part of the palace of the Rajah of Kerangasem (modern Amlapura), with Mount Agung behind. ABOVE: Rice terraces near Ubud. Bali's intricate terracing system, one of its many glories, is best seen in the center and east of the island.

arid west is almost deserted, and that there are no cities to speak of, this represents a considerable population density.

Life on this favored tropical island has probably never been particularly hard. So easy has it been for Bali's farmers to grow two crops of rice a year, there has always been time to spare for other activities. The result is Bali's celebrated dance dramas, temple festivals and generally easygoing way of life that had the early tourists from the West, back in the Thirties, concluding they had at last discovered the earthly paradise.

AN EQUABLE CLIMATE

Bali enjoys a benign climate. Situated on the southern edge of the equatorial belt, it does not experience the yearlong rainfall that produces the rain forests of the Amazon or the Congo. Instead, Bali has a long dry season, roughly from April to October, and a short wet season, November to March.

These seasons are caused by the relative heating and cooling of the great continents to the south and north of Indonesia. In the Australian summer that continent becomes hotter than its surrounding seas. Hot air rises, and so winds are ultimately drawn in from the cooling continent of Asia to the north. Deflected sideways by the rotation of the earth, these winds, wet because they have crossed the seas to the north of Indonesia, become Bali's wet season northwest monsoon. By contrast, in the Australian winter, winds blow northward from the cooling continent and, coming from so dry a place across a relatively narrow ocean, become the southeasterlies of Bali's dry season.

Records show that the south of the island receives annually 78 percent of the maximum possible sunlight (and 63 percent even in January, the wettest month), as a result, even during the rainy season skies are often clear for days on end. Furthermore, though it is often hot, temperatures never equal the heights they can reach, for example, during a Greek or North African summer. Cooling breezes attracted inland from the sea by the high volcanoes ensure a climate where on the coast the average monthly temperature does not exceed 31°C (89°F), yet where the average monthly mini-

mum never drops below 24°C (78°F). Day and night, wet season and dry, the temperature remains warm and equable. It is much cooler, and with a greater difference between day and nightime temperatures, up in the mountainous regions.

The relatively high humidity — 75 percent on average — prevents the Balinese climate from being ideal. Humidity can make temperatures that are not excessive in themselves at times extremely wearying.

A TROPICAL LANDSCAPE

The physical shape of Bali is a product of the forces that created it.

The volcanoes that form its central spine fall steeply to the sea in the north, leaving

only a few valleys and a narrow coastal strip where agriculture is possible. To the south and east of the mountains, however, because the land has been lifted by the deeply burrowing edge of the Australian Coastal Plate, the slopes are gentler and alluvial plains have been deposited. This area of rich volcanic soils cut into by fast flowing streams is the Balinese heartland and the home of its great kingdoms and their highly developed cultures.

The same lifting that produced lush South Bali also raised from the sea bed the large limestone island of Nusa Penida, and the peninsula south of the airport, probably also once an island, known as the Bukit.

West Bali tapers away toward Java as the land-creating volcanoes, which now seem extinct, decrease in size.

Bali's coral reefs and silted up estuaries mean that the island is without natural harbors. During the dry season the south-easterlies produce the heavy surf for which southern Bali is famous, but which makes landing any kind of boat difficult. During wet months the northwest monsoon makes access to Singaraja in northern Bali (the closet thing Bali has to a natural harbor) all but impossible. Nowadays large ships use Benoa in the east, but even here liners have to anchor offshore and off load their passengers by lighter. Southwest Bali, protected by Java from the worst of the weather, is the home of the island's largest fishing fleets.

Rice harvesting is done by the whole village and entirely by hand. OVERLEAF: If Kuta is known for its sunsets, then the north coast has its sunrises.

Volcanoes in the Sea

Bali's fauna and flora are similar to those of Java. The roar of the old Balinese tiger has probably been silenced now forever, even in its last refuges in remote West Bali. Similarly, crocodiles are no longer on show in the Prancak River. Wild monkeys, though, are still common, as are various kinds of bats. Turtles are regularly caught and slaughtered for temple feasts. The domesticated Balinese pig can be seen in every village, and so can the beautiful faun-like Balinese cattle. Water buffalo can be seen lugging carts along the roads in the northern parts of the island.

Bali's forests consist of the spectacularly tall and skeletal coral tree, the erect and unbranching *pala*, teak, mahogany and, high on the mountains, pine. A sacred banyan tree stands somewhere in every village, and huge *kepuh* are frequently found growing round cemeteries. There are several species of palm —coconut, *lontar* (providing leaves for making books in the traditional style), *sago* (providing sap for palm beer and material for thatching) and *salak* (yielding the fruit of the same name). The waxy white and yellow flowers of the frangipani (*kamboja*) spread their sweet scent around many a temple precinct, and protect the buried sections of wooden building posts from rot.

FROM JAVA MAN TO GOLKAR

It's almost certain that humans originally spread outwards from the tropical regions of the world, and specimens of early man have been found in Java. The basic Malay-type population of modern Indonesia appears to have been there for several thousand years at least, and the evidence of the wide extent of peoples speaking Malayo-Polynesian languages points to a large ethnic group extending from peninsular Malaysia in the west eastwards to the Philippines.

To this population, with its belief in spirits that inhabit all places and all things, came Indian Hinduism, in about the second century AD. The reasons for this are easy to see: To travel from India to China without crossing the highest mountain ranges on the

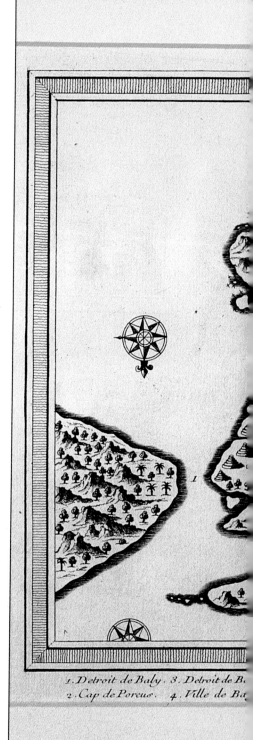

1. *Detroit de Baly* . 3. *Detroit de B.*
2. *Cap de Porcus* . 4. *Ville de Ba*

And old French map of Bali. The island is seen from the north, with Java to the right and Nusa Penida to the left. The number "4" marks Denpasar, "Ville de Baly."

Volcanoes in the Sea

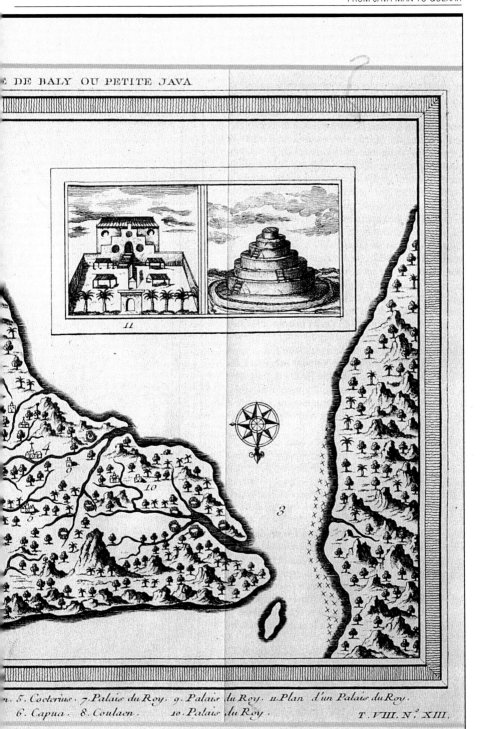

E DE BALY OU PETITE JAVA

11

5. Cocterius. 7. Palais du Roy. 9. Palais du Roy. 11. Plan d'un Palais du Roy.
6. Capua. 8. Coulaen. 10. Palais du Roy.

T. VIII. N.º XIII.

planet, you must sail south down the coast of Myanmar (Burma) and through the narrow Straits of Malacca that lie between Peninsular Malaysia and Sumatra.

Once trade became established along this route, it cannot have been long before the desire of the Indian merchants to trade with the islands, and especially with rich Java to the south, combined with the ambitions of the Sumatrans to exert some measure of control over the trade sailing past their shores — all factors which contributed to extensive cultural interaction. Then the natural tendency of the more complex and highly organized culture to dominate the simpler and less sophisticated one meant that both Indian and Chinese influences on the tropical islands south of the Asian mainland began early.

Along with Hinduism, the Indian merchants and priests brought with them their complexly interrelated culture — Sanskrit, the caste system and Hindu mythology. Remnants of all these aspects are still found even in Moslem Java, where the shadow puppet plays and the dance dramas continue to portray the characters of the great Indian epics.

Under these influences, and with a naturally rich soil, Java eventually produced a series of powerful Hindu, and later Buddhist, civilizations, from the Mataran to the Majapahit. Sumatra, less easy to cultivate, concentrated on the control of trade, and its Srivijaya empire too flourished. At their most extensive, the maritime trade routes stretched from China to Arabia and East Africa, and all through the Straits of Malacca. Bali, rather on the edge of things, and lacking both the natural resources and harbors of Java, joined and left empires as they waxed and waned.

These old Hindu empires, with connections as far west as Madagascar, must have been quite exotic. How far their imported culture penetrated into the lives of the ordinary people is another matter. The immense Buddhist temple at Borobudur in central Java and the nearby Hindu one at Prambanan are, however, evidence both of extraordinary dedication and exceptional powers of organization.

Just as trade with India and China had brought Hindu and later Buddhist priests to Indonesia, as well as Chinese scholars, so

trade with Arabia eventually led to the arrival of Islam in the archipelago.

Everywhere along the coast of Java in the fifteenth century, rajahs were becoming sultans, and the final outcome of this expansion of Isla was the fall of the great Majapahit empire and the flight of its aristocracy, priesthood and community of artists and scholars across the narrow strait from east Java onto the neighboring island of Bali.

The emperor became the king of Bali and rajah of Klungkung, and the rest of the island was divided up into seven diminutive

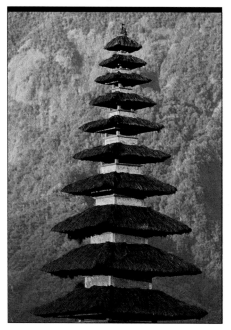

kingdoms — Bandung, Tabanan, Bangli, Gianyar, Karangasem (Amlapura), Buleleng (Singaraja) and Jembrana (West Bali) — and given to members of the ex-Majapahit royal family to rule. Men used to ruling an empire now began to focus their attention on a medium- size island.

These Balinese kingdoms vied with one another over the centuries, first one becoming dominant, then another. But culturally, and, more important, religiously, the island was a whole. On great festival days the Balinese traveled to the Mother Temple at

OPPOSITE: Turn-of-the-century Balinese. Western influence on the East Indies began early, but Bali was largely left alone because of its lack of ports and mountainous interior. ABOVE: A *meru* at Ulu Danu temple in Candikuning.

Besakih irrespective of the kingdom they resided in. Though there were wars between them from time to time, it seems likely these kingdoms were largely the playthings of the rajahs who ruled them. Their boundaries form the basis for the island's modern administrative districts.

Why Islam never moved into Bali remains something of a mystery. Islam certainly extended further east into Sulawesi and the Moluccas. The root reason is probably that the faith spread with trade, and Bali, with little to offer and no harbors, was consequent-

ly ignored. Nevertheless, prolonged interaction with Islamic and other cultures did leave its mark on the island. There are Moslems in the east-facing ports of Padangbai and Kusamba, and Buddhist priests work alongside the Hindu ones. Up in the mountains, the Bali Aga, who never accepted the caste system and other Hindu imports, continue their intransigent existence.

Thus Bali (with a section of western Lombok) became what it remains today, the only predominantly non-Islamic territory in the archipelago, and an isolated outpost of Indian Hindu culture gorgeously stranded in the tropical seas south of the equator.

Rather than fade away, cut off from its source, Balinese culture has flourished,

apparently intact, and continues to do so today, even in the presence of an unprecedented influx of tourists and consequent Western influence.

It could be argued that the Balinese were well trained in keeping foreign influences at bay by three hundred years of contact with the Dutch. Improved ship production brought the various European powers to the East in the sixteenth century. Acquiring spices quickly became the prime object of their expeditions; these were used not only to flavor meat but, far more importantly, to preserve it. Soon cloves, cinnamon, nutmeg and the rest were fetching staggering prices in Lisbon and Amsterdam. It was the Dutch who eventually came to dominate this immensely lucrative business and, as the British were later to do in India, soon began administering the territories they were exploiting. The former trade of what became known in Europe as the East Indies was suppressed, surplus clove trees (which threatened to lower prices in Europe) were burned down, and the islands were made to grow an ever-increasing proportion of crops marketable back in Amsterdam. Cloves were sold there for approximately 15 times the price paid for them. The old Arab-Chinese-Malay monopoly of the trade was at an end.

The Dutch first set foot in Bali in 1597, taking home glowing reports. Despite this aesthetic appreciation, the search for profits led them to Java and the eastern spice islands of the archipelago. Again, Bali was ignored. The Dutch had enough on their hands in the more profitable corners of the region. The trade in spices, it is true, ceased to be the license to print money that it had been, and control of the islands was even temporarily lost to the British during the Napoleonic wars when the French occupation of Holland was taken as an excuse for seizing all Dutch possessions in Asia as war booty. Nevertheless, the peace treaty saw the Dutch colonies return, with minor adjustments, and interest in the region revived by the introduction of American cash crops such as cotton and tobacco into the islands.

One export Bali had traditionally been valued for was slaves. By the end of the eighteenth century up to two thousand Balinese were being shipped abroad into slaverly, annually. The slave trade was finally abolished in 1830.

The nineteenth century, like the centuries before it, saw several revolts against Dutch rule. The most notable was the so-called Java War of 1825–30 where Javanese resistance was led by Prince Diponegoro. Major streets in Denpasar and Klungkung are now named after him.

The first Dutch attempt to occupy, as opposed to keep an eye on, Bali came in 1846 when the Balinese plundering of a wreck was used as a pretext for moving in and eventu-

on September 20, 1906. A similar heroic but suicidal last stand took place in Klungkung, and then it was all over and the Dutch were masters of the island.

Their rule was not popular. A rigid policy of white supremacy was enforced and little was done to benefit the Balinese.

The early Thirties was the time when the first Western artists began arriving in Bali, men like Walter Spies, who lived in Ubud, and Miguel Covarrubias and Le Mayeur, who settled near Denpasar and in Sanur respectively. They lived with, or at least alongside,

ally controlling the northern and western districts of the island. From then on a policy of divide and rule set the remaining Balinese kingdoms against one another until one side made the tactical error of appealing to the Dutch for assistance against its neighbors. This was what the Dutch had been waiting for and they promptly annexed the kingdom they were helping, Gianyar, in 1900.

Another instance of the looting of a wreck, this time off Sanur, led to the completion of Dutch control. This, however, did not become final until after the massacre of 4,000 Balinese in Denpasar where the aristocracy presented itself in full ceremonial dress for ritual *puputan*, or resistance to the last man, against what were clearly superior forces. This was

the local people, and made a point of being independent of the Dutch administrators. They were in Bali because of the idyllic existence to be had there, in which culture and an easy life seemed to go hand in hand, and they had no use for the distinctions deemed necessary by the colonial masters for the perpetuation of their system.

Wealthy tourists, too, began arriving at this time despite the difficulties; it's estimated that about a hundred a month were visiting Bali by the middle of the decade.

A good account of the period is K'tut Tantri's *Revolt in Paradise*. An American

ABOVE: Twentieth century colonists and visitors recorded in stone and OPPOSITE in the temple at Kubutambahan, North Bali.

citizen, she settled in Bali in 1933, adopted local dress and a Balinese name, and stayed in Bali and Java until the late forties. Her book is also a good guide to the events that followed the outbreak of the Second World War.

The Japanese entered the war in 1941 and proceeded quickly to overrun Singapore, Malaya, Burma, the Philippines and the Dutch East Indies. The Dutch colonial army finally surrendered to them on March 7, 1942. Japanese anti-colonial propaganda did not win the support of the Indonesians for long, but the opportunity was taken by some of the emerging nationalist leaders to advance their cause, and on the defeat of Japan the independent Republic of Indonesia was proclaimed on August 17, 1945.

The Dutch, however, had other ideas. In association with British forces they landed in Indonesia with the ostensible purpose of disarming and interning the Japanese there. Before long, however, troops of both nations were fighting armed Indonesian volunteers, and in November 1945, Surabaya was shelled from the sea and bombed by British forces.

Eventually the British fell back on the role of go-betweens, but the guerrilla war against the Dutch continued until, on December 27, 1949, when, under international pressure, The Hague agreed to recognize the sovereignty of the Republic of Indonesia.

The country's first president was the long-established leader of the independence movement, Sukarno (who had a Balinese mother). He held power until the combined effects of a declining economy, militant anti-Americanism and the increasing influence of the Indonesian communist party (PKI) led to an alleged coup attempt by the PKI on the night of September 30, 1965. This was swiftly put down by the army, and since that date Major General (now President) Suharto has been in control. Policies have been pragmatic and pro-Western, and the PKI has been declared illegal. A degree of democracy has been restored but to date the power of the ruling Golkar party has nowhere been effectively challenged, and it is they and the army who essentially control the country.

This turnabout in the nation's political orientation was not effected, however, without a terrible purge of communists, suspected communists, and, most notably, Chinese in

the last months of 1965. The total number of victims has never been agreed on — indeed the account of this period is now the subject of what ideological debate is still permitted. In Bali alone the number of dead almost certainly exceeded 100,000; the killing there was more extensive and brutal than anywhere else in the country. According to one observer, "Whole villages, including children, took part in an island wide witchhunt for communists who were slashed and clubbed and chopped to death by communal consent." It's a sobering thought when considering a culture dubbed by so many as one characterized by beauty, harmony, and a serene adherence to the will of the gods.

Today Bali basks in the relative prosperity brought to it by tourism. Eighty-five percent

of all Indonesia's tourists come here and only here. For the rest, the economy remains agricultural, dominated by rice production. The new "miracle" rice means the island now produces a surplus for export. Other exports include copra and coffee. The Chinese are back and running restaurants, clothes shops and travel agencies in Kuta and elsewhere.

LANGUAGE

Bali has its own language, Balinese (see LANGUAGE in TRAVELERS' TIPS, page 247). Though part of the Malayo-Polynesian family of languages, it is as distinct from Malay (Indonesian) as English is from German. It exists in three forms: High, Middle and Low. Lower ranking people use High

Balinese when speaking to their superiors; high-ranking people speak Low Balinese amongst themselves or when speaking to inferiors, except in formal situations. Middle Balinese is used in delicate social circumstances.

Bahasa Indonesia, the official language of Indonesia, is virtually indistinguishable from Malay. It is taught in all schools as part of Indonesian government policy. Most young Balinese can speak it when necessary.

The ancient Javanese tongue of Kawi is used by the priests, and it is the language of the gods in the shadow puppet dramas.

Bali is extraordinary in the continuance of Hinduism there thousands of miles away from its Indian home. Processions to the temple such as this one are a reasonably common occurrence.

Balinese
Culture

A VILLAGE UPBRINGING

Banjar and Subak

With the exception of the Bali Aga settlements, Balinese villages all follow a similar pattern.

The village is invariably on either side of a road. Along this road run thatched walls with somewhat higher roofed gateways, also thatched, leading into the family compounds. Side roads at right angles to the main road lead to the rice terraces, while immediately behind the family compounds are kitchen gardens where crops such as green vegetables and corn are grown.

Somewhere in the center of the village stands the communal buildings: the village temple *(pura desa)*, the assembly pavilion *(bale agung)*, the *kul-kul* tower and, more often than not, a sacred banyan tree.

Some distance away from the village is the village cemetery, a rough grassy field surrounded by trees where cremations take place and bodies are buried temporarily prior to cremation. A small temple of the dead *(pura dalem)* also stands there.

Low bellied pigs forage freely round the village and mangy dogs hang out, despised but tolerated. Fighting cocks in round bamboo cages are often placed on the ground where they may be seen and admired, and where they can peck at the earth before being moved on to a new patch.

Chickens, too, wander at will, but ducks are herded daily into the rice paddies where they are kept together by means of a tall pole topped with a white cloth. The ducks never stray far from this marker.

Balinese villages are shady, well tended places where gardens, and the communal manipulation of running water, give a strong sense of security and order.

Villages are run by a council *(krama desa)* of which every married householder is a member. This council elects one of its members as leader *(klian desa)* and meets in the *bale agung*. It orders the life of the village and makes arrangements for festivals. The council can also administer punishment, essentially expulsion. This is a serious punishment in Bali as, once expelled from his village, a man will find no refuge anywhere else on the island.

It isn't long before the visitor realizes that every hotel worker he comes into contact with identifies strongly with his village and hurries back there whenever he has a couple of days off, even if it's on the opposite side of the island.

Large villages and towns are subdivided into *banjar*. These operate much as the villages do, each with its own temple, council, *bale agung* and the rest. In this way, village organization continues, even in the capital of Denpasar. Each *banjar* has its own festival on its temple *odalan*, or anniversary, and on the night before Nyepi — a great island wide festival — each *banjar* in Denpasar parades its own lovingly made monster through the central streets without any hint of rivalry.

In many cases Balinese aristocrats still live in their palaces *(puri)*, and these are situated within villages rather than outside them. These large walled compounds are like miniature villages in themselves, containing houses for different family members, each with its own garden and subdividing wall. There is no real middle class in rural Bali. The Chinese businessmen and the shopkeepers of Kuta, together with the other self-made people, tend to live in or just outside of Denpasar.

Although rice fields are nowadays owned by individual villagers, the old cooperative system of agriculture still continues to exist. One of the reasons for this is that irrigation is necessarily communal, and the flow of the water, the careful provision of exactly the right amount of water for all the fields before it is allowed to flow away downstream to the next village, requires careful cooperation and management.

The organizations that oversee this operation are known as *subak*; everyone who owns a rice field is a member. The *subak* meets monthly, sometimes more often, at the shrine in the rice field dedicated to the deities of agriculture, where they makes decisions about what repairs or improvements are needed, and who will be responsible for carrying them out.

Rice is central to the island's life. Some of these beautifully terraced fields have been flooded for the planting of the young shoots.

THE CULT OF RICE

For the Balinese, to eat is to eat rice. As elsewhere in Indonesia — which indicates the cult is pre-Hindu — the rice plant is treated as a woman, and the stages of her birth, growth, pregnancy and final fruition are all celebrated. She is Dewi Sri, the rice goddess.

First comes the laying out of the seed to germinate. This is considered worthy of a small offering and done on a propitious date by the Balinese calendars. Some 45 days later the shoots are planted out in the waterlogged paddies, first in a ritual pattern — nine seedlings in the shape of a star — then in rows one handspan apart. Nowadays, such ceremonies are usually preceded by an application of trisodium phosphate, a government recommended fertilizer.

Forty-two days later the Dewi Sri's "birthday" is celebrated with altars in the fields. When the grain first appears, she is said to be with child. Altars are again erected in the fields and foods that pregnant women have a taste for are presented as offerings. Rites are performed to ward off the vermin (or evil spirits) that might attack the grain.

Four months after the planting (five months for traditional strains), comes the harvest. Effigies are made of Dewi Sri and her husband Wisnu from the first sheaves and taken to the cultivator's household temple. A Rice Mother is declared and placed to oversee the harvest to the end.

The ingenuous look on the face of the little Dewi Sri figures called *cili* can often be seen in Balinese art, and in unexpected places everywhere. With their primordial simplicity, *cili* represent the impish soul of the island.

Only men plant and tend the rice, but everyone takes part in the harvest. It's a collective activity, too, and the harvesters go from one irrigation cooperative to another till the work is finished.

The rice cultivated in Bali is these days almost exclusively the new "miracle" rice, a shorter, less elegant plant than the old rice depicted in paintings from before the seventies, but yielding at least a 50 percent larger crop, and over a shorter growing period. The older kind, however, is said to taste better

and fetches a higher price in the markets than the new variety.

WHERE DO YOU SIT?

Caste is more deeply embedded in the Balinese psyche than it may first appear.

In the same way that the Hindu religion was brought, in the Majapahit invasion, to a people previously content with worshipping spirits of place and of their ancestors, so too the age-old Hindu distinction between people born to different roles in life

was superimposed on a culture that was essentially collective and probably relatively classless. Just as the Balinese have taken to the one, so they have accepted the other. Despite the fact that 93 percent of the population has to be content with membership of the lowest of the four castes, the Sudra, they appear to accept uncritically the claims of the other three castes, and at times, even when away from their home villages, seek to adopt their status for themselves. Some commentators have judged that caste in modern Bali represents little more than a pleasant diversion. Perhaps this is the impression the Sudras would like to give, and that the top-dog Brahmanas can afford to give (seeing as they are often also the richest people around). Nevertheless, the complexities of an inter-caste marriage have not lessened with the arrival of a few hundred thousand tourists on the beaches of Kuta and Sanur.

Essentially, the Brahmanas were the priestly caste; the Satrias, the warriors; the Wesias, the merchants; and the Sudras, the ordinary people. A long-standing struggle between the Brahmanas and the Satrias over which of them was the senior group seems to have been resolved in a de facto victory for the Brahmanas.

do you sit?" (referring to the custom of always sitting lower than someone of a higher caste) remains a question strangers will often ask each other on first acquaintance.

NAMING OF NAMES

Balinese personal names usually refer to the position of the child in the family order. The firstborn is Wayan — or, in the higher castes, Putu or Gede. The second is Made — or Nengah or Kadek. The usual name for the third born is Nyoman, with Komang as an

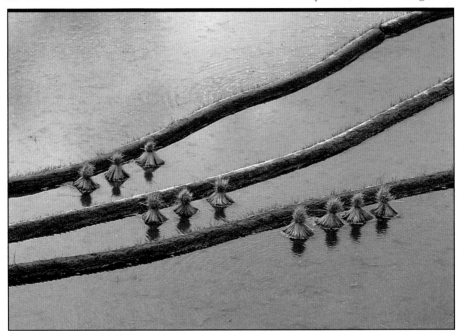

The following titles are used by the four groups as prefixes to their names:

Brahmana men: Ida Bagus; women: Ida Ayu (Dayu for short). Both these mean "highborn and beautiful."

Satrias men: Cokorde, Anak Agung, Ratu, Prebagus; women: Anak Agung Isti, Dewa Ayu.

Wesia men: I Gusti, Pregusti; women: I Gusti Ayu.

Sudra men: I; women: Ni.

Legally, feudal discrimination according to caste is forbidden. It is true that Brahmanas can be found waiting tables in restaurants and Sudras occupying reasonably important government positions. Nevertheless, socially the habits of deference persist, and, "Where

alternative. The fourth child is Ketut. These names are used for boys and girls indiscriminately. After four, the cycle is repeated, with the fifth child Wayan again and so on.

SEX ROLES

Distinction according to sex is more rigorous than that according to class.

Only men work as craftsmen (weaving excepted), climb coconut trees, tend cattle or cultivate the fields (though women invari-

OPPOSITE: Weeding between the growing rice plants; note the low banks between fields and the subtly varied water levels. Such terraces are maintained, and the water flow controlled, by close cooperation between and within villages. ABOVE: Rice shoots waiting to be planted.

ably help with the rice harvest). Only women do the housework, look after the chickens and pigs and prepare offerings for temples.

It often surprises Westerners is to see women doing all the heavy labor on construction sites and roadworks. The principle here is that whereas it's the men who build the traditional Balinese wooden houses, the women do the dirty work in Western style building.

Also, it is the custom for women to carry goods on their heads, men to carry them slung at either end of a pole they carry on their shoulders. It's normally women who carry offerings to the temple, but when a man does this he too must carry them on his head.

Nevertheless, Balinese women do enjoy a measure of independence by Asian standards, keeping the profits from their economic activities for themselves and also easily obtaining a divorce from an unsatisfactory husband without incurring any serious social disapproval.

BIRTH, CHILDHOOD, LOVE AND MARRIAGE

Family life is particularly important to the Balinese. The existence of offspring to ensure an adequate cremation is essential, and the more children there are to bear the cost of this expensive ceremony the better. In earlier times, and possibly still, Western contraception devices were considered akin to black magic. Failure to bear children is an acceptable ground for divorce (as is male impotence) in Balinese society.

Three months into pregnancy the mother-to-be is subject to a ceremony, and during the gestation period she will probably wear one or more amulets to protect her from the attention of *leyak* (witches) anxious to feed on the entrails of the unborn child. After the birth itself, the mother is considered unclean *(sebel)* for 42 days (and the father for three days).

The newborn child is considered to be accompanied by four "brothers" ("sisters" in the case of a girl), the *kanda empat*. These have their physical manifestation in the placenta, blood, skin-coating and amniotic

Threshing rice in North Bali — a common sight any time of year as Bali's climate allows crops to be planted and harvested year round.

fluid, all of which are saved and buried with great solemnity, the place being marked with a shrine.

Not so long ago the birth of twins of the opposite sex was considered a disaster by the ordinary people, necessitating, among other things, the removal and eventual destruction of the family's house and the impoverishment of the father of the ill-begotten unfortunates. Among the upper castes, however, the twins were considered the reincarnations of two souls previously happily married, and their birth the occasion for great rejoicing. The situation probably represented the continuance of ancient Balinese beliefs among the ordinary people and the more successful dissemination of Hindu ideas among the upper classes, many of whom descended en masse on Bali in the sixteenth century from Java.

After 14 days, the newborn is named, but it's only after 105 days (three months of 35 days each) that the child is allowed to touch the ground for the first time, the occasion being marked, not unexpectedly, with a ceremony. Another similar ceremony takes place after one Balinese year (210 days; see TIME PASSES, page 101) and in practice the two ceremonies are frequently combined on the later date to reduce the expense of the necessary feasting of guests and hiring of priests.

The Balinese allow their children to live an unusually natural life. They are suckled for as long as they want, often over three years, and allowed to eat — as their parents do — whenever they're hungry. They are held in permanent bodily contact with either the mother or another woman of the family for every moment of the first three months of life, and throughout early childhood fathers cuddle or carry their children almost as often as their mothers. Not surprisingly, Balinese children rarely cry.

Once they're able to walk, the children live a free and easy life in the village in the company of other children of their own age. They are never beaten, and little in adult life is hidden from them so that they appear to enter the world of sex at adolescence without surprise, guilt or neurosis.

Sexual relations between Balinese teenagers are left to proceed in a natural way

without interference from the parents, at least in the Sudra class that makes up the vast majority of the population, and there's no expectation that early affairs will necessarily lead to marriage. Love charms and magically potent amulets are often used when the girl seems reluctant. Homosexuality is frowned on but seems rare.

The relaxed attitude to sex continues on into marriage. Parents have a minimal part to play in the arrangements, and in the commonest form of marriage the ceremony doesn't take place until several days after the announcement of consummation. Even in upper caste arranged marriages, the couple may sleep together for an agreed period before the wedding.

The commonest form of marriage ceremony in Bali is kidnapping (ngrorod). The boy seizes the girl in some public place and, after token resistance, the couple speed off to a prearranged hideaway where offerings are set out for the gods and the union consummated. It's considered vital this happens before the offerings wilt in order for the union to be valid. This is the real marriage, performed in the sight of the gods, and the subsequent public celebration is merely a recognition of the couple's new status.

Arranged marriages (mapadik) are commonest among the aristocracy, but only with the full agreement of both parties.

The wedding ceremonies take place at the home of the boy's father. A toothfiling ritual (see below) will be incorporated if this operation hasn't been performed already. There's much feasting and music, but the actual ceremony is a simple one with the priest blessing the union amid much throwing of flowers, ringing of bells and dashing with holy water.

In the past, a Balinese woman could not marry a man of lower caste than herself, thus keeping daughters from descending the social scale when marrying. If this is changing nowadays, it is changing slowly. Marriage with divorcees and widows, however, is freely allowed.

A young girl takes an offering to the temple. Under a very liberal system of child rearing, the Balinese mature early and retain a natural dignity throughout adult life.

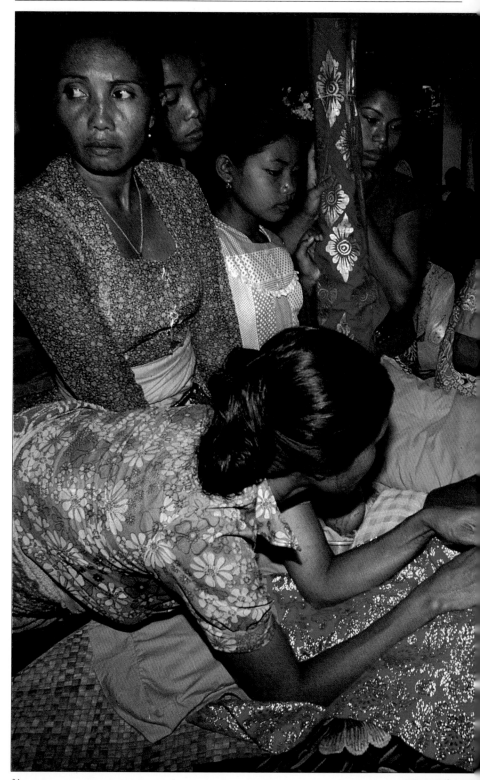

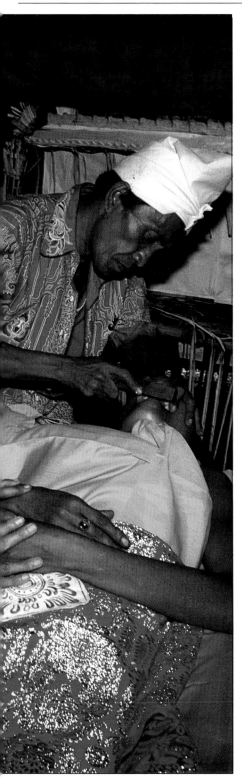

Balinese women can divorce their husbands — for cruelty, impotence or failure to support them — by simply walking out of the house. The divorce is then confirmed by the village council; this is generally a formality as there are no set criteria by which "support" or "cruelty" can be judged.

Tooth Filing

It is considered essential for every Balinese adult sooner or later to have his or her teeth filed — so much so that in the event of accidental death in youth the teeth of the body will be filed before cremation.

The purpose of the ceremony is to reduce the power of the vices of greed, jealousy, anger, drunkenness, lust and "confusion" that are considered more appropriate to animals than to humans. Consequently, the two upper canine teeth, and the four incisors between them, are filed down amid feasting and general celebration. Because of the cost of the hospitality involved, toothfiling ceremonies are often held in conjunction with other rituals. Because it's thought desirable to have had your teeth filed before you get married, the ceremony is frequently held in conjunction with a wedding.

Ideally, the six teeth are filed down by someone of the Brahmana cast, perhaps the upper-caste patron of the family concerned. The patients, dressed in their finest, lie down in a pavilion, usually two at a time, surrounded by offerings. They are then wrapped in a white cloth while family and friends gather round.

The extent to which the teeth are filed down depends largely on the wishes of the subject, but as filed teeth are considered beautiful as well as an aid to virtue, it's not uncommon for a thorough job to be requested. The filing usually takes between 15 and 30 minutes. The mouth is held open by a short piece of sugarcane and from time to time the patient spits out the filings into a yellow coconut which is later buried in the family temple. A small mirror allows the

Tooth filing — a custom that is still rigorously observed by all Balinese, and no young man or woman can be married before the ceremony has been completed. Groups of adolescents often have their teeth filed together, and marriage and tooth filing rituals frequently take place together.

the Rig Veda, is certainly the oldest religious text known anywhere in the world.

The central tenets of Hinduism fit in well with a system of beliefs that holds that the world is everywhere populated by spirits. A people who believed from the start that in every tree, animal, bush, volcano — and in every fortunate or disastrous event there was an invisible intelligence at work — cannot have found it difficult to take to a philosophy that taught of a World Soul of which we, and all other living things, are temporary embodiments.

victim to inspect the work and request improvements. Often hundreds of young men and women have their teeth filed together in one ceremony to save on expense.

MEN AND GODS

BALINESE HINDUISM

Every Balinese will describe himself to you as a Hindu, but the reality is that the elements of Hinduism found in Bali are rather like the Catholicism found in the remoter parts of the Philippines. For some it may be a genuine presence, and its philosophy a real foundation for faith and action, but for the majority it is a dressing applied to the more fundamental and essential spirit-based religion found everywhere in the Malay archipelago.

Nevertheless, it is an extraordinary phenomenon to find, isolated on one South Seas island, manifestations of a religion originating somewhere near the Caspian Sea and brought into north India nearly four thousand years ago. Even then the tenets of Hinduism were far from new. The origins of the Vedas, the holy books of the Aryans who brought Hinduism to India, are lost in the mists of antiquity, but the oldest of them,

To the educated Hindu, the universe is ordered by a controlling spirit, Brahman. Your inner essence, the silent core of your being that remains when all the lusts for money, sex and power are stilled, is your Atman. The innermost secret, the core of the mystery, is that the two — your "soul" and the vast spirit of the universe — are one and the same thing. You are a part of it, manifested for a brief time in matter. So is a mouse, a tree, a grain of corn.

The cycle of birth and death, creation and destruction, goes on forever, the essence of all things constantly embodying itself in matter. In just the same way that all things are part of the great World Spirit, so their death is no tragedy, merely the returning of the part to the whole, a whole from which innumerable new manifestations will be born.

This constant rebirth of the spirit, at a higher or lower level of creation according to the place your actions have brought you to in your last incarnation, is natural and inevitable. But it's wearisome to the high-aspiring soul who longs for permanent rest, for final union with the creating spirit itself. Because the spirits of all things and the great universal spirit are essentially one and the same, this ultimate union, or reunification, is possible. Reject all desire, which holds you down among the world of material things, and you might attain that final fusion with the ineffable and unimaginable that is known as *moksa*. You at last realize the potential that has been in you all along and become one with Brahman.

This is the philosophic heart of Hinduism. Over the millennia, innumerable manifestations of it have grown up in India and elsewhere. In Bali, orientation of temples toward the volcanoes and the use of cock's blood (obtained at cockfights) in temple rituals seem remote from the pure spirituality of the Chandogya Upanishad. Still, these practices reflect the yearning of all people have to see and touch, to develop local sanc-

tities and hold on to the practices of their ancestors.

Despite differences, the influence of the Hindu vision in Bali is remarkably pervasive. Balinese cremations are genuinely cheerful affairs, and the numerous rituals preceding them, symbolizing the cutting off of attachment to the soul of the dead, are living parts of ordinary village life. The soul must be allowed to go free, and not be held back by grief — so teaches the religion; and the result is that, remarkable as it may seem to Westerners, the ordinary Balinese at a cremation do not mourn. Despite all the animist belief in spirits and blood sacrifice, the essence of Indian Hinduism has entered into the people's souls.

The variety of religious practice, the number of places and things that can be venerated, is astonishing. There's hardly a field, a large tree or even a discotheque on the island that doesn't have its incense-burning shrine. The same is true, it might be argued, of Hong Kong or Bangkok, but in Bali the constant attention to these household shrines, and the frequency and elaborateness of the various temple festivals, are unparalleled.

The charm of the Balinese is the charm of a people whose natural grace has been sustained and augmented by a religion that is based on respect and reverence for the life of all things.

Every village *(desa)* has its temple of origin *(pura puseh)*, its temple of the dead *(pura dalem)*, its temple for the irrigation system *(pura subak)*, and any number of temples and shrines dedicated to local streams, lakes, springs, hills and waterfalls. All must have their offerings on their holy days. In addition, evil spirits, thought to occupy their own special sites, but proliferating at crossroads, must be placated with offerings too, thrown down casually and quickly crushed by the first passing car (but not before the greedy spirits have wolfed up their meager essence).

Thus the spirits of goodness are constantly being invited down into the world of everyday life and feted at festivals, and the evil spirits kept at bay by what amount to derisory, but regular, bribes.

For the Balinese, the volcanoes are the seat of the gods. Every structure in Bali is to some extent influenced by this sense of "to the mountains" *(kaja)* being pure and the opposite direction *(kelod)* being impure. Thus, a house will have its shrine in its most *kaja* corner, and its pigpen and garbage area in its most *kelod*.

This doesn't mean that to the Balinese the sea is impure, though some Western writers have inferred this. It is true the Balinese historically have not been seafarers, but the sea itself is seen as a purifying element, used for cleansing symbolic items from the temple *(arca)* and one source of holy water.

The mountain-oriented temples of Bali often have a deserted, even shabby look. They contain no idols, and no priests are in attendance. Only the temple keeper *(pemangku)*, dressed in white, is usually somewhere around to keep the place tidy and accept the donations of visitors. On festival days, though, things are very different.

The principal festival of any temple is its anniversary *(odalan)*, occurring every 210 days from the date of its founding. Then bamboo altars and tables are put up, and offerings of fruit, cakes and flowers, piled high on the heads of the women, are brought from nearby houses. The *pemangku* receives them, pours holy water onto the hands of the villagers and places grains of rice on their temples and brow. The villagers take flower blossoms and, holding them between the tips of their fingers, raise them to their foreheads

three times before throwing them toward the shrines.

The high caste priests *(pedanda)* are said to be the direct descendants of the Indian Brahmins who officiated in the old courts of Java. They only attend temple ceremonies on the most important occasions, such as aristocratic weddings, at which they sit on a high platform ringing their bells and reciting their mantras. They can be either Buddhist or Hindu *(pedanda bodda* or *pedanda siwa)*, the former going bareheaded with long hair, the latter wearing a gold and red miter

crowned with a crystal ball. The chief use of these learned *pedanda* as far as the ordinary people are concerned is to bless the holy water used in all temple ceremonies.

At these temple anniversary festivals, male and female figures, the *arca*, made of sandalwood, or of old Chinese coins *(kepeng)*, are deemed to symbolize the gods and are taken during the day to a river or the sea and symbolically washed. In addition, cockfights are sometimes staged in the afternoon. *Gamelan* orchestras play, and

ABOVE: Traditional life goes on even in the midst of the tourist invasion — a purification ceremony at Kuta. OPPOSITE: Partly for the gods, partly for the aesthetic, stone statues such as this one at Poppies, Kuta, are decorated daily with fresh flowers.

dance dramas may be performed. As the evening wears on, coffee and cake are offered to everyone present, and certain villagers will go into a trance (during which they may also perform a sword dance) when a spirit, it is believed, will speak through them and report on how the offerings have been received by the gods.

At dawn, the women dance in honor of the rising sun and the elaborate offerings, their essence judged to have been devoured by the gods, are taken back home and eventually eaten by the weary devotees.

HOTELS FOR THE GODS

Walk into any Balinese temple and you'll find the same mixture of diversity and similarity you find amongst Christian churches. A typical Balinese temple, however, might present itself to you as follows:

You pass from the street into the first, or outer, compound through two carved stone structures, the inside (facing) walls of which have been left smooth. The general effect is of a structure, tapering upwards, that has been split down the middle. This split gateway is known as a *candi bentar*.

The first compound is spacious and almost empty. It does, however, contain a *pemangku* clad in white who asks you to sign

a visitors' book and pay a donation of a couple of hundred rupiahs. The compound also contains some ordinary-looking pavilions (roofs resting on four posts, with a waist-level floor) and a brick tower. Climb the tower and you will find hanging at the top some hollowed out tree trunks with slits cut into them: these are called *kul-kul*, and they are hammered in times of emergency to summon the villagers to the temple compound. The pavilions are used by the *gamelan* orchestras, and for preparing offerings and cooking food, on festival days. If the temple has a

second, outer compound it will simply contain further pavilions.

At the top end of the outer court, oriented directly towards the mountains, there is a wall with a door in it. Around this door are ornate decorations, and the door itself is intricately carved. It's called the *padu raksa*. The door stands half open, and you can climb the few steps up to it and walk through. You can't go straight ahead, however, as a short wall, an *aling-aling*, bars your way. It's actually meant to bar the way of evil spirits which are thought to travel in straight lines, as well as to be rather stupid — seeing their way barred, it's hoped, they'll reverse direction and fly back out again. Turning left or right and going down the steps into the inner courtyard, you find yourself in the holiest part of the temple.

There are a considerable number of shrines along two walls, either the eastern and northern walls in South Bali or the eastern and southern walls in North Bali, as the shrines must face the mountains. Some of these shrines are small structures a couple of meters high, little more than high tables with roofs of black thatch (*ijuk*). Others are high towers with multiple roofs. These are known as *meru*, and the roofs are always of an odd number. The number signifies which

Sanghyang Widhi Wasa, the supreme deity in the Balinese pantheon. The support for the chair is carved to represent the world as imagined in Balinese mythology, mountains supported by a turtle entwined with snakes. When there are three chairs instead of one, they are for the godhead in the form of the trinity Siwa, Wisnu and Brahma.

TIME PASSES

The Balinese use three different calendars: a Javanese calendar based on 210-day cycles,

deity they are dedicated to, as follows: three roofs means it is dedicated to Dewi Sri (the rice goddess), five to Isawa (an incarnation of Siwa), seven to Brahma, nine to Wisnu, and 11 to Siwa. The finest *meru* in Bali can be seen at Besakih and Mengwi.

Close to the eastern wall there is a sounder structure with locked doors. This is the *gedong pesimpanan* and contains various dusty items — masks for *barong* dances, for instance — communally owned by the villagers and occasionally used in festivals.

Situated in the corner between north and east in South Bali or south and east in North Bali is a stone throne placed at the summit of an elaborately carved structure also of stone. This is the *padmasana*, the chair for Ida

an ancient South Indian lunar calendar and the Western — and now international — Gregorian calendar.

The old Java calendar is the basis for the calculation of the dates of all temple anniversary festivals, all of which consequently recur every 210 days. This period of time is made up of 30 weeks of seven days each — but also, superimposed on them, a string of other "weeks" of one, two, three, four, five, six, eight, nine and 10 days each. As not all of these numbers divide exactly into 210, vari-

Purification ceremony on Kuta Beach — RIGHT: Facing the ocean, the devotees venerate a temporary bamboo shrine. Such ceremonies take place after, for example, a cremation. OPPOSITE: A *pemangku* distributes holy water.

ous extra days of the week of the four, eight and nine-day weeks are discreetly added at fixed points in the cycle so that all the weeks can come to an end together on the 210th day.

The result of this system is that any particular day has ten different day of the week names. In practice, however, it is only the three, five and seven-day weeks that interest the Balinese. These, though, are very important, and special coincidences between their cycles are used as auspicious days for ceremonies and rituals. For instance, when the third day of the three-day week coincides

with the fifth day of the five-day week, it's a good day for just about anything.

Used in conjunction with this calendar (called *pawukon*) is the lunar system known as the *saka* calendar. Being based on the moon, this calendar features months, *sasih*, each of 30 days. Each month is deemed to begin on the day following the first appearance of the new moon *(tilem)*. Halfway through each month, of course, is the full moon, *purnama*. The 12 months are named after the Sanskrit words for one to ten, with names derived from other sources for the last two.

The phenomenon of "possession" — entering a trance during a temple festival. While these men are possessed, they can endure extremes of pain without any apparent ill effects.

The innumerable possibilities offered by the combinations of these two systems are not lost on the Balinese, and the inter-chiming of these celestial rhythms is no doubt as much a manifestation of serious play, of variations within an overall unity, as the shifting rhythms and sudden harmonies of the *gamelan* orchestra. Life to the Balinese, at least in theory, is in large part the observing of earthly rhythms and harmonies that reflect imagined — and possibly actual — heavenly ones.

The most common as well as the most important temple festivals are the ones that celebrate the *odalan,* or anniversary, of the temple. The majority of these are calculated according to the *pawukon* 210-day calendar.

Certain major temple festivals are fixed according to the lunar, *saka,* calendar. To obtain dates, contact the Badung Tourist Office in Denpasar which publishes a monthly list of temple festivals, large and small, throughout the island.

THREE FESTIVALS

Nyepi celebrates the solar New Year for Bali. Despite the island's being in the southern hemisphere, it is a kind of spring-cleaning of bad spirits. On the day before Nyepi, evil spirits are attracted down with special offerings, then terrified out of their wits as night falls by a veritable orgy of firecrackers dropped in garbage cans, gongs, beating of *kul-kul,* yelling and parading gigantic, hideously grotesque monsters. It's a great night to be in the streets of Denpasar.

Nyepi is celebrated the day after the new moon of the ninth Balinese lunar month, a date that usually falls in March (see FESTIVE FLINGS in YOUR CHOICE, page 60).

Galungan, and the festival which follows it ten days later, **Kuningan,** are celebrated every 210 days, like the temple anniversary festivals, and so can occur at any time of the year. Galungan is the time when the spirits of the ancestors return and revisit the homes of their offspring. *Barong* (giant monsters) roam the streets, everything is brushed clean, dance dramas of great length are performed and a party atmosphere prevails everywhere.

Kuningan, by contrast, is a festival of purification and is closely associated with the

Holy Spring at the temple of Tirta Empul at Tampaksiring, the *odalan* or anniversary festival of which is on the same day. The day after Kuningan there is a festival on Turtle Island (Serangan).

A VILLAGE CREMATION

It's a hot morning. A tour organizer wakes you early and you set off down one road then another, down a lane, down a track and you're there.

A high bamboo tower and a bamboo bull, richly adorned and shining in the early morning light, are standing ready in an open space in the middle of the village. Under a blue and orange canopy, the special cremation *gamelan,* the *gambong,* is playing its old style instruments, bamboo-keyed and struck by players holding four hammers apiece. You engage a young man in conversation.

The dead man was his grandfather. Aged 60, he'd died 12 days ago in the hospital. They'd waited for an auspicious date for the cremation — there are perhaps two in a month. This cremation, together with the ceremonies beforehand, will cost the family the equivalent of US$3,000; they'd had to feed the whole village since the day of his death.

An elegantly dressed man comes out from the nearby lodgings. He's wearing sarong, waistband, headdress and tennis shoes. He photographs the bull and, by means of an attached string, tweaks its extremely virile phallus. Great laughter from the *gambong* players. He proceeds to photograph the various different groups of villagers present. The tower *(wadah)* can have anything from one to eleven roofs, like the temple *meru.* This one has seven. The number, always odd, depends on the caste of the deceased.

Everyone is dressed in their best, but even "Kuta Beach" T-shirts are acceptable, so long as they're neat and new looking.

The bull is moved forward, and a bamboo ramp placed against the tower. Young men in white headbands do the work. The *gambong* music becomes more excited.

Entrance of the *rangda* mask for a temple dance. Almost all of Bali's dances are religious in origin, the only exceptions being those created in modern times for the benefit of foreign visitors.

Women go up the ramp and rub their hair on the bier.

A procession of women carrying offerings on their heads leaves the lodgings and lines up in front of the bull, waving their hands a bit in recognition of friends in the crowd. Then they proceed down the track to its intersection with the lane.

The music gets more frantic as the young men go into the lodgings; the *gambong*, previously playing in two sections, is now together. Here and there people smoke cigarettes. A well-dressed woman comes out of the lodging carrying a plastic shopping bag. She takes up a position next to the musicians.

There is expectant silence now from the *gambong*. Scattered smiles and some laughter ruffle through the crowd.

Two live chicks are brought out from the lodging and placed in the tower — then a long white cloth is unwound from the lodging doorway to the ramp, followed by some sausage-like bundles. The music has now resumed and is vigorous and strong.

The bull is lifted off the ground and sets off on the shoulders of the youths. There's some argument, then it's turned round and bounced up and down. Someone has the job of jiggling the genitals with the string.

Suddenly the body emerges. It's shrouded in white at the end of the sheet, and it's bundled quickly into the tower, just under the lowest roof. The *gambong* is now ringing out as the cloth is wound up and stuffed into the tower at great speed.

Away down the track, at the junction with the lane, the bull is being wildly bounced and circled round. The body is tied securely into the tower. A man climbs onto the tower carrying a bird on a stick. The ramp is removed.

Bearers lift the tower, and run round and round in a circle with it, laughing as they go.

Off you go, with the musicians and their cymbals, gongs and drums. Down the track and left into the lane. Everyone follows, the old men with the little children (the young men are all assisting at the ceremony). The sun disappears behind a cloud.

The village cremation. These days the fire is largely kerosene sprayed onto the bier from a portable tank. The actual cremation takes place at a burning ground just outside the village.

Along the lane, you pass paddy fields reflecting the now dull sky. School children dressed in white are lined up with their teachers to witness the event. Great red flowers like gladioli glow in the hedgerows. Several immobilized motorcyclists wait on the verge for you to pass. People chat quietly amongst themselves as you all walk along. Tourists walk with the villagers. No one seems to mind them — if anything, they seem honored.

Finally you are there, and the tower is rushed into the rough field surrounded by high trees that is the burial and cremation place. The man on the tower throws grain on anybody within range. The tower is set down, and the ramp moved up to it.

The two chicks are untied, chirruping wildly. There's much argument as the body's half moved out and the white cloth unwound.

Clearly this is a much-used site. Burned straw lies around, and little bamboo shrines stand precariously here and there. The *gambong* sets up, and strikes up again.

The body of the bull — a tree trunk with a lid cut into it — is opened up to receive the corpse, which is brought across and placed on top of the bull, supported on bamboo poles. The musicians stop playing. All but a few strips of stained cloth are removed. A sour aroma drifts across the grass. The bamboo poles are removed and the body slowly lowered into the wooden sarcophagus.

A lengthy wait begins now as the family and a priest sprinkle holy water and place items inside the bull. The people hang around, chatting quietly and smoking their clove cigarettes. A drink seller toots his bicycle horn. It's like an English village fete, sociable, and pleasant and relaxed. This final placing of offerings is drawn-out. The penultimate, in life as in art, is always long.

Finally the cloth goes in, the *gambong* strikes up, and the lid is replaced in the bull's back. Plastic tubes are unwound, attached to blackened metal burners. The burners are put underneath and the taps opened. Kerosene (paraffin) begins to spring onto the bull and is lit by a match.

The burning is strangely non-ritualized, a technical problem. The *gambong* doesn't play. The work is done by two men in yellow plastic safety helmets.

The fire spits and roars. The body shifts position. There are explosions, bones cracking. The cloths are now burned and the dead man grimly visible. The people are quiet.

Then suddenly the musicians start up again, lively and even cheerful. The people relax, and your tour driver comes across and says it's time to be off.

What about the ceremony by the sea? Tomorrow. The burning of the tower? Also tomorrow (actually later that day, but the driver wants his lunch). The village cremation is over.

About Cremations

Bodies are often buried for some considerable time before what's left of them is exhumed for cremation. If a Balinese dies far from home, or at sea, an effigy is usually burned in the village cemetery as a substitute for the cremation proper.

The bamboo *wadah* is decorated with colored paper, tinsel, cotton ornaments and small mirrors. Sudras are entitled to only one roof, but are usually cremated in large groups, victims of the cut-price, even in death. Three to eleven are reserved for the three senior castes, while a Brahmanic priest or priestess has no roof at all but an empty chair akin to a temple *padmasana*. The tower and the bull are rotated frequently, and especially at crossroads, both to deceive the evil spirits and to prevent the soul of the deceased finding its way back home again. The giant head on the back of the more splendid towers is called a *bhoma*, a fanged monster with wings outstretched, decorated in colored cotton.

In the case of high caste cremations — the kind that visitors to Bali are almost invariably taken to — there will be elaborate ceremonies too on the previous day. A procession bearing effigies *(adegan)* of the deceased will go to the house of the high priest to receive his blessing. There will be *baris* dances (see DANCE AND DRAMA, page 117) and singing in Sanskrit, together with various small ceremonies in which members of the family symbolize their breaking of emotional ties with the dead man, ties that might oth-

OPPOSITE TOP: "Suddenly the body emerges. It's shrouded in white at the end of the sheet, and bundled quickly into the tower..." (page 106).
OPPOSITE BOTTOM: Cremation bulls.

erwise keep him in this world and prevent his soul from the freedom it desires.

In the evening prior to the cremation there will be shadow puppet performances or displays of the *barong landong* dance.

The actual burning usually takes around three hours, during which time the family goes home to rest. When they return to the cremation ground in the late afternoon it is for a more private, small scale ceremony. The ashes have now been gathered and placed in a yellow coconut. They are taken in procession to a local river, or to the sea, and are there scattered on the water after another brief ritual.

MAGIC AND WITCHCRAFT

The Balinese won't talk about it much, but they all believe in witches. Certain people become witches *(leyak)* by undergoing a series of rituals, reciting mantras backwards and the like, and the disembodied spirits of these people can, it is believed, be seen as green lights hovering in graveyards or at crossroads, or as animals encountered in the dark.

Though these beliefs certainly have their origins in the pre-Hindu past, they nevertheless are embraced by the Hindu world view. Negative forces are simply the opposites of the positive ones used by the temple priests. Each is a part of existence, and security is best safeguarded by ensuring a balance between the two natural sets of forces. It's the left and right of the shadow puppet plays in another form.

Most Balinese drama originates in temple ceremony (just as Western drama originated in religious performances in ancient Greece), and these dramas often involve possession, or are staged as rituals of exorcism. Whether it's a performance of the *barong* dance, the provision by a *balian* (herbalist/witch doctor/faith healer) of an amulet against illness, or the rituals surrounding *kanda empat* (see BIRTH, CHILDHOOD, LOVE AND MARRIAGE, page 91), life in Bali proceeds according to spiritual tenets.

The *barong* dance at Batubulan. This good natured monster overcomes the powerful *rangda* in ritual conflict, with a little bit of help from his friends. This popular dance is an exorcism ritual aimed at limiting the power of the *rangda*, or witch.

HEROES AND VILLAINS

Ideally, anyone hoping to come to grips with Balinese culture on a serious level ought to read something of the great Indian romance, the *Ramayana*, beforehand. (Though this is akin saying a visitor to England should read *A Christmas Carol* or *Hamlet*; whereas this too would undoubtedly be worthwhile, it's unlikely many visitors, even those with cultural aspirations, will actually take the trouble.)

The ancient Sanskrit poems, the *Ramayana* and the *Mahabharata*, do still have a pervasive influence on the Balinese, even though not one in 10,100 will have read a single line of them. Reading isn't the main means of cultural transmission in Asia; the epics were passed on for millennia by recitation before they were ever written down. In Bali today it is through the shadow puppet plays and the dance dramas that the people make contact with these ancient symbolic stories. It's comparable to the Middle Ages in Europe where few read the scriptures, but everyone followed the religion and knew the stories of Adam and Eve, Abraham and Isaac, David and Goliath, Noah's ark, and the birth and death of Jesus through church festivals, street dramas, paintings and stained-glass windows.

As the average visitor is only in Bali for a short time, and the shadow plays (for instance) are in several unfamiliar languages, it will perhaps be useful to give a brief description of these two great works, and the crucial episodes returned to time and time again by Balinese dancers and puppeteers.

The *Ramayana* (The Romance of Rama) is an immensely long poem, 48,000 lines, completed probably around BC 300 by Valmiki, a sage who himself appears as a character in the poem.

Prince Rama, the perfect ruler and an incarnation of Vishnu (Wisnu in Bali) wins Sita to be his wife by bending the bow of the god Shiva (Siwa in Bali) at a tournament. Rama is heir to the throne of the kingdom of Ayodhya but is disinherited and forced into exile in the forest with his wife and his half brother Laksmana.

One day, while Rama and Laksmana are pursuing a golden deer, the demon king

Ravana (who has sent the deer specifically to distract Rama) seizes Sita and carries her off to his island kingdom of Lanka.

But Rama is helped by the forest monkeys, by their king Sugriva and especially by their warrior-general, the white monkey Hanuman. It's he who discovers where Sita is and leads Rama to her. In the inevitable battle that follows, Rama wins back Sita, and also, by and by, his own throne.

But the people suspect poor Sita of infidelity to Rama while she was on Lanka, and Rama is forced to place her in a hermitage.

There she gives birth to Rama's twin sons and meets the sage Valmiki.

Eventually, when her sons are grown, Sita is accepted back by the people and by Rama, but, weary of life, asks the earth to take her, which it duly does.

From this brief outline, many Balinese echoes are apparent. There's a *losmen* called Ayodhya at Lovina, there's a Hanuman statue at the entrance to the Sangeh Monkey Forest, and the story of Rama and the deer is at the heart of the Balinese Ramayana Ballet.

OPPOSITE: The figure of an official in the *barong* dance. The courts of the old Hindu rajahs of Java and Bali have left their mark on a number of Balinese dramas. ABOVE: Balinese dancers' costumes are made and maintained with an extraordinary care and attention to detail.

If the Ramayana is long, the Mahabharata (The Great Epic of the Bharata Dynasty) is positively sprawling. It's three times the length of the Old and New Testaments of the Bible put together, 200,000 lines of Sanskrit verse. Like the Bible, it is a storehouse of the history, laws, poetry and moral principles of a people. It was probably only revised by its supposed author, one Vyasa, any time between BC 400 and AD 400, and it's the longest poem known anywhere in the world.

The main channel in this vast and complex river of words is the story of the feud between the rival branches of a royal family, the Pandavas and the Kauravas.

Who should rule has been rendered unclear by the eldest son of the previous generation being passed over for the succession because he's blind. The next in line gives up the throne to become an ascetic and the blind son is subsequently brought back to rule. Upon his death, his five sons are forced to flee the court and go into exile, together with the wife they all share, Draupadi. They are joined by their cousin Krishna. Eventually they return, but are forced to flee a second time when the eldest brother loses everything in a dice game with his cousin.

War becomes inescapable, and battle rages for 18 days on the field of Kuruksetra, north of modern day Delhi. Only seven individuals survive the immense conflict, among them the five brothers and Krishna.

Krishna is later shot, mistaken for a deer, and the five brothers set out to seek the heaven of Indra in the company of a dog, actually the god Dharma in disguise. Only the eldest, Yudhisthira, eventually completes the quest.

Part of Book Six of the Mahabharata is the celebrated *Bhagavadgita* (Song of the Lord). It's a dialogue between Arjuna, one of the Pandava brothers, and Krishna before the battle. Anticipating the terrible destruction that is certain to take place, Arjuna asks if it is right that he should fight to kill his own kith and kin in this way. Krishna replies with the doctrine of the disinterested discharge of one's duty, and in the process reveals himself as a reincarnation of the god Vishnu.

But far from endorsing a militaristic ethic, the *Bhagavadgita*, goes on to encompass the heart of Hindu belief as to the nature of God and the means of approach for the awakened soul to this supreme reality.

What is notable about the poem as a whole is the way it manifests the values of a warrior society and then proceeds to add to these religious values that finally supersede the heroic ones, and even point the way forward to the later Indian principles of nonviolence and philosophical pacifism.

The stories contained in these two poems spread, alongside Indian religion, east into Cambodia and south to what is now Indonesia. That incidents from these epics are still

alive and popular, not only in India itself (where they form the material for the *kathakali* dance dramas) but as far south as Java and Bali, is surely one of the most remarkable spiritual wonders of the world.

THE BALINESE AT PLAY

SILVER RAIN

Old Balinese princes used to pay for the formation of large and splendid orchestras in which they then performed themselves, no doubt with considerable display of self-congratulation, rather as the princelings of eighteenth century German courts would commission works from Bach or Mozart with prominent, but not too difficult, parts for the instruments they played.

This patronage by the rajahs of old, dividing their time between *gamelan*-playing

Balinese *gamelan* musicians. Almost entirely percussive, it has been described by one writer as "a shining rain of silver", by another as "the muffled laughter of forgotten gods".

and the demands of their innumerable wives, has given way to support by the local community associations *(banjar)* and a competitive ambiance fostered by the training courses in *gamelan* music given by the colleges of higher education in Denpasar.

Though the *gamelan* derive from the indigenous orchestras of old Java, the music they play in Bali today is altogether more lively and progressive than anything you'll hear on the larger island. Though it may seem at first that what you're hearing is a highly stylized and traditional art form, the truth is that new styles within that form are constantly evolving, and Balinese *gamelan* music is very much a living and growing genre.

What characterizes the Balinese *gamelan* is its brilliance of sound, its sudden changes of volume and pace and its virtuoso displays of precise, fast playing.

Two key features should be understood: As with Balinese drama, the performers are not professional, and the music exists primarily as an accompaniment to rituals and dance performances (themselves also accompaniments to rituals) rather than as an entertainment in its own right. Of course, there are exceptions nowadays, such as the uprooted-looking performers seated in the lobbies of some big hotels playing with commendable spirit for a set portion of every hour. But the overwhelming majority of the musicians in Bali are farmers during the day, and *gamelan* artists after sundown.

If you want to judge how genuine the *gamelan* you're seeing is, count the number of performers. A real *gamelan gong*, the commonest type of modern band, will have around twenty players and feature the following instruments:

Xylophone-like instruments known as *gangsa*. These consist of bronze keys over bamboo resonators that are beaten with a mallet held in the right hand and their reverberation immediately cut short by the thumb and index finger of the left.

A *riong*, a frame holding bronze "pots" which four players strike with sticks.

A *trompong*, an instrument similar to the above but played by a virtuoso solo player.

A *ceng ceng*, a frame with many cymbals suspended from it — these are struck by another, hand held cymbal.

Kendang, drums. These are the heart of the *gamelan*, the only instruments, the dancers need attend to, and they are played by the seasoned maestros of the orchestra. The first drummer is like the first violinist and conductor of a Western classical orchestra combined, the leader and controller of the *gamelan*.

The musicians will all be male, seated on the ground and dressed in the colorful uniform of their particular orchestra.

The instruments are of invariable pitch, fixed forever at the time of manufacture. Where instruments are paired, there is often a slight and deliberate difference between their respective pitches designed to set up a deliciously thrilling dissonance that is an essential component in the brilliant, metallic cascade of sound that is Balinese music.

Here, then, is a music that, unless extra instruments are added, is entirely percussive. Nothing could be further removed from the Western classical tradition where the timpani have the lowest status of all the instruments in the orchestra. In Bali, they are everything, and the result is a music that injects energy into the sultry night air, a music so vibrant and electrifying that the name *kebyar gamelan* says it all. *Kebyar* means bursting into flower, flaring up suddenly into jagged, passionate brilliance.

The American Colin McPhee, author of *A House in Bali* (see RECOMMENDED READING, page 250), can be credited with first bringing this unique music to the notice of the West. He must have known his own attempts to transcribe the music for two pianos were doomed from the start, but the influence persisted nonetheless, in America especially, and found its first major flowering on the international scene in the Sixties with the music of such artists as Steve Reich, Terry Riley and, later, Philip Glass.

DANCE AND DRAMA

While only men play in the *gamelan* orchestras, the dance dramas are truly androgynous, with women and men dancing a wide variety of roles, sometimes as the opposite

Musicians, *gamelan*-players at Besakih Temple BOTTOM and Tanjung Benoa TOP.

sex, sometimes as their own and sometimes as animals. The style is essentially Javanese, and before that Indian, but with Balinese spirit ritual elements added.

Training is intensive and begins young. Balinese dance has always made great use of children; girls destined for the *legong* dance start at age six or seven with training that includes special massage to make their limbs supple. Hand and head movements are especially important, leg movements — in contrast to Western dance of all styles — less so. Facial expressions and the movement of the eyes are most important of all. Despite the long training, dancers are not paid, at least not when performing traditional festival dances at the temples.

The wide repertoire of Balinese dances is always being added to, old styles falling out of favor and new ones coming into fashion. In this, Balinese dance contrasts with the unchanging classical dance of Java from which it derives. The reason for this is simple: Dance in Bali is a popular art form, rooted in collective social organizations, whereas in Java it was for centuries something performed under the patronage of the rajahs and nowadays is staged almost exclusively for tourists.

Balinese dances were originally, and are generally still, sacred, performed to greet the gods as they descend from their mountaintop homes into the temples to attend the temple ceremonies.

However, special abbreviated dance shows are now put on specifically for visitors. These take place either at the bigger hotels at Sanur or Nusa Dua or in villages such as Ubud, Batubulan or Bona.

There won't be any Balinese in the audience at these tourist shows, apart from the odd child selling soft drinks or "programs" who might stay on to watch. Raked seating will be provided so that everyone gets an uninterrupted view, there'll be an attempt at modern theatrical lighting, and the shows will begin at a convenient time. What you will see, however, will not be the dance drama, performed in the crowded forecourt of a temple attended by the entire village population dressed for a high festival, that

Gamelan music and street processions often combine to add delight to the most oppressively humid day.

made Bali famous in the Thirties. Any performance done as a routine for an audience which the artists know is unfamiliar with the art form will inevitably lack fire. In addition, the context will be missing, and what you will be witnessing will be an art torn up from its roots and presented in a vacuum.

Nevertheless, there are of course varying levels of artistry in these tourist shows, and it should be said at once that the dances at **Ubud**, the large village north of Denpasar that is the "cultural capital" of Bali, are usually of a high quality, and only the original social context is missing.

At Ubud, a different program is offered each night of the week, either at the Ubud Palace or elsewhere. Where the performances are outside the village itself, transport is provided and the cost included in the price of the ticket.

The *legong* performance, currently presented on Monday and Saturday at the Palace, is a kind of revue. It features a number of different dances, with the *legong* itself some two-thirds of the way through. The standard is high and, despite the fact that this performance is put on exclusively for the benefit of foreigners, this is an excellent introduction to Balinese dance.

Danced against a background of the temple, the combination of the hard, precise music, the rich costumes and the dedication on the faces of the young performers is powerful. That the lighting is improvised, some of it consisting of domestic light bulbs with biscuit tin reflectors, only adds to the authenticity and excitement of the performance.

At **Bona**, half an hour's drive east of Denpasar, shows are given nightly at various sites. The village is not easily accessible by public transport after sunset, and audiences are almost invariably brought in by the various tour agencies in Kuta and Sanur. The performance areas, lit by torches in preparation for the *kecak* dance, make a picturesque sight as you drive past them in the early Indonesian dark. The performances themselves, however, can be less impressive.

The standard fare at Bona is a *kecak* dance followed by two spirit possession dances, the *sanghyang dedari* and the *sanghyang jaran*. The convenience of this arrangement for the

organizers is that none of these dances requires a *gamelan* accompaniment.

At **Batubulan**, north of Denpasar on the road to Gianyar, *barong* dances are performed, again exclusively for visitors, at 9:30 AM every morning. The show lasts an hour.

Bali's Dances

The following are the main dances and other dramatic performances you are likely to encounter on the island:

Arja Sometimes referred to as "Balinese opera," this is ballet and opera combined. Four women, playing male characters, sing and dance simultaneously. Clowns and servants provide the lowlife commentary.

Baris Gede A warrior dance for a group of a dozen or so middle-aged men, its purpose is to protect the visiting gods at temple festivals from evil spirits. The dancers wear headdresses with a triangle of white cloth at the back with pieces of shell attached. They carry spears tipped with peacock feathers, and during the dance they divide into two groups and engage in mock conflict.

Baris Pendet A solo form of the above. In this demanding virtuoso dance, the performer goes through all the emotions of a warrior before, and then in, battle.

Barong Essentially an exorcism dance, the *barong* features a benign monster—the *barong ket*—like the lion in the Chinese lion dance, but with long white hair and fitted with leather saddles. Its mouth opens and closes noisily. Its opponent is the *rangda*, a witch with long white hair, drooping breasts, bulging eyes and twisted fangs, flourishing a magically powerful white cloth.

The full version begins with introductory dances unconnected to the main action—a comic confrontation between the *barong* and three masked palm-wine tappers, and a short *legong* dance.

The play's essential feature is a battle between the good-natured *barong* and the *rangda*, with the *barong* assisted, not very effectively, by a group of men armed with *kris* (short swords). What leads up to this is a plot involving a queen who has to sacrifice

All the sultry, languid beauty of the tropics is suggested by this young performer in the *barong* dance. Children are trained in the art of dance from an early age, and often continue to perform throughout their adult lives.

her son to the goddess of death. The son is saved, being given immortality by the god Siwa, but takes on a variety of heroic tasks which quickly prove too much for him. He calls on the *barong* for help, and the *barong* in turn calls on the armed warriors.

The *rangda* puts a spell on the men so that they try to kill themselves. The *barong*, however, renders their swords harmless; the impotent frenzy of the entranced warriors is a big feature of the show.

The *rangda* is finally defeated, but real magic is considered to have been brought forth by the performance — and indeed the warriors are often in a trance by this stage — and so a chicken is sacrificed and water sprinkled on the warriors by a resident *pemangku* as a conclusion to the dance.

Barong Landong The name means "tall barong." This performance features two large figures, twice life size, manipulated by actors inside them. They enact a comic slinging match between a black giant, *jero gede*, and his woman, *jero luh*. The little chanted drama is accompanied by a few musicians and is a rite to dispel evil which is performed on important occasions such as the night before a cremation.

Calon Arang An exorcism drama aimed at the local village witches (*leyak* — see MAGIC AND WITCHCRAFT, page 110) and usually performed when a new temple is dedicated.

Staged at the full moon, and continuing until dawn, the drama features the witch *rangda* who, at the climax of the performance, after comic interludes and dances by young girls, emerges from her house and advances in a frenzy on the audience.

The part of the *rangda* is taken by an experienced older actor because the performance involves the witch going into an entranced rage, possessed — so the Balinese believe — by the spirit of the actual *rangda*. The end of the event is unpredictable, and the *rangda* can on occasion run amok. Only an actor of long experience can hope to control so powerful a spirit entering into him. The purpose of the performance is to placate the *rangda* by demonstrating her power, and

A gorgeously clad figure from the *kecak* dance approaches the flaming lamp that is this dance's only illumination. The dance has no instrumental accompaniment and is based on a story from the Indian *Ramayana* epic.

thus gain her cooperation against the lesser witches in the village.

The performance raises many profound questions, such as the extent to which any acting anywhere is a form of self-imposed possession, and the reasons for the world-wide obsession with solitary women past the age of childbearing as agents of evil (*rangda* means widow).

Gambuh This is an ancient Balinese dance performed to entertain visiting gods at temple festivals. Speaking in Kawi, a prince and his beloved undergo various trials to the

accompaniment of an antique orchestra featuring bass flutes. Comic servants provide a commentary in Low Balinese.

Janger Twelve girls and twelve boys sit on four sides of a square with a leader in the middle. They perform a variety of dances, comic sketches and acrobatic displays.

Jauk A short dance by a masked dancer displaying the sinister convolutions of a demon.

Joged A non-temple dance that was much appreciated by early visitors to the island anxious to penetrate the ceremonious reserve of the Balinese. A solo girl dances flirtatiously with men she selects from the audience. Sometimes it is performed by a boy dressed as a woman, in which case it's called *gandrung*.

Kebiyar Duduk The Balinese emphasis on eyes, head and arms in dance, as opposed to legs, is highlighted in this dance for a solo seated performer. It's essentially an abstract interpretation of Balinese music and was invented in the Thirties by the famous Balinese dancer known as Mario — his career

is described by Covarrubias in *The Island of Bali.*

Kecak There is no accompanying orchestra in this dance. Instead, a large group of men provides a continuous vocal background, something like a sound picture of an ocean in all its moods. They are dressed only in a black and white checked sarongs, with a red flower behind the right ear and a white one behind the left.

They move around on their haunches, sometimes swaying from side to side, sometimes bouncing up and down, sometimes flinging themselves forward in a circle, with arms outstretched toward the center. All the time they chant, sometimes in unison, sometimes contrapuntally, between sections of the group.

The central performance area is lit only by a flaming lamp, but the gorgeously clad characters in the drama to which the group of men provide an accompaniment usually arrive on the scene through a temple gateway, dramatically lit from behind.

The story is of Rama's trip to the forest with Sita to seek the golden deer. Rawana, king of the demons, kidnaps Sita, but Hanuman, the white monkey, comes to her aid by telling Rama what's happened. A son of the demon king fires an arrow (that turns into a snake) at Rama, but Rama calls on Garuda, the bird god, to save him. The king of the monkeys, Sugriwa, then arrives on the scene and the drama ends with a fight between the monkeys and the demons, with the *kecak* chorus dividing in support of the two sides. Rama is reunited with his beloved Sita.

Kupu Kupu Carum A dance in which a prince manages through meditation to overcome the temptations offered him by a band of nymphs. The actor playing the prince remains motionless throughout most of the performance.

Legong This most classical of all Balinese dances used only to be performed by girls who had not yet reached puberty. It is performed by three dancers, two of them en-

acting the principal characters and the third playing the *condong* or servant.

The dance is so formalized, with the dancers portraying first one incident then another without any change of style, that it is difficult to follow what's going on. The plot involves a princess, Rangkesari, who has been forcibly abducted by a prince, Lasem. She refuses to have anything to do with him, and when she hears her brother, the crown prince of Kahuripan, is coming to save her, she appeals to her captor to release her and so avoid a battle. He refuses, and on his way out to fight sees a raven, an omen of his imminent defeat on the battlefield.

The dance tells only a fragment of this brief story. It begins with the *condong* dancing a prologue, then shows the two identically dressed girls as the prince and princess. The prince is already about to leave for the battlefield when they first appear. He is sad that the princess has rejected him; she asks him not to fight her brother; he refuses and leaves. The *condong* then closes the performance by appearing with little gilt wings attached, representing the bird of ill omen.

Such highly stylized dramatic forms, showing only the climax of a story already well known to the audience, and even that symbolically and without any actual confrontation, has characterized highly developed forms of theater elsewhere, in ancient Greece and in Japan, for example. Here in Bali, the *legong* has a particularly remote quality given to it by its being played by (originally) young girls dressed in exceptionally elaborate costumes.

There is no mention of the *legong* in the ancient *lontar* (palm leaf books) referring to dance, and the form was probably created as recently as the nineteenth century.

Mendet (also known as *Pendet*) A dance to welcome the spirits to the temple, performed by a group of older women carrying offerings in their right hands.

Oleg Tambulilingan A dance representing the flirtation between two bees gathering honey among the flowers.

Panyembrama A welcoming dance performed by a troupe of girls who scatter flowers on the spectators. It was evolved in the Sixties as an introductory dance for the *legong* revue performances.

Prembon A masked dance showing the defeat by Sri Krishna Kapakisan of rebellious subjects using a magical sword given him by Gaja Mada.

Ramayana Ballet Imported to Bali recently from Java, this dance tells the story of Rama and Hanuman (the white monkey) from the *Ramayana* epic. It's the same story told by the *kecak* dance.

Rejang A stately, processional movement performed by women bringing offerings to a temple.

Sanghyang Dedari (also called the Virgin Dance) A possession dance in which two young girl dancers are put into a trance. The only music is chanting by unaccompanied voices.

Sanghyang Jaran (also called the Fire Dance) This is an event rather than a dance, in which a young man enters riding a hobbyhorse and proceeds to trample with his bare feet a pile of smoldering coconut husks. The performer is in a trance and sometimes kicks the glowing shells around violently. They're raked back into a heap by an assistant. Afterwards, the entranced youth is brought back to normal consciousness with water. He then drinks holy water three times and offers blossoms three times in the direction of the temple.

Topeng Pajegan A masked dance in which a solo dancer performs in a series of different masks to portray a variety of characters in a story.

Topeng Panca A masked dance in which a number of dancers, each wearing a different mask, act out a story.

Topeng Tua A solo masked dance, slow and deliberate, in which the dancer imitates the uncertain and painful movements of a very old man.

Wayang Wong A rare form of drama where players enact the stories from the shadow puppet plays.

In addition to attending performances, you can take **dance classes**, held in the mornings, at two colleges in the capital (see under DENPASAR in THE BROAD HIGHWAY, page 160).

The *wayung kulit*, or shadow puppet play. The *dalang*, or puppeteer, sits behind his screen and selects his puppets from a collection in a large wooden box. The stories are well-known to the local audience — they have to be as only the jokes are in a language the ordinary people understand.

Each year the six-week **Bali Arts Festival** is held in Denpasar from mid-June to the end of July. It features a much music and dance.

The **Badung Government Tourist Office** (23399 or 23602 on Jalan Surapati in Denpasar, issues an up-to-date broadsheet coming temple festivals, many of which will include dance performances.

The *wayang kulit,* or shadow puppet play (*wayang* — puppet, *kulit* — leather) you are

most likely to see will have been staged specifically for tourists. But there are at least a couple of dozen practicing puppeteers in Bali staging performances on request for weddings, temple anniversaries and the night before cremations.

The *wayang kulit* is, like almost all art in Bali, ceremonial in origin, and the puppeteer *(dalang)* a kind of magician.

The artist as seer is an old idea, and it's no surprise that the Indonesian puppet play — it's also found in Java — is seen by many as a form of metaphysics. Sukarno, the country's first president, used to gather his ministers together in his hill station retreat and tease them with puppet shows obvious prefiguring of their advancement or fall from grace.

Even now there are commentators who attribute the blank passivity of the people in the face of the massacre of leftists in 1965 to a fatalism rooted in the mythology of the *wayang,* a belief that, in the eternal battle between good and evil, there was no hope for you if, in the episode of the drama which happened to constitute your life, you were unfortunate enough to be caught on the wrong side of the stage.

The "stage" in the *wayang* is a cloth screen about one meter by three. The right of the stage as viewed by the audience is the side of the bug-eyed villains, the left of the strangely emaciated aristocratic heroes.

On a low platform behind the screen sits the *dalang,* cross-legged and formally dressed as if for a religious ceremony, which in a way this is. To his left is the puppet box containing a large selection of the puppets in regular use. Behind him, dressed in sarong and headdress, sit the musicians of the *gender wayang* behind their *gangsa,* the xylophone-like instruments of the *gamelan.* No gongs or drums are used, and the *gangsa* are struck by hammers held in each hand. Consequently the reverberation has to be stopped by the knuckles rather than the left hand as in the *gamelan* proper.

The performance begins with an overture by the musicians during which the puppeteer sprinkles holy water and makes offerings to sanctify the show and "bring the puppets to life." The show itself begins with a kind of skeletal leaf (but actually the sacred Tree of Life) dividing the screen. It will be used again later to indicate changes of scene.

The stories are all taken from the *Ramayana* and *Mahabharata* epics (see HEROES AND VILLAINS, page 113) and are well known to the Balinese, just as the story of Cinderella is known in advance by Western audiences at a pantomime, or *Don Giovanni* to the opera-goer. The attraction of the performance is both the retelling of an old tale and the up-to-date and local references the *dalang* will manage to incorporate into it.

It's as well the stories are known already because the actual narration is chanted in the dead Javanese language of Kawi, and the language of the ordinary people will only appear in the sarcastic and debunking remarks of the four lowlife clowns.

At every *wayang* play, not only does the audience witness a highlighting and a confirmation of the established social order, it also is made conscious of the interplay of this world with that of the gods, and in a way that makes life seem a small part of a greater enactment over which it is foolish to think we have any measure of control.

Spectators have every right to go backstage and watch the show from the other side. There'll even be a couple of benches provided, one on each side of the performers. It's here, behind the scenes, that the real

An assistant sits on either side of the puppeteer and prepares and then hands him the puppets as he needs them from a banana tree trunk into which they've been stuck ready for use. The puppets' traveling box stands away to the puppeteer's left and, sitting cross-legged, he beats on the box with a peg held between the toes of his right foot, providing rhythmic excitement and special effects for the innumerable fights into which the stories always quickly descend.

The puppeteer does all the talking, telling the story and acting all the speaking parts.

atmosphere of the *wayang* can best be flavored.

It's an enclosed, primordial scene. The flaming lamp, clearly visible even from the front of the house and giving the flickering effect of early film to the show as a whole, can be seen backstage as being a giant kettle with flames leaping from its stubby spout.

The puppets themselves are intricately shaped, and painted in great detail, with much gilt — quite unnecessarily for their function as casters of shadows, but appropriately for sacral adjuncts. A string, worked by the *dalang*'s index finger, moves the puppet's jaw, while a thin stick, manipulated with the puppeteer's other hand, operates the arm of any character that appears solo.

Sweat running down his face from the hot night and the heat of the lamp, he pours out a stream of jokes, chants and heroic invocations, beating the screen with his flimsy puppets and simultaneously hammering the box with his foot.

The guttering flame is replenished by the "evil side" (puppeteer's left) attendant pouring oil into the lidless kettle. A shield behind concentrates the light onto the screen and keeps it out of the eyes of the puppeteer. The costumed musicians hammer away, interweaving their arpeggios and changing

The *wayung kulit.* ABOVE: The puppeteer, both magician and priest, both jester and guardian of an ancient tradition. OPPOSITE: The primordial scene backstage — spectators are welcome to go round and take a look.

rhythm for every new scene and facet of the immemorially ancient story.

It's an extraordinary scene, these stories from far-off India being reenacted in the tropical night and with such a combination of relish and formality. The eager, laughing faces of the audience, the constant reversing of the puppets, so that they appear first facing this way and then that, and each change accompanied by a clack with the toehammer. The old tackle, the flaring light, the relish of the exuberant puppeteer... it's akin to the Sicilian puppets of Palermo reenacting stories of

the crusades based on the rhyming epics of Ariosto or Tasso. It has the same enclosed quality, the same intensity.

Here in the tropics it's older still. What you're seeing is something so ancient that scholars are unable to ascribe a place of origin to it. Yet here it is being recreated in this wall-less village hall, by the sweating, laughing puppeteer.

It's the magic of the old Javanese night. The puppeteer, as well as being a priest, is a magician, able to bring to life these ancient stories with his two-dimensional dolls. He stirs the naturally symbolic imaginations of the people, warming their easily welcoming hearts with his gusto and his mixture of heroism and broad popular comedy.

The popularity of these night entertainments shows how deep they go into the consciousness of the people. These flickering images in jungle villages beside elaborately wrought Hindu temples have for centuries molded the souls of an artistic people with stories of magic, power struggles, good and evil, and seemingly pointless heroism.

When in 1909 the Balinese aristocracy presented themselves before the Dutch army for certain destruction in long lines of bejeweled and costumed splendor, the images and patterns of the heroic tales of the *wayang kulit* cannot have been far from their hearts. Like the Pandavas and the Kouravas at war in the *Mahabharata*, they could never surrender.

THE AFFRIGHTED SUN

The gamecock clipped and armed for fight
Does the rising sun affright. — William Blake,
Auguries of Innocence (1805)

The tending and care of fighting cocks is one of the most visible parts of Balinese life, and men sitting in circles preening their birds is one of the most common sights on the island.

Gambling has been illegal throughout Indonesia since 1981. In Bali, however, where the letting of blood is deemed a necessary part of temple festivals, permits are issued by the police allowing three cockfights on the days of temple anniversary celebrations. Both the restriction on the number of fights and the general prohibition on gambling are regularly ignored on these occasions.

Bets are placed nominally in the ancient currency of the *ringgit* though in reality in the rupiah equivalent. A lay priest (*pemangku*) gives offerings to both the good and evil spirits before the fight begins.

The Balinese word for cockfights is *tajen* (blades), the razor-sharp knives that are attached to the cocks' left legs.

Cocks naturally fight each other over the female birds. But it's only with the lethal blades attached that they slash their opponent almost to death, often in a matter of

ABOVE: A fighting cock and its master. OPPOSITE: Men preening and matching their fighting cocks — a common sight all over Bali. Cock fights are nowadays only permitted before temple anniversary ceremonies as a precaution against excessive gambling.

seconds. They are not armed with blades in the trial bouts, of course, but in the fight itself, nature becomes hideously armed, a flurry in the air becomes a flashing of steel, with the defeated bird lying bleeding in the dust.

The blade becomes the property of the specialist *(pekembar)* the owner has employed to fix it in place. As soon as the winner has been declared, the legs, blade attached, are chopped off the losing cock, almost invariably while it is still alive.

CRICKET FIGHTING

The Balinese also bet on crickets; it's a sort of poor man's cockfighting. The creatures are caught in the cracks of the dried out rice fields after harvest and fed on grains of rice and flower petals. They are exercised and bathed, and kept in tubular cages made of sections of bamboo. The fights take place inside a pair of cages placed together end to end. The winner is the cricket that forces the other to retreat to its furthest corner. Bets are in the region of a few thousand rupiah — on cocks they can be millions.

BIRD ORCHESTRAS

Bells and small flutes are attached round the necks of doves so that when they wheel overhead they produce a delicious tinkling and humming. Covarrubias says in *The Island of Bali* that these aerial musical instruments are a protection against birds of prey. It is true that if this is not the case, then bird or-

chestras are the only form of Balinese music created purely for pleasure.

Even so, it would be very Balinese to make them for fun, and then say they were to accompany the gods on their way down to the temples. Whatever their original purpose, the unexpected sound of these tiny instruments borne on the breeze is one of the real delights of the island.

ART AND CRAFTS

PAINTING

Balinese art acquired some celebrity before the war due to the publicity given it by artists from the West coming to live on the island. They found a prolific but static local tradi-

tion and encouraged the practitioners to experiment along semi-Western lines. The results proved exotic yet familiar, just the thing the well-heeled tourists wanted to take home as mementos. It's a different story today.

It may well be true that you can resell Balinese pictures in the Gulf States and elsewhere for a handsome profit, if you know where to take them. But there is a vast amount of substandard work being produced these days in Bali merely to satisfy tourist market.

Much of the worst can be bypassed by going direct to Ubud, the center for Balinese painting both good and mediocre. Here at least you will have a chance to inspect a wide range of work — particularly conveniently at the gallery set apart across a rice field to the left of the Puri Lukisan Museum where paintings by many artists hang with prices (not necessarily final) attached. A visit here will allow you to compare styles and going rates before you begin looking at the galleries showing a single artist's work.

Balinese painting before the Thirties was exclusively concerned with the production of hangings and calendars for temples. Production was centered on Kamasan, south of Klungkung, and work of this kind is now referred to as being in the Kamasan style. Subjects were scenes from the epic stories, painted in hand-ground paints, and the final result was not unlike a colored version of the *wayang kulit* shadow puppet plays. These types of paintings are still available and are still being produced in Kamasan.

For the rest, styles are nowadays divided into "traditional" and "young artists." By traditional is meant the style of painting encouraged in the Thirties by the Western artists Rudolf Bonnet and Walter Spies, painters who settled in Bali and lived in Campuhan, down by Ubud's suspension bridge. These paintings depict daily scenes as well as legendary ones, in restrained colors or even in monochrome. They are comparatively realistic, filling every corner of the canvas with detail, and lacking any real attempt at light and shade effects.

ABOVE: A Balinese painting from a private collection. The rural scene, and the crowding of the canvas with largely decorative detail, is very typical of the traditional Balinese school of painting.

The so-called young artists were set to work by the Dutch painter Arie Smit in the Sixties and are based in Penestanan, an extension of Ubud just over the bridge from Campuhan. Their pictures are vividly colored naive versions of daily life scenes.

Of course there are some fine pictures among all these, though originality is not a strong suit in the Balinese hand. But prices are not low, whatever the quality — you will have to start thinking in terms of at least US$200 as an absolute minimum for a small sized production if you want to acquire anything of reasonable quality.

The booklet *Different Styles of Painting in Bali* by Drs. Sudarmaji, available at the Neka Gallery in Ubud (not to be confused with the Museum Neka) is helpful in getting an idea of what to expect.

WOODCARVING

Balinese woodcarving is renowned because a natural local aptitude has allowed itself to be influenced by Western styles, and the resulting hybrid artifacts consequently differ from anything found anywhere else in the world. The main place to see woodcarvings in Bali is the village of Mas, south of Ubud.

The craftsmen of earlier times were occupied with carving figures of gods and heroes for the adornment of the palaces of the local rajahs. The depiction of animals and trees, as well as nontraditional fantasy figures, came with the arrival of Western artists. A particular style involving smooth surfaces and elongated human bodies has become common, and is often looked on as quintessentially Balinese, but actually evolved in the Thirties under the influence of the European art nouveau style.

As with all art objects, the only advice that can be given is to buy what pleases you and what you consider to be of high quality. Despite the endless duplication, there are some wonderful craftsmen at work. Fashioning the wood with delicate steel tools and a light-weight hammer, and working with extraordinary speed, they have gained the reputation of being among the finest woodcarvers anywhere in the world.

Painted carvings, made from local soft woods, are inexpensive and produced in huge numbers. Carved fruits — bananas in particular — almost all produced in the village of Pujung, can be found all over the world.

Hardwood carvings are produced using imported wood as Bali's climate does not give rise to equatorial rain forests. Ebony, for example, is imported from Kalimantan and Sulawesi in eastern Indonesia. Beware of imitations of these woods. To be sure your ebony is ebony, there's a surefire test: Ebony doesn't float. Whether your retailer will allow you to test it is another matter.

The famous shop for woodcarvings is Ida Bagus Tilem's — where presidents and millionaires buy their Bali souvenirs. Quality is guaranteed, but prices are high; this is a place to see the best, then perhaps seek out comparable specimens in the numerous smaller establishments elsewhere in the village.

MASKS: THE OTHER FACE

Masks (*topeng*) are an important element in Balinese dance, and foreigners have been quick to see them as eminently desirable items.

Balinese silverware — the subjects are usually sacred and the technique invariably superb. The center for silverware is the village of Celuk.

Every actor knows the power of a mask. Hanging on a wall, it's merely decorative. Put it on and it comes alive, a part of the actor — but different — an altogether new being. Mask and actor combine to become something neither was before.

The Balinese interpret this psychological phenomenon as a sacred power that inhabits the mask. Many masks represent gods, and as the head is considered the most sacred part of the body, the special status of masks in Bali is assured.

Masks are made primarily at Mas and Singapadu out of the wood of the *pule*, the tree called in Australia the milky pine.

STONECARVING: PORTABLE SHRINES

Carved stone is everywhere in Bali. Bug-eyed monsters with lolling tongues and long fangs cohabit happily with figures on flowery motorbikes. In temples they are everywhere, but also few public buildings or private houses don't boast at least some examples of the art.

Stonecarving is unlike woodcarving in that Western stylistic influence has been minimal, though figures from nature, as opposed to mythology, have long been incorporated into the designs. Balinese wit, with wry comments on modern fashions, is common.

Stonecarvings also differ from woodcarvings in that the ordinary Balinese can afford to buy them. Prices are often low, as little as Rp5,000 for the smallest pieces. The only problem for the visitor is weight — even so, small items, a few centimeters in height, can be found depicting just about any animal, bird, mythological or fanciful character you could wish for.

Most Balinese stonecarving goes on at Batubulan, home of the tourist version of the *barong* dance and on the road from Denpasar to Gianyar. Shops and workshops are one and the same, and all prices are negotiable.

The stone used in carving is a soft sandstone, extremely easy to work but friable. So pack your purchases carefully when taking them home, and remember they'll weather fast if kept outdoors. To some, though, the temptation to have a mock Balinese shrine in the garden may be irresistible.

WEAVING: *ENDEK, IKAT* AND *BATIK*

Weaving enthusiasts will be eager to seek out the local handmade cloth, *endek*, where a pattern has been dyed into the weft by tying it here and there with strips of plastic. The cloth is made on old European style hand looms in small factories, and is sold for local consumption in markets all over Bali.

Ikat, a cloth for which both warp and weft have been dyed before forming a pattern, is produced and sold in the Bali Aga village of Tenganan. The creation of *ikat* cloth is an astonishingly complex and time-consuming procedure, and you naturally pay for this when you buy the finished product.

Most visitors, however, will be content with the better known batik from Java. Batik is not a Balinese product (though "Bali patterns" are always on offer), but both the brilliant "new" and the more delicately shaded "old" batik are on sale in all the main towns, and more or less everywhere that tourists frequent.

All three types of cloth — *endek, ikat* and *batik* — are sold either direct from the bolt or made up into attractive, if not always modern, articles of clothing.

GOLD AND SILVER

Despite the claims on the front of shops in Celuk, the center for gold in Bali is a small area of Denpasar, at the junction of Jalan Sulawesi and Jalan Hasanudin. Here, items of jewelry are sold by weight, prices follow the current price of gold, and the shops cater primarily to rich Balinese rather than to visitors and foreign tourists.

Celuk, just past Batubulan coming out from Denpasar on the way to Gianyar or Ubud, is the silverware center. Intricately worked items — anything from rings to tableware — are a specialty, the smaller pieces virtually solid silver, the larger ones silverplated. You can even watch the silversmiths at work. Prices, however, tend to be

OPPOSITE: Balinese temple stonecarving — a sense of humor is frequently in evidence, while some happily display eroticism in the Hindu tradition. Stone carving is one of the less expensive art objects to acquire, and almost all Balinese homes display some examples.

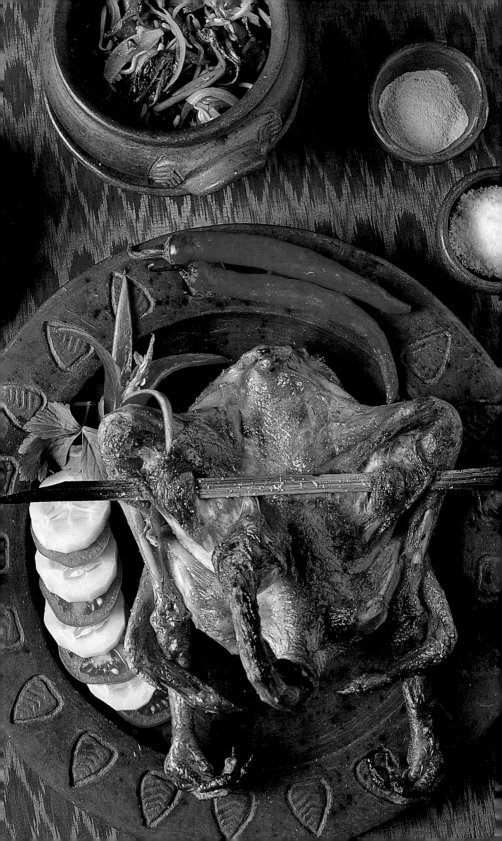

high; they are far more reasonable at the next village of Singapadu.

FOOD AND DRINK: FROM *RIJSTTAFEL* TO *KRETEK*

FESTIVAL FARE

Local Balinese fare on ordinary days is very basic. Daily food consists of cold boiled or steamed rice *(nasi)* with a side dish of chopped and highly spiced vegetables. This is prepared early in the day and left out, covered with squares of banana leaf, for members of the household to help themselves to whenever they feel hungry. It's eaten, with the right hand and preferably alone, on a banana leaf plate that is then thrown to the pigs.

At festivals, however, far more complex dishes are prepared, and these, together with the tasty bits and pieces the Balinese love to eat at street stalls, are what the visitor is most likely to come across in the hotels and local restaurants. Only in the villages, or in the smaller eating places such as in Kuta's Night Market (see under KUTA in THE BROAD HIGHWAY, page 172) will you encounter daily Balinese fare.

Among the festive dishes, the best known is *be guling*, roast pork. It'll be labeled as *babi guling*, and you'll be told this means Balinese roast suckling pig. But the animal you'll be eating will have been three to six months old, barely a suckling, and *babi* is anyway Indonesian, not Balinese. *Be* means meat and *guling* turned.

Next is *bebek betutu*, roast duck, the least difficult to come to terms with of the Balinese festival foods.

Thirdly, *lawar*, or *ebat*, is a mixture of raw, finely chopped meat (usually turtle or pig) and fruits and spices, endlessly ground.

Of the humbler local dishes, *nasi goreng* (fried rice) is the commonest, and what most visitors, uncertain of what other options might imply, tend to fall back on. It can be anything from sumptuous to little more than greasy rice with the odd shrimp, egg and spring onion mixed in.

Nasi campur is another cheap filler, consisting of steamed rice with bits and pieces of everything on top. *Gado gado* is steamed beansprouts and vegetables, all under a sticky peanut sauce.

By contrast, the *rijsttafel* was the Dutch colonial standby — a wide variety of different side dishes served separately with steamed rice. It's usually ordered by a group, everyone taking what appeals to him.

Nasi padang is also a set of side dishes with rice, but it's truly Indonesian (from the region of Padang in Sumatra). You order the things you fancy from a wide choice on the counter, and they all come highly spiced but cold.

Satay is a popular Indonesian specialty, tiny kebabs — usually ordered by the half a dozen or more — served with peanut or hot pepper sauce.

It won't be long before, having mastered some basic terms, you can begin to combine them, and recognize the combinations on menus. Thus, once you know chicken is *ayam*, coconut sauce is *opor*, noodles are *mee* and bananas are *pisang*, you won't have any problems identifying *ayam goreng* as fried chicken, *opor ayam* as chicken cooked in coconut sauce, *mee goreng* as fried noodles and *pisang goreng* as banana fritters. Rice cakes, the usual Balinese breakfast, are *jaja*.

On offer with virtually everything is *kecap*, not ketchup (though the pronunciation is identical) but soy sauce; *manis* is sweet, *asin* is salty.

In the resort areas of Bali, Western food is as common as or more common than Indonesian. Menus are self-explanatory — though perhaps non-Australians will need to be told that *jaffles* are toasted sandwiches sealed at the edges so that the contents come molten and gently bubbling.

DRINKS

Cold drinks assume a new and vital significance in the Balinese climate. Supreme among these are the exquisite mixtures — made everywhere but especially delicious on beaches — of fresh fruit, ice, syrup and a dash of canned milk whisked together in a blender. They're called simply *es jus*, iced juice, and the going rate on Kuta Beach is US$.25 (US$.35 if they're brought to you

Grilled chicken doesn't always look the way you expect it to! Lombok-style chicken is served whole.

where you're lying on the sand). You can choose any combination of the listed fruits, or else tell them to put in something of everything. These gorgeous drinks sometimes seem to be the essence of Bali. The silky property given them by a high proportion of avocado or papaya takes them within range of paradise itself.

Everything else is in a lower class, though the flavored yogurt drink, *lassi*, isn't far behind.

For the rest, *air jeruk* is lemon (or orange) juice, made with fresh fruit, while *stroop* is fruit cordial.

Much has been written about the danger of taking ice in the tropics. The cogent argument is that if the water the ice was made from wasn't boiled, the ice will contain any infection that was present in the water. True, and a point worth remembering in many places. But for some years now the ice in Bali has been produced in approved factories and is, if not one hundred per cent safe, widely accepted.

Ordinary tap water is *not* drinkable. The better-off Balinese drink a commercial brand of bottled water called Aqua, and you should do the same.

Commercially produced ice cream is completely safe, but avoid the homemade variety peddled from street carts. Anything containing milk products needs careful handling and constant refrigeration in the tropics.

When it comes to alcohol, you are faced with the choice of expensive bottled products, similar to things you'll already know, and the inexpensive local brews.

The latter are essentially three — *brem*, a sweet wine made from black rice; *tuak*, a semisweet beer made from the sugar of the coconut palm; and *arak*, a deceptively tasteless brandy distilled from either *tuak* or *brem*. A beverage made of *arak* and *brem* mixed is excellent.

As for non-Balinese alcoholic beverages, imported wine is usually expensive, and consequently not much consumed, spirits are available but soon dropped in favor of *arak* by many visitors, while beer comes in four

---

Satay is popular all over Indonesia. Here the tiny kebabs are waiting to be grilled on a street side stall. They're usually served with a spicy peanut sauce.

brands, Bintang, Anker, San Miguel and Bali Hai. Foreign residents usually consider Bintang the beer of choice.

For the rest, tea is *teh* and coffee *kopi*. Each can be taken with milk (*susu*) and will come sweetened unless you specifically request it without sugar, in which case add the word *tawar*. Thus, coffee with milk but no sugar is *kopi susu tawar*.

TROPICAL FRUITS

The range of fruit available in Bali is almost a reason for going there in itself. Pineapples, papayas, coconuts, bananas, avocados — all are common and cheap. In addition there are a number of fruits you might encounter here for the first time — and you should definitely give them a try. You don't want to find yourself tasting them for the first time on your last day and discovering, too late, that you were made for each other.

The following are the main attractions:

Salak has a texture not unlike a Brazil nut but tastes like a lichee.

Rambutan is also similar to the lichee but with a hairy red skin.

Mangosteen is a fruit that travels badly and so is little known outside the tropics. The outside is black, brown or purple and the inside stunning.

When cut cross section, **Blimbing** forms a five pointed star, hence its Anglo-Saxon name star fruit. You can eat all of this refreshing pale green or yellow fruit.

Jambu-sotong are guavas.

Markisah are passion fruit. You'll see them on sale in the mountains. Break them open and eat everything you find inside, seeds and all. Exquisite is the only word for them.

Nangka is jack fruit. They're so big you'll only want to buy a segment. You eat the yellow inner part and discard the white outer layer.

Jeruk refers to all citrus fruits, but the pomelo, or *jeruk bali*, is the most common. It's like a grapefruit but bigger, and the taste is much sweeter. Lemons are *jeruk nipis*, ordinary oranges *jeruk manis*.

Durian — love it or loathe it — is the infamous fruit that stinks, but tastes to some people like heaven. You can even get durian-

flavored ice cream — a good means of judging whether or not you want to brave the real thing.

There are many more fruits from which to choose. If you see them for sale, give them a try. If you're worried you don't know which part to eat, ask the tradesman — street sellers in Indonesia will normally do just about anything to encourage you to buy. Just ask him to open one up for you, and if you don't trust his standard of hygiene, buy a couple and give him one, then eat them in tandem.

COCONUT PALMS

The Balinese venerate the coconut. The tree is such a generous provider and is considered such a friend to man, that, when I asked one hotel worker whether people were ever killed by coconuts falling to the ground, he said the tree was so kind he was sure it would never happen.

The coconut palm provides oil for cooking and lamps, sweet water to drink, flesh to eat or to make "milk" from for use in cooking, wood for house building and furniture,

OPPOSITE: Vividly colored rice cakes, *jaju*, the most popular breakfast with the Balinese. ABOVE: *Salak* is available everywhere, along with many other tropical delights such as mangosteen, durian, custard apple and mangoes.

leaves for offerings, the "palm cabbage" (just below the head) for food, and gum from its flower buds for palm beer *(tuak)*. Copra, the dried meat of the nut from which oil can easily be extracted, has been one of the main exports from the tropical belt for over a century.

SALT IN THE WOUNDS

An insight into the realities of the Third World life among which the tourist will find himself is provided by the economics of the salt making business.

Salt in Bali is made from sea water, a process involving the carrying of large amounts of water from the sea onto the sand, carrying the wet sand into vats, the water from the vats into troughs and the final sludge from the troughs into filtering baskets. It's a family business, and an average family will produce 25 kg (about 55 lbs) of salt a day during the dry season. The day's salt, the product of at least two adults' labor, is sold for about Rp950 — about US$0.60. During the rainy season the family can produce nothing at all.

BETEL

Often, in the Balinese countryside, you'll come across what seems at first a terrifying spectacle—an older woman with lips stained scarlet, black teeth, a bulge in one cheek and dribbling what looks like blood.

This is merely someone indulging in the ancient and widespread Asian habit of chewing betel.

It's actually a combination of three basic ingredients folded together inside a betel leaf. Together they form a mild stimulant, aid to digestion and antiseptic all in one. But what is extraordinary, though hardly surprising, is that the Balinese have made it into a symbol of the three persons of God — Brahma, Wisnu and Siwa — and it is inconceivable for any temple offering to be made that doesn't include at least one sample.

JAMU

Jamu is a quintessentially Indonesian product, a herbal medicine marketed by a wide range of outlets, from teenage girls with ready

mixed concoctions on their backs doing the rounds in the early mornings to giant wholesalers and distributors of their patented, albeit traditional, medicines. Air Mancur is not an Indonesian domestic airline but the biggest name in this huge *jamu* trade.

The science of *jamu* originated from the Javanese city of Solo, and virtually everyone connected with the industry is Solonese.

Jamu's most celebrated claim is that it increases sexual potency. If you're interested in putting this claim to the test, and are not sure whether your Indonesian is up to explaining what you want in the local supermarket, try the itinerant vendors. They'll probably be round far too early for you even to catch sight of them, but everyone else in Bali is up around 4 AM and your room boy

will undoubtedly be able to procure you a foul tasting glassful. It will cost you around US$0.18. At that price, it's probably worth a try.

KRETEK

The first scent the arriving visitor receives on walking from his plane to Immigration at Denpasar Airport is of cloves. This is altogether appropriate for what were once known as the Spice Islands, but the reason for the aroma today is that chopped cloves constitute 50 percent of Indonesia's most popular type of cigarette, the *kretek*.

They're big business, and not least for the Indonesian government. The great Eiseman (see RECOMMENDED READING in TRAV-ELERS' TIPS, page 250) once estimated income from the tobacco industry constituted 80 percent of all the country's tax revenue. He further revealed that, in one of the biggest tobacco companies' largest factories, every *kretek* cigarette was — believe it or not — rolled by hand.

The Balinese, too, sometimes find time to enjoy the beach. Their snacks, though very inexpensive, are an acquired taste. Note the fully clad bathers. The Balinese have no tradition of sea going, and until recent years the people tended to be fearful of the sea.

The
Broad
Highway

WITH ITS HIGH MOUNTAINS and low-lying coastal plains, Bali divides itself naturally into surprisingly self-defining areas. Not all, however, are of equal interest to the visitor. We have consequently dealt with those districts of most historical or contemporary interest at some length and considered West Bali and the offshore islands more briefly under OFF THE BEATEN TRACK (see page 226). The areas where most of the tourist accommodation is situated are in the south-eastern corner—Sanur, Nusa Dua and Kuta. East Bali, the area around Ubud and the mountain locations are popular either for day trips or for excursions with one or two overnight stops. The same applies to the district we begin with, North Bali, nowadays somewhat neglected but once the gateway through which all visitors arrived on the island.

NORTH BALI

Northern Bali is in many ways distinct from the rest of the island. Whereas to the south the land falls away from the central mountains gently, creating the extensive fertile plains where most of the island's population lives, to the north the land drops more steeply to the coast, affording little easily cultivable ground. Temperatures, too, are slightly higher than in the south and the rainfall approximately half that of the southern plains.

Nevertheless, the very fact that the area is somewhat different from the rest of the island is in itself an attraction. The abrupt descent of the land to the sea provides excellent views northward from temples perched on projecting spurs of land, the drier climate allows the cultivation of grapes and the seven-kilometer (four-and-a-third-mile) beach resort strip immediately to the west of Singaraja provides fine snorkeling and a peaceful ambiance that is very much to some people's taste.

Nowadays it is southern Bali that gets all the tourists' attention. With Denpasar as the island's administrative center, the airport at Tuban and Kuta Beach a mecca, now that surfing has become the premier beach pleasure, North Bali hardly attracts a look.

It wasn't long ago that everything was based on Singaraja. But, when K'tut Tantri, the American expatriate who "went native," first established her glamorous and quickly famous international hotel at Kuta in the Thirties, the site she chose was as far as it was possible to be from the center colonial Dutch operations. Singaraja was their power base and capital, largely because they had subdued northern Bali before they extended their control to the south. International liners used the northern port (they now dock at Benoa) and almost all foreign visitors arrived there.

GETTING THERE

Almost everyone arrives in North Bali by road from Denpasar via Bedugul. Fifteen-seater buses leave from the Ubung terminus; the fare from Denpasar to Singaraja is Rp3,000, and the journey takes two hours. Travelers should leave Denpasar by late afternoon — buses are frequent until 5 PM, but less so after. Check in advance at Ubung if you want to depart in the early evening; there are no night buses. There are no set timetables for the buses; they depart when they have a full complement of passengers.

North Bali is remote from the rest of the island — poorer, hotter and quieter. There are few tourists and all the accommodation is simple.

BALI'S OLD CAPITAL: SINGARAJA

Singaraja can seem an attractive enough place on a sunny morning, particularly from its upper streets, which command views to the sea. But Bali is not a place that excels in its urban environments, and there is very little to see in the town. The library, **Gedong Kirtya**, is said to contain a collection of Balinese manuscripts, sacred and other texts inscribed on palm leaves (*lontar*), but no one I know has ever found the place open. The **Tourist Information Bureau**, next door to the library on Jalan Veteran, seems a superfluous institution but is open most mornings.

Best is to see the town by night when the **Night Market** provides a dimly lit spectacle and adds a touch of glamour to a town that has little to offer in the way of sightseeing by day. When electricity is available, the market operates from 6 to 10 PM. On the frequent occasions when they have to make do with kerosene lamps, it tends to end earlier. The many fruit sellers who set up at night along the main streets stay in business until midnight, however. The market operates seven days a week, the two days of Nyepi (see THREE FESTIVALS in BALINESE CULTURE, page 105) being the only exception.

Virtually no foreign visitors stay in Singaraja as the attractive beachside *losmen* and hotels of Lovina are only a 15-minute *bemo* ride away. Anyone intent on spending a night in the northern capital, however, might try the **Wijaya Hotel** (21915 FAX 25817 (moderate prices). It is situated at Jalan Sudirman N°74. Eleven of its 19 rooms have air conditioning.

There are three *bemo* stations in Singaraja —**Sanket** for Denpasar, **Penarukan** for eastern destinations such as Air Saneh and Amed as far as Amlapura and **Banyuasri** for western destinations such as Banjar and Pulaki as far as Gilimanuk.

LOVINA'S BLACK SAND BEACHES

Lovina is the general term covering the black sand beaches that extend from just before

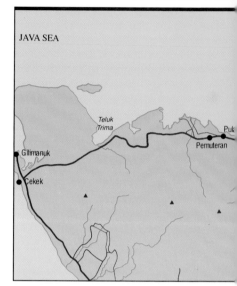

The celebrated Pura Beji at Sangsit: "sublime cosmic harmonies have become modulated into beautifully wrought shapes of pink stone".

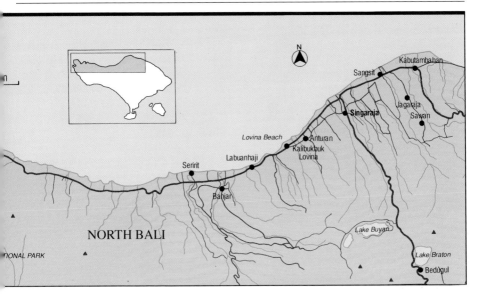

Anturan village, five minutes' drive west of Singaraja, to the far end of Kalibukbuk another couple of kilometers further down the road.

Ever since the development of Kuta, Sanur and Nusa Dua, Lovina has been a tranquil and almost forgotten retreat where visitors snorkel by day and reread a classic paperback by night. Today Lovina is expanding, but more slowly than the other tourist destinations on the island. It still retains a quiet, though no longer quite forgotten, air. In many ways it is reminiscent of what Sanur must have been like a couple of generations ago. Yet while many of the smaller homestays still have no phone, at the Singaraja end, several new luxury hotels have opened, standing incongruously among the rice paddies.

Despite these changes, the charm of Lovina for the moment still lies in its tranquil–lity and its twin offshore attractions, snorkeling along the reef and the spectacle of dolphins at dawn just beyond it. Boatmen will be only too keen to take you out to experience either of these wonders.

General Information

Shuttle buses run to Denpasar, departing at 10 AM and 2 PM and at 10 PM leave for just about everywhere else in Bali as well. Long-distance buses leave for Jogyakarta at 1 PM and for Surabaya at 7 PM.

For car and motorcycle rental plus driver, ring **Marga Sakti Transport** (0362-41061 or 0362-411570 and ask for K'tut Sutarwan.

Money changing rates are not good in Lovina. It is far better to buy rupiahs in Kuta or Denpasar before you arrive. If you do need to change money, the best rate is probably to be had from **Kunti Rental** (0362-41341, on the main road at Kalibukbuk village.

What to See and Do

DOLPHINS AND DIVING

His delights/ Were dolphin-like, they showed his back above/The element they lived in.
— Shakespeare, *Antony & Cleopatra* (1608)

You will have no problem seeing the dolphins in Lovina. Everywhere and all day long boatmen will ask you if you'd like to go with them the next morning to see these magnificent creatures. See WATCH DOLPHINS AT PLAY in TOP SPOTS, PAGE 18, for a full description of this not-to-be-missed experience.

As for diving, **Spice Dive** (0362-41305 FAX 0362-41171, will arrange everything for you, including trips to Tulamben and Menjangan Island and instruction courses, either basic or advanced. See SPORTING SPREE in YOUR CHOICE, page 32, for details on diving in this and other regions in Bali.

Where to Stay

The two upmarket places that today dominate the eastern end of Lovina, the end nearest to Singaraja, are the **Palma Beach Hotel** (0362-41775 FAX 0362-41659 (45 rooms; average and above) and the **Hotel Aneka Lovina** (0362-41121 FAX 0362-41827 (59 rooms; average and above). The former offers a tennis court, and both hotels have swimming pools. Less expensive, but nevertheless aimed at the better-off visitor and still at this end of the beach, is the **Banyualit Beach Inn** (0362-41789 FAX 0362-41563 (20 rooms; moderate).

Excellent value can be had at the **Ansoka Hotel** (41841 FAX 41023. Of its 38 rooms, the best are moderate in price, while the rest are inexpensive, but all rooms include access to the hotel's facilities — notably a swimming pool. Of the many budget-category places on offer, the **Palestis Beach Cottages** (0362-41035 (20 rooms; inexpensive) is outstanding, friendly and clean and has a brand new swimming pool. The **Padang Lovina Seaside Cottages** (0362-41302 (13 rooms; inexpensive) can also be recommended.

These last three are in the center of Kalibukbuk village, where a large statue of a dolphin now dominates the shoreline.

Also in this area are the **Bali Lovina Beach Cottages** (0362-41285 FAX 0361-233386 (34 rooms; average and above), a smarter place overlooking the beach.

Note that accommodation in Lovina tends to be cheaper than in Kuta or Legian, and spacious fan-cooled rooms with attached bathrooms can easily be found for US$4.

Where to Eat

An excellent beach restaurant is the **Sea Breeze Café** (0362-41138, offering such unexpected delicacies as cauliflower cheese, lemon meringue pie and mango crumble. Many visitors from Singaraja consider it the best eating place in Lovina — informal but comfortable and offering a varied and imaginative cuisine. Well-patronized by visitors and also offering good, reasonably-priced meals is the **Warung Kopi Bali** (0362-41361, in the center of the village and often full at dinner time. Also popular, the **Bali Apik Bar and Restaurant** (0362-41050 is known for its wide range of drinks and hearty pizzas.

SPRINGS AND TEMPLES

North Bali has several attractions in addition to the beach — where the choices are

and places a tiny wicker tray of flowers and food there. The monkeys of Pulaki, sitting as often as not all over the road eating grapes and pineapple, are happy beings on the receiving end of the same pious devotion.

The **Hot Springs** at **Banjar**, 18 km (just over 11 miles) west of Singaraja, is one of the nicest places in the north. Whereas before 1985 there were only muddy pools fed by water falling through bamboo pipes, now there is a modern complex worthy, albeit on a small scale, of Budapest or Baden-Baden. There are two tiled pools, one set above the

limited, anyway, to the pleasures of snorkeling and dolphin watching.

Fifty-six kilometers (35 miles) west of Singaraja on the coast road to Gilimanuk there is the **Pulaki Monkey Temple**. Situated on the road overlooking the sea, it is the home for hundreds of monkeys. Don't imagine, though, that you're doing them a special favor when you buy them nuts from the ever-ready vendors — every local farm vehicle that passes empties out onto the road sacks full of fruit leftovers for them, an operation that makes the temple an inevitable slowing down point for all traffic. It's in the nature of a religious offering, just as when *bemo* drivers pull up at shrines — no one is getting off, but the conductor jumps down

other, into which a warm and slightly sulfurous stream of water gushes through magnificent dragon (*naga*) mouths. There is a restaurant up above, and the ambiance, with its flowering shrubs and terraced garden overlooking the baths, is utterly delightful. It's like coming across the Emperor Nero's private retreat right in the middle of a tropical jungle.

To get there, ask the *bemo* driver for Air Panas at Banjar. You will be put down at a road junction where several horse drawn traps (*dokar*) will be waiting to take you the two-kilometer (one-and-a-quarter-mile) drive up to the nearby village, from where

The lonely coast of North Bali — black sand, fishing nets; the shoreline serves as a major footpath.

The Broad Highway

you'll have to walk; or you can go on the back of one of the many motorbikes waiting at the junction all the way from the main road.

There's a hotel at Banjar, too, a couple of hundred meters from the pools. It's the **Pondok Wisata Grya Sari** (0362-92903 FAX 0362-92966 (14 rooms; moderate).

A privately negotiated ride on the back of a bike is also the best way to get from the springs to the **Buddhist Temple**, Banjar's other attraction and something not to be missed. It's a walk of under a kilometer (around half a mile) through jungle but it's possible to lose your way; the motorbikes go by the road the long way round.

The temple is a beautiful mixture of Buddhist and Balinese Hindu elements. Set on a steep hill overlooking the sea, it contains a lily pond, a yellow Buddha and numerous red-tiled roofs at different levels that make a most attractive combination. It's an easy walk back down to the coast road.

The falls at **Labuanhaji** are of less interest. A river forces its way through a cleft in the rocks and falls some six meters (20 ft) into a murky pool. There is another fall and pool above, accessible by a slippery path.

It's certain that after heavy rain these waterfalls would be more impressive, nevertheless, given their modest scale and the lack of any facilities (in contrast to Banjar), they are barely worth the one-kilometer (just-over-half-a-mile) trudge from the road. If you do go, boys will press their services on you as "guides," in effect showing you where to turn off the lane and take the short brick path beside the paddy.

PURA BEJI'S UNHEARD MELODIES

Eight kilometers (five miles) east of Singaraja is the celebrated **Pura Beji** at **Angsit**. It is one of the most elaborately carved temples in all Bali. Here carved wings stand right out, all but free from the mother stone.

In the clammy silence, the smiling faces of the men and gods gaze out in voluptuous ease, caught forever in a moment of serene resignation. The peace and infinite generosity of Balinese Hinduism is wonderfully expressed here in this gorgeous place. "Heard melodies are sweet," wrote the English poet Keats, "but those unheard are sweeter." Here at Pura Beji the most sublime cosmic harmonies have become modulated into beautifully wrought shapes of pink stone.

The temple is not difficult to find. A small sign points the way downhill off Sangsit's main street, but anyone will show you the way — it's the only place in this little agricultural market any visitor ever goes to.

SAWAN'S GONGS

Sawan, another nine kilometers (five and a half miles) east, is an attractive village. It's

known as the place where gongs for *gamelan* orchestras are fired — just say "gong" and any child will lead you up a lane and through a barn door, and there you will discover a couple of men and a woman hammering, polishing and working bellows for the fire.

The primary charm, however, lies in simply wandering through this restful place, taking lunch at a streetside *warung* and watching the easy, tranquil village life go by. Sawan is reached by *bemo* from the main road between Sangsit and Kubutambahan, passing the village of **Jagaraga** on the way up.

The **temple** at **Kubutambahan** is at the junction of the road from Kintamani and the coast road. Most visitors give the place only a couple of minutes — time enough to photograph the carving of a man on a flowery bicycle: The guardian will show you where it is once you have signed the visitors' book and made your donation.

YEH SANIH

At Yeh Sanih, another six kilometers (four miles) east, freshwater springs have been diverted to create bathing pools between the road and the sea. There's an accompanying restaurant and accommodation, **Bungalow Puri Sanih** (15 rooms; moderate). Frogs croak, mosquitoes bite and boys flop into the cool water.

The coast, as elsewhere in North Bali, has a bleak appearance, but it's certainly peaceful, and there's a place to stay right on the beach called the **Air Sanih Seaside Cottages** (0362-23357 (seven rooms; inexpensive). There's also a small temple up a short path on the other side of the road. You might be lucky enough when you visit it to hear a strange and beautiful whistling and tinkling in the air — a few members of a local bird orchestra out for a quick run through of a small part of their repertoire.

SEMBIRAN: VILLAGE WITH A VIEW

Sembiran is a large village three kilometers (two miles) up from the road. The road is good, and transport is by motorbike; a group of them wait at the junction for prospective customers (US$1 is a reasonable fare).

The village itself is neglected, though it clearly was once important. Visitors are few, and children run away startled as you approach. What is fine about Sembiran, though, is the temple perched on the hillside one kilometer (just over half a mile) before you get to the village proper. Your transport will wait for you while you take a couple of pictures, but don't linger too long as other fares are waiting and he will be quick to urge you on. It may be preferable to walk back down from the village (the temple will be on your left) and inspect it at your leisure.

Characteristically of North Bali, the site commands an excellent view out over the sea, though technically, like all Balinese temples, it is oriented upwards to the mountains. Trimly kept, the place has an almost

Greek atmosphere, and its gray stone and green grass give it a classical simplicity.

SANUR

Sanur is altogether a comfortable place — not cheap, but long-established, leafy and reassuring. The beach, placid and sheltered behind a reef, is not up to Kuta's standards (but then no other beach in Bali is).

All the hotels, except the Grand Bali Beach and the Bali Hyatt, are of the bungalow type and are often set in shady tropical gardens,

most of them facing the (generally safe) beach. Snorkeling is available off a sheltered reef that stretches out from the yellow sands dotted with colorful fishing boats. There are fine views east with the mountains of central Bali rising grandly across the bay.

All of the tourist facilities available in such profusion in Kuta are here too, but presented in a more genteel, affluent way. Sanur is a lush garden where visitors lie on beach beds under palm trees sipping their Camparis or flop splendidly into a pool. (Hotels without pools can't compete in Sanur.) Leather

OPPOSITE and ABOVE: The Buddhist temple at Banjar. Buddhism coexists with the dominant Hinduism — there are, for example, Buddhist *pedanda* (high priests) as well as Hindu ones.

traveling bags replace canvas ones. It's as discreet, worldly and wise as Kuta is fresh, brash and youthful. You pay your money — more than in Kuta, but less than in Nusa Dua — and you take your choice. Sanur is, incidentally, the place where many of the foreigners resident in Bali opt to live.

WHAT TO SEE AND DO

Hydrotherapy and Massage

In keeping with Sanur's ambiance of genteel comfort there is a sauna, spa and mas-

sage club known as **Sehatku** (0361-287880, N°23 Jalan Danau Tamblingan, where you can relax and have all those worries kneaded away by expert hands. It isn't as inexpensive as the massages on Kuta Beach, but it's undoubtedly more congenial to its clients and very much in the gracious Sanur style.

Pedicures, manicures, facial and body massages are the specialty at **Peruna Beauty Line Salon** (289536 further down the same street.

An Explosion of Paint

One of the few historical sites in Sanur is the house, now known as the **Museum Le Mayeur**, where the Belgian painter Le Mayeur lived from 1932 to 1958. The place has been left more or less as it was, with his books still on his desk and so on. What is so striking about the house is that his painting explodes from the framed pictures onto the walls and eventually all over the window frames. Fantastic scenes from the *Ramayana* epic in augmented Balinese style feature prominently.

WHERE TO STAY

Almost all of the more exclusive hotels in Sanur are right on the beach. Starting from the north and working south, the first hotel you'll come across is one of the great institutions of the island:

The **Hotel Grand Bali Beach** (0361-288511 FAX 0361-287917 (574 rooms; expensive) has every facility anyone is likely to require. It's the only hotel outside Nusa Dua built upwards rather than in the more usual bungalow/garden style, but it also has its low-rise wing and cottages. You approach the hotel down a long drive with a nine-hole championship golf course on the right, where figures in white tropical suits swing their clubs with Balinese caddies in attendance. A *gamelan* orchestra celebrates your arrival for lunch, and many of the airlines have offices in the hotel to facilitate your smooth departure.

The **Segara Village Hotel** (0361-288407 FAX 0361-287242 (150 rooms; expensive) with two-story cottages in garden surroundings, is quiet and relaxing and faces the beach. It has children's programs and facilities.

A slightly less expensive hotel, still on the oceanfront, is the **Natour Sindhu Beach Hotel** (0361-288351 FAX 0361-289268 (59 rooms; average and above).

Continuing south, you'll come to the **Tandjung Sari** (0361-288441 FAX 0361-287930 (26 rooms; expensive) the preferred hideaway for celebrities and jetsetters in Sanur. For many, it is the only place to stay in Bali. Meanwhile **Santrian Beach Resort** (0361-288009 FAX 0361-287101 (31 rooms; average and above) offers the usual one- and two-story bungalows in the usual verdant, tropical gardens.

The **Bali Hyatt** (0361-288271 FAX 0361-27693 (390 rooms; expensive) set in an astonishing 15 hectares (36 acres) of land, combines very Balinese public areas with four-story accommodation. High thatched roofs rise over restaurants serving food from Indonesia and Italy, and a sauna and discotheque complete the international part of the ambiance.

At the far end of the beach is the **Sanur Beach Hotel** (288011 FAX 287566 (425 rooms;

expensive), which claims to be the friendliest of the big Sanur hotels. It's usually booked solid by tour groups.

Back in the center of things, just behind the Grand Bali Beach, is the new **Radisson Bali** (281781 FAX 289168 (325 rooms; average and above).

WHERE TO EAT

Sanur teems with fine restaurants. Many are along the road running parallel to the beach one block inland, Jalan Danau Tamblingan. Two of Sanur's most famous eating places are here: the Italian restaurant **Mamma Lucia** (288498 and the fine Chinese establishment **Telaga Naga** (281234, extension 8080. The latter is run by the Hyatt, though it is situated a short distance away from it in an enchanting Chinese style garden. Both Szechuan and Cantonese dishes are served.

On the same street is the **Kul Kul Restaurant** (0361-288038, offering Western and Indonesian food, with traditional Balinese dishes available if ordered in advance. Similar in style is the **Balimoon** (0361-288486, specializing in seafood and pizzas.

Other popular places include the **Italian Terrazzo Martini** (0361-288371, the **Legong Restaurant** (0361-288066, with European, Chinese and Indonesian food and Balinese dancers performing nightly at 8 PM and the amiable and cozy **Mandelo's** (0361-288773. **Café Batu Jimbar** has become the most popular place for health-conscious eating; the owner grows his own vegetables up in the mountains and produces some of the most delicious meals in Sanur.

The further south you go along Jalan Danau Tamblingan the cheaper the restaurants get. Once past the Hyatt there are a number of very reasonable *warung* bars and small restaurants to be found.

There are also some fine eating places on the main road known as Jalan Bypass. One of the most unusual is Bali's only Korean restaurant, the **Chong Gi-Wa** (/FAX 0361-287084. Hearty servings of magnificent northern food, cooked up on your table, are accompanied by the unique Korean pickled cabbage known as *kimchi*. Nearby, there is also an elegant Japanese place, the **Chiku-Tei** (0361-287159 FAX 0361-287290.

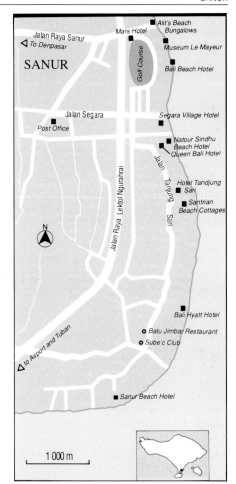

SANUR

Alit's Beach Bungalows
Jalan Raya Sanur
◁ To Denpasar
Mars Hotel
Museum Le Mayeur
Golf Course
Bali Beach Hotel
Jalan Segara
Post Office
Segara Village Hotel
Natour Sindhu Beach Hotel
Queen Bali Hotel
Jalan Raya Lektol Ngurahrai
Jalan Tanjung Sari
Hotel Tandjung Sari
Santrian Beach Cottages
N
Bali Hyatt Hotel
to Airport and Tuban
Batu Jimbar Restaurant
Sube'c Club
△ to Airport and Tuban
Sanur Beach Hotel
1 000 m

NIGHTLIFE

Nightlife is not a prominent feature of Sanur as young people make for the charismatic venues at Kuta and Legian, only a 15-minute drive away. There are, however, a number of pubs and relaxed drinking places at Sanur. Among these are **La Taverna**, right on the beach, **Koki** on Jalan Bypass and the Hyatt's **Grantang Bar** with live jazz every evening from 8 PM until 1 AM, except Wednesday.

For dancing, there is **Pirates** at the Segara Village Hotel (8 PM onwards) and the rooftop **Bali Hai** at the Hotel Grand Bali Beach.

SHOPPING

Sanur is a good place to shop if you are looking for quality. You won't find many bargains

Enjoying a ride on a *prahu* off Sanur.

here, but for that special present, try Sanur's smart boutiques and art shops, almost all of which are on Jalan Danau Tamblingan.

For ceramics, there's the **Miralin Collection** (/FAX 0361-286061 and **Earth and Fire.** Puppets (some originals, some reproductions) and Javanese terra cotta figurines are on offer at the **Lama Gallery** (0361-286809 FAX 0361-751468. For leather you might try **Rafflesia** (0361-288528. For *ikat* and hand-woven fabrics there is **Nogo** (0361-288832; this company has five shops in Bali, but the Sanur outlet is their main one. For clothes in general there is the **Mama Leon Boutique** (0361-288044 FAX 0361-288150. It's a beautiful showroom and shop, and the factory is just behind.

BALI'S CAPITAL: DENPASAR

Denpasar is emphatically not an attractive place. It is Bali's capital, but few tourists have any need to go there, and there are few good reports of it from people who have been and escaped back to Kuta or Sanur to tell the tale. There are, for instance, numerous small hotels and *losmen* there, but it's rare that anyone other than Indonesians from outside Bali and on business in Denpasar stays in them.

It's a crowded, noisy, polluted town, the very antithesis of everything people come to Bali to find. Like many another Asian city, it's caught between two moments in history; it was built for an age of horse drawn and pedestrian traffic and now endures the full force of modern mechanized transport.

So great is the tourist concentration in Kuta and Sanur that even shopping and such services as banks, telex offices and travel agents are as good there as in Denpasar, or better. A visit to the Immigration Office, or the Denpasar Police Office to get a license to drive a motorbike on Bali (if you don't have an international driver's license) is the most likely reason for paying a visit to the town.

Nevertheless, Denpasar does have one or two places of interest, and these will be dealt with briefly below.

GENERAL INFORMATION

The **Badung Government Tourist Office** (0361-234569 or 0361-223602, at Merdeka

Building, Jalan Surapati N°7, provides maps, lists of festivals (valuable as these go by the Balinese calendar and so vary from year to year) and details of dance and other performances. It's not the full service provided by some countries, but the attendants are helpful and do respond to personal inquiries. The office is open from 7 AM to 2 PM daily, except on Friday when it closes at 11 PM and Monday when it is closed all day.

The **Bali Government Tourist Office** (222387 (/FAX 226313, by contrast, is difficult to find, being located in a complex of government buildings and not oriented to the needs of the individual traveler.

Should you happen to hold a visa of the kind that can be renewed (see TRAVELERS' TIPS for information on visas), then you may need to go to the Immigration Office (Kantor Imigrasi) (0361-227828. It's in the Renon Complex, Niti Mandala; open from 7 AM to 1 PM, except on Friday when it closes at 11 PM, Saturday when it closes at 12 noon and Sunday when it's closed.

WHAT TO SEE AND DO

Heroic Last Stand

The center of Denpasar is a large grassy square known as the **Tanah Lapang Puputan Badung**. Its notable feature is a heroic, three figure statue standing in pools amid fountains, a memorial to the four thousand Balinese who died defending the city against the Dutch on September 20, 1906.

Standing facing the monument from the center of the square, the building on your right is the **Museum Bali**, with the Pura Jagatnatha next to it on the left. Over on the opposite side of the square is the military headquarters for the island.

The museum is a bit of a joke. The basic concept, that its very buildings should in themselves be exhibits of Balinese temple and palace architectural styles, is attractive. Unfortunately, the contents have neither the range nor the organization to make them the major resource that such an institution ought to house. Exhibits include a model of a toothfiling ceremony, some interesting masks, some paintings and woodcarvings and a display of agricultural tools and implements. There is no catalog available in

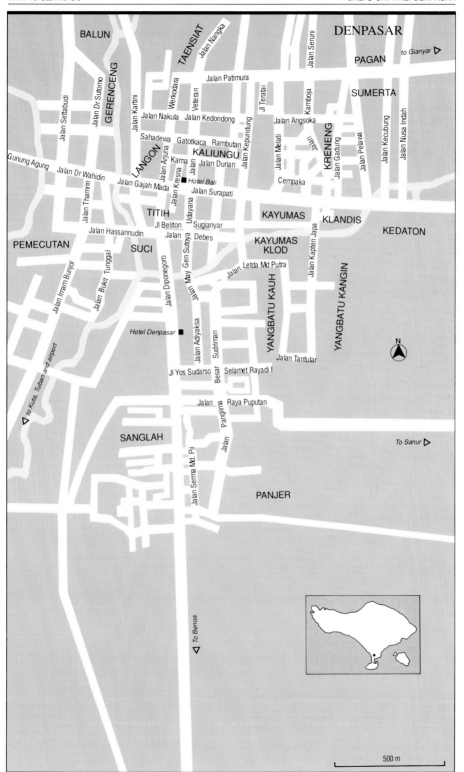

DENPASAR

BALUN

TAENSIAT

Jalan Nangka

Jalan Seruni

PAGAN

to Gianyar ▷

GERENCENG

Jalan Dr Sutomo

Jalan Settabudi

Jalan Kartini

Werkodara

Jalan Patimura

Veteran

Jalan Nakula Jalan Kedondong

Jl Teratai

SUMERTA

Kamboja

Jalan Angsoka

Jalan Nusa Indah

Jalan Kecubung

Sahadewa Gatotkaca Rambutan

Jalan Kepundung

Jalan Melati

KRENENG

Jalan Pelawa

Jalan Gadung

LANGON

KALIUNGU

Gunung Agung

Jalan Dr Wahidin

Jalan Arjuna

Karna

Jalan

Jalan Durian

Cempaka

Jalan Thamrin

Jalan Gajah Mada

Jalan Kresna

Jalan Surapati

■ Hotel Bali

Udayana

TITIH

Jl Beliton

Sugianyar

KAYUMAS

KLANDIS

KEDATON

PEMECUTAN

Jalan Hassannudin

Jalan

Debes

KAYUMAS
KLOD

Jalan Imam Bunjol

Jalan Bukit Tunggal

SUCI

Jalan Diponegoro

Jalan May Gen Sutoya

Jalan Letda Md Putra

Jalan Kapten Japa

YANGBATU KANGIN

to Kuta, Tuban and airport

Hotel Denpasar ■

Jalan Adiyaksa

Sudirman

YANGBATU KAUH

N

Jl Yos Sudarso

Besar

Selamet Rayadi I

Jalan Tantular

SANGLAH

Jalan

Jalan Raya Puputan

Panglima

To Sanur ▷

Jalan Serma Md. Pil

PANJER

▽ To Benoa

500 m

English. The museum is open from 8 AM to 3 PM daily and closed all day on Monday.

The **Pura Jagatnatha** is a modern temple dedicated to the whole of Bali. Unlike most Balinese temples, it is closed to the public except at festival times.

Art Centers

Two art centers provide useful indications of what riches the island has in store. The **National Art Center**, between Jalan Abiankapas and Jalan Palawa Pagan in the east of the town, contains exhibits of shadow puppets and the giant *barong landong* puppets, silverware, carvings, basketry, paintings and weaving. Further east — you'll need to take a taxi — is the government-run, fixed price art shop; ask the driver for **Sanggraha Kriya Asta**. It not only has a wide range of items, but it also provides a convenient indication of the kind of prices to be paid for similar objects elsewhere when you will be expected to bargain for them.

You can attend lessons in Balinese dance at two places in Denpasar: the **Academy of Dance Indonesia** (ASTI) on Jalan Nusa Indah and the **Conservatory of Performing Arts** (KOKAR) on Jalan Ratna. Lessons take place in the mornings.

There is an annual six-week-long Bali Arts Festival between mid June and the end of July at the **Werdi Budaya Arts Center**, Jalan Nusa Indah.

WHERE TO STAY

The best hotel in town is the **Natour Bali** (0361-225681 FAX 0361-235347, located at Jalan Veteran N°3 (77 rooms; average and above). It's the old Dutch colonial hotel (Charlie Chaplin and Noel Coward among many other celebrities stayed here) and though now over 60 years old, it has been tastefully modernized and has a swimming pool and an ambiance that manages to be both efficient and relaxed.

WHERE TO EAT

Food in Denpasar tends to be Indonesian as foreign tourists are not common. The Natour Bali, however, provides a varied cuisine, and along Jalan Teuku Umar there are several small but interesting places offering food from different parts of Indonesia.

SHOPPING

If you want to buy sarongs and Indonesian fabrics in Denpasar then there is nowhere better to go than the local **cloth market** on Jalan Sulawesi, where prices are far lower than in tourist outlets. Note that taxi drivers are more likely to know the street by its old name of Jalan Kampong Arab.

Almost opposite the Natour Bali Hotel (see below) on Jalan Veteran there is an outdoor **bird market** and a covered **jewelry market** (at N°66).

If orchids are your interest, you will be in paradise at the **Flora Bali Orchid Farm** (0361-225847 FAX 0361-232877, Jalan Noja N°102. You can inspect acres of infant plants at your leisure. It's not the place for spectacular floral shows, but specialists will not be able to drag themselves away. Note that only vacuum-packed specimens can be taken out of the country legally.

GETTING AROUND

There are three main *bemo* stations in Denpasar: **Tegal**, **Ubung** and **Batubulan**. Each serves a different area of the island, and small light blue vans shuttle back and forth between them for around US$.25 (but don't expect to have room to breathe). The shuttles also run to **Kereneng**, the home station for *bemos* plying routes within Denpasar.

Tegal serves Kuta, the airport, Ulu Watu and Nusa Dua (should anyone staying at Nusa Dua ever want to use a *bemo*). Ubung serves the west and north; full-sized buses both ordinary and air conditioned, leave from here to Gilimanuk, plus minibuses to Singaraja/Lovina. Batubulan is the station for services to Ubud, Kintamani and East Bali. For a *bemo* to Sanur, go to Kereneng.

A further small station, **Sanglah**, serves Benoa Harbor.

One final point — all over Bali you will hear *bemo* drivers touting for passengers calling out "Badung!" In fact, "Badung, Badung!" rings through the dusty evening air from Klungkung to Kuta and from Ubud to Tabanan. You won't find it on any map, but just as Karangasem is the old Balinese name for Amlapura and Buleleng for Singaraja, Badung is the name by which all Balinese know the Denpasar area, and these tired and hungry drivers are looking for their last fares of the day before finally heading home.

NUSA DUA AND THE BUKIT

The region south of the airport is generally referred to as the Bukit. It is the Balinese word

Dua (literally "Two Islands") for development as a major tourist complex has done little to alter the traditional life of the region. The area includes the five-star complex of Nusa Dua itself, the fishing village of Tanjung Benoa situated at the end of a five- kilometer (three-mile) sand strip directly to the north of Nusa Dua, the village and bay of Jimbaran (located on the neck of the isthmus immediately south of the airport) and the upland area itself that culminates in the magnificently situated temple and surfing venues of Ulu Watu.

for hill and strictly refers only to the high ground southwest of Nusa Dua. Nevertheless, the peninsula is of a piece, and the reason is that whereas the rest of mainland Bali is made up of volcanic rock and soils, the Bukit, like the nearby offshore island of Nusa Penida, is entirely limestone. Indeed, it is probable that at one time the Bukit was once an island too. Even today it is only connected to Bali proper by a low-lying and narrow isthmus.

Rainwater runs straight into the ground in limestone country, and the consequent lack of surface streams means there is no water available for irrigation during the dry season. As a result, life in the Bukit has traditionally been hard. The selection of Nusa

NUSA DUA: FIVE-STAR LUXURY

The development of Nusa Dua only truly got under way in the early eighties. Prior to that, the area was an infertile coastal patch featuring the two small "islands," connected to the mainland by sandy strips, which give the place its name.

Nusa Dua's hotels are all five-star rated and each is, in its own style, the last word in luxury; all meet the highest international standards. They stand in their own ample grounds complete with several restaurants,

The Nusa Dua Hotel, one of the many five-star hostelries in this ultra-exclusive enclave; all have international-standard facilities and top-notch sports facilities.

swimming pools and more. Indeed, each of them is a self-sufficient holiday environment and anything that might be thought to be missing — Balinese local culture, for instance — is brought in and presented for the hotel guests' exclusive delectation.

Nusa Dua's beaches may not be the finest on the island, but they are safe and adequate for many people's needs. They are sheltered behind reefs and thus are shallow and placid, and they have white sand. Rocks and seaweed become more common as you move south, so that Club Meditérranée enjoys the best beach and the Grand Hyatt the least pleasant. On none of them are you likely to meet people other than fellow guests at the Nusa Dua hotels. To some people, however, this is an advantage, and certainly anyone concerned about security can be confident that here they are staying in a place specially designed with their safety in mind. Along the long avenues of palms that link the access roads to the hotels, security men are stationed on their motorbikes, lolling in boredom across the handlebars of their machines. Their main function in normal times seems to be to keep hawkers away from these wide acres in which are concentrated many of the richest people staying on Bali.

The atmosphere created by well-trimmed verges and impeccable tarred driveways is more that of a presidential golf course than somewhere given over to free-and-easy relaxation. Indeed the **Nusa Dua Beach Hotel** (771210 FAX 772617 (450 rooms; expensive) is where heads of state stay when they visit Indonesia, government officials flying down from Jakarta to meet them here rather than having to face the security nightmare presented by the nation's capital. The Reagans stayed there, in a presidential suite "with special security features," in 1986 and in many ways the entire district, with access confined to a narrow bottleneck close to the airport, is ideal for such uses. Nusa Dua as a whole was conceived as a place in which world statesmen could meet, and tourists subsequently pay for the honor of breathing the air of the same prestigious environment. The architectural style of the Nusa Dua Beach Hotel is solidly generous, while its rooms are in four-story blocks.

The **Melia Bali** (0361-771510 FAX 0361-771360 (500 rooms; expensive), by contrast, mixes Balinese style and Spanish ownership, with daily cabarets and flamenco played by Balinese musicians. It too has rooms in four-story blocks.

The **Putri Bali** (0361-771020 or 0361-771420 FAX 0361-71139 (384 rooms; expensive) is the other big, traditional hotel at Nusa Dua. The name means "Balinese Princess."

The Bali **Club Meditérranée** (0361-771521 FAX 0361-771835 (402 rooms; expensive but including all meals, sports and entertainment) offers a unique vacation experience. Three extensive buffet meals a day, all sports equipment and instruction and supervised activities for children (see FAMILY FUN in YOUR CHOICE, page 49) plus a lively cabaret show every night, are provided for in the all-inclusive price. Yet you can ignore it all if you like and simply use the place like any other luxury hotel — and this is the most luxurious of Club Med's Asian properties. Note that nonguests interested in savoring the distinctive Club Med style can come in for lunch or dinner and use all the facilities over a four-hour period.

The forecourt of the **Bali Hilton International** (0361-771102 FAX 0361-771616 (37 rooms; expensive) resembles a grandiose pleasure palace Ghenghis Khan never had time to build. Statues gesture extravagantly across multilevel waterfalls in a determined attempt to outdo even Nusa Dua's opulence.

The **Grand Hyatt Bali** (0361-771234 FAX 0361-772038 (750 rooms; expensive) similarly opts for the grand hotel style, though on a slightly more human scale. A swimming maze, including slides and chutes, makes up for the less than ideal beach.

The **Nusa Indah** (0361-771906 FAX 0361-771908 (367 rooms; expensive) doubles as Indonesia's most up-to-date convention center, while the smaller **Sheraton Lagoon** (0361-771327 FAX 0361-771326 (250 rooms; expensive) offers an intimacy that tends to be missed elsewhere.

The smallest of Nusa Dua's hotels is the **Hotel Bualu** (0361-771310 FAX 0361-771313 (50 rooms; expensive). It is well suited for children, has a PADI-certified diving instructor and free sporting facilities.

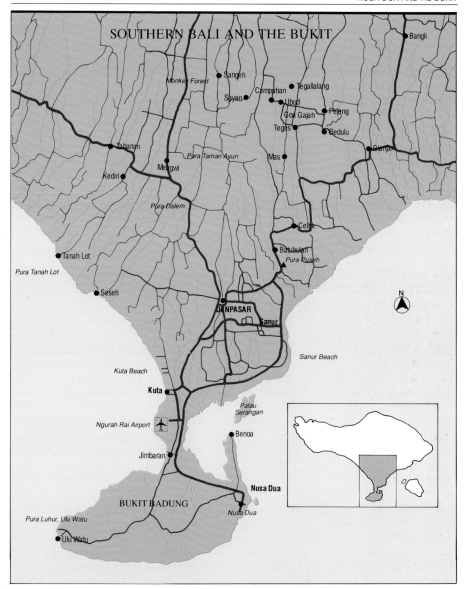

SOUTHERN BALI AND THE BUKIT

On the edge of Nusa Dua is the Japanese-owned **Nikko Bali** (0361-773377 FAX 0361-773388 (300 rooms; expensive) with dramatic sea views.

Finally, overlooking Nusa Dua from a nearby hilltop is the ultra-luxurious and exclusive **Amanusa** (0361-772333 FAX 0361-72335 (35 suites; expensive, starting from US$460), the sister resort of the Amandari at Ubud and the Amankila near Candi Dasa. The Amanusa is classically beautiful and you are treated like the royalty who may well prove to be your fellow guests.

Where to Eat

All of the Nusa Dua hotels have extensive restaurant facilities. In addition the area boasts several classy establishments such as the Japanese **Matsuri** (0361-772269, the Mexican **Poco Loco** (0361-773923 and the seafood restaurant **Makuwa Pakuwa** (0361-772252.

Nusa Dua has a large shopping complex, the **Galeria**, and several restaurants, such as the excellent Spanish **Olé Olé** (771886 and the new **On the Rocks**, where your food is cooked over hot rocks, Polynesian style.

Sports

The **Bali Golf and Country Club** (0361-771791 FAX 0361-771797 is an 18-hole golf course of championship standard. It stands on a lush swathe of land overlooked by the Amanusa. Some Nusa Dua hotels include use of its facilities as part of a package.

TANJUNG BENOA

Benoa is actually the name for the port of Denpasar; the fishing village that faces it from the other side of the bay is Tanjung Benoa.

It's a longish way round from one to the other by road, but a short trip by boat. Between the two, sheltering the entrance to the bay, lies Pulau Serangan, commonly known to tour operators as Turtle Island.

It is the fishing village of Tanjung Benoa that's most likely to interest visitors — with its raffish, freewheeling air, like a place long forgotten but determined to survive. The development of Nusa Dua to the south has seen a string of new hotels along the road joining the two places, and Benoa is now becoming an important center for diving, parasailing and windsurfing.

Dominating the place is the new, bizarre but wonderful **Beluga Marina** (0361-771997 FAX 0361-771967. This glittering venue boasts

Italian food, live jazz in the afternoons and Western pop from the same Javanese musicians in the evenings, a diving center and a jetty where two huge silver catamarans wait to transport you over to Nusa Penida, a former penal colony of the Kingdom of Klungkung. The imagination is simultaneously ravished and stimulated to crazed laughter by the sheer audacity of the place. Shining stained glass, Martini bottles winking from behind the bars, the brilliant blue sky outside — the Beluga Marina is a cheeky marvel of the latest in Italian kitsch and is not to be missed. Entirely in keeping with the sheer chutzpah of the place, the management stages *kecak* dances every night right in the middle of one of its two extraordinary restaurants.

The other half of Tanjung Benoa is equally astonishing. From a beachside establishment called **Lingga Sempurna** (0361-771457, you can be taken parasailing, jet skiing, SCUBA diving and snorkeling, among many other activities. Parasailers whoop through the air and jet skiers slice the waves in the hot afternoon.

Transport can be arranged from the beach over to Turtle Island for around US$1.50 per person, each way. In addition, the village has an important **Chinese temple**, open from 6 AM to 9 PM daily. There is a wonderful view across the strait to the sun-and-shadow-etched cliffs of Nusa Penida in the late afternoon.

There are several hotels situated along the short stretch of road connecting Tanjung Benoa and Nusa Dua. Conspicuous among them are the **Grand Mirage** (0361-771888 FAX 0361-772148 (312 rooms; expensive) and the spectacularly original **Novotel** (0361-772239 FAX 0361-772237 (92 rooms; expensive) built to resemble a village of straw-roofed Balinese huts.

TURTLE ISLAND

Pulau Serangan, also known as Turtle Island, is a low, sandy spit cut off from the mainland to the north at high tide. Variations in tidal levels, however, make it inadvisable to cross other than by boat. The island is

ABOVE and OPPOSITE: Pura Luhur, Ulu Watu and its sacred monkeys.

covered by palm trees and at its one village, turtles are kept in a small arena ready for inspection by visitors — a holdover from the days when they arrived spontaneously on the beach in huge numbers. Formerly they were kept on a much larger scale for eventual sale for food to the "mainland."

It has been 50 years since these mass arrivals ceased. The blame, for this loss anyway, cannot be put on the major construction program underway at the time of writing, which aims to extend the area of the island from its current 112 to 491 hectares (269 to 1,213 acres). Luxury villas, an 18-hole golf course, a marina and a hot water spa are under construction. Nevertheless, informed local opinion is that the island's ecology, and even its physical structure, cannot survive this sort of onslaught.

For the time being the island remains a popular destination for half-day tours. Travelers visiting individually will have a nicer time if they visit early in the morning or at the end of the afternoon to avoid coinciding with the tour groups.

For the Balinese the main significance of the island lies in the important temple **Pura Sakenan** which attracts thousands of worshippers during the festival of Kuningan.

JIMBARAN

The village of Jimbaran straddles the road running south from close by the airport to Ulu Watu. Ten years ago this was a fishing beach virtually unknown to tourists; today it is the site of five major hotels.

Coming from Kuta, after passing the stalls of the village market, a road leaves off to the right where tall *kepuh* trees mark the site of a cemetery where bodies awaiting cremation are buried. This leads to the beach and the friendly yet modern **Puri Bali** (0361-752277 FAX 0361-752220 (41 rooms; expensive), five years ago the only hotel in this area.

Now, however, there is also the **Keraton Bali Cottages** (0361-701961 FAX 0361-701991 (99 rooms; expensive), a luxurious establishment facing the road and with its back to the beach, the resplendent **Four Seasons** (0361-701010 FAX 0361-701020 (147 villas; expensive), the huge **Intercontinental** (0361-701888 FAX 0361-701777 (425 rooms;

expensive) and the latest addition, the **Ritz Carlton** (0361-702222 FAX 0361-701555 (323 rooms; expensive).

Jimbaran Bay itself is sandy, with the airport runway visible at the northern end, the waiting planes silhouetted against the sky. At night it is the venue for excellent beachside restaurants with trestle tables set up under awnings and serving a wide variety of seafood. These establishments, and there are many from which to choose, attract a fashionable clientele. The **Ramayana** (0361-702859 is recommended.

After crossing level country, the road from Jimbaran begins to climb up onto the limestone plateau itself, and before long there is a fine view backwards over the airport and southern Bali. Immediately, piles of white stone, destined for roadworks, can be seen at the side of the road. With its dry stone walls and scanty vegetation, the landscape looks like what geographers refer to anywhere in the world as "karst country". Underground there may be secret rivers and caverns measureless to man, but on the surface the soft dry contours present a terse, tight-lipped picture. In place of lush rice terraces and coconut palms is a waterless landscape more reminiscent, with its chirping crickets and scent of herbs, of the south of France than the tropics.

The red-tiled buildings you pass on the left are the premises of Denpasar's **Universitas Udayana**. Two kilometers (one and a quarter miles) further on, take a left turn at a small junction to get to the **Hotel Bali Cliff** (0361-771992 FAX 0361-771993 (175 rooms; expensive) with its spectacular clifftop location and a swimming pool that appears poised to plunge down to the seaweed-covered rocks far below.

If your destination is Ulu Watu, ignore this crossroads and carry straight on. The road offers beautiful glimpses of the sea

Luhur Ulu Watu probably means "above the stone," for this is just what it is. The temple is built on a high ledge of rock extending out over the sea 76 m (250 ft) below. Nothing could be more dramatic or more beautiful. On three sides, the Indian Ocean rolls in with some of the biggest waves in Asia. Java is barely visible straight ahead. The gods stare out in sublime comprehension, but here, with all the power of nature at their feet, their serenity is doubly authentic. The white of the carved limestone and blue sea combine unforgettably in this pure and special place.

ahead, until finally it arrives, 21 km (14 miles) from Kuta, at its destination.

TEMPLE ABOVE THE STONE

After passing a *warung* on the right, the road swings sharply to the left and terminates in a car park where food and drink is also available. This car park serves **Pura Luhur Ulu Watu**, one of Bali's six Temples of the World and one of the finest places on the island (refer also to SEE ULU WATU in TOP SPOTS, page 10).

A wide path takes you down an incline, and then the long flight of steps of the temple itself is ahead of you. The silence, the dry, scented air and the proximity of the sea fill you with an almost unbearable expectation.

The temple's history goes back at least 1,000 years and probably more. The sixteenth century Buddhist sage Wawu Rauh is said to have achieved *moksa* (or attained Nirvana) here. Nothing could be less surprising.

The temple was struck by lightning in October 1996, but since then has been renovated. It reopened in March 1997 after a month of ceremonies designed to placate the gods after such a terrible reprimand.

There is one practical note that needs to be sounded in the general air of ecstasy and sublime transcendence of the temple area. The temple is inhabited by a small band of mischievous monkeys. They will not pause for a moment's thought before jumping

High up on Bukit Badung, the Hotel Bali Cliff has a spectacular outlook over the Indian Ocean.

down and seizing any item you leave unguarded, knowing that you will try to trick them into letting you get it back with offers of food. In the process your camera or wallet could well be dropped from one of the trees where the monkeys usually retire, into the sea water. The temple attendants say that this is a common occurrence. So be warned. But don't allow an excessive concern for your possessions to distract you from the full wonder of the place.

SURFING MECCA

The **Ulu Watu** that is such a special place for Bali's surfers is hardly less impressive. To get there, take the road from the car park as if you're heading back to Kuta, but at the *warung* a couple of hundred meters down on your left take the lane that leads off at a right angle towards the sea. Motorcyclists still wait to take you, claiming there is no car park at the other end. Seasoned surfers know better, however.

The road descends slowly between prickly pear cactus hedges. Shortly after the place where the bikes wait to bring people back, you go down some concrete steps into a dry valley. From here you can climb down a short bamboo ladder into the so-called cave (actually its roof has collapsed) that leads to the cove, or follow the path up to the line of *warung* and souvenir stalls that enterprising Balinese have established on the steep sides of the slope overlooking the ocean.

There's not much to be seen from the little cove itself, just to the left of where the cave meets the sea. The sand is gritty and the sea bed rocky, but at least it's a place to get wet and cool off, and someone may try to sell you a silver amulet.

The wonderful place is the highest of the *warung*. This is perched on the edge of a ridge running up the cliff and commands a stupendous view out over the incoming surf. The spectacle is extraordinary. The sea is spread out before you in all its majestic fury. Away to the right Mount Agung is outlined — on a good day — against the blue. You can sit there under the thatched roof of the *warung* and sip your iced fruit juice and watch the figures far below skimming along the great glassy slopes as if they were on skis, playing

with the ocean like children in the vast lap of the gods. As the sun goes down, straight ahead of you, it shines through the waves like light coming through the green stained-glass windows of a cathedral.

KUTA: YELLOW SANDS AND TECHNICOLOR SUNSETS

Kuta Beach extends in a long and gentle curve from just north of the airport through Kuta proper, then through Legian to the Bali Oberoi Hotel at Seminyak and beyond. The sand is fine, hard and yellow, and the surf that breaks along the length of the beach originates somewhere near the Antarctic and is famous worldwide. So too are Kuta's sunsets. It is far and away Bali's finest beach.

GENERAL INFORMATION

Kuta has metered taxis. With a flag-fall of less than US$1, they provide the cheapest way of getting around, other than on the back of one of the ever-ready motorbikes, or, during the day, in a *bemo*.

When getting in a taxicab, make sure the meter is turned on, and be certain to have plenty of small rupiah notes with you, as you could all too often find that the driver has no change.

There are many places for car rental. One you could try is **Jaya Mertha (** 0361-751233 on Jalan Padma.

If you need to send or receive a fax, a useful place to know about is the **Krakatoa Café and Business Center (** 0361-730849 FAX 0361-730824 on Jalan Raya Seminyak. They have typewriters for your use, too. More important, though, is that the place is a major center for Westerners living in this part of Bali, and its large notice board is one of the best ways of finding such things as houses for rent. There's also a health food shop attached.

For e-mail messages and access to the Internet, there is **Impian Nusa (**/FAX 0361-761326 E-MAIL hchua@idola.net.id or hchua@singnet.com.sg, a cyber café on Jalan Pura Bagus Taruna.

Access to the Internet is also available at **Wartel Kambodiana (** 0361-753330 FAX 0361-753331 E-MAIL kambodiana@denpasar.wasantara.net.id, located on Kuta Square.

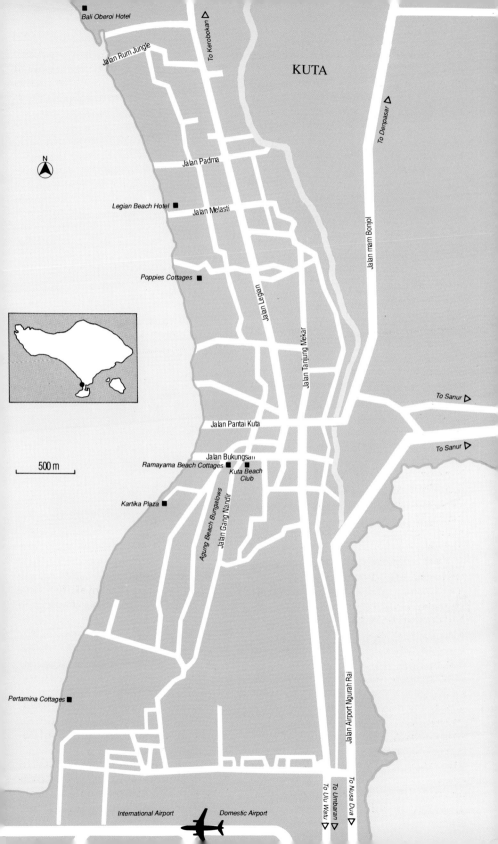

braiders, hair beaders, massage artists, runners bearing iced beer from the beach restaurants, sellers of Dyak elixirs fresh from the jungles of Borneo — add an Italian tenor and it would be the opening scene from the opera *Der Rozenkavalier.*

Yet a few hundred meters away a hundred or more Balinese may be performing a post-cremation ceremony involving a procession in full traditional dress and the scattering of ashes on the waves accompanied by the release onto the waters of ducks, chickens and doves.

AN EXOTIC FAIRGROUND

Kuta is in every possible way the diametric opposite of Nusa Dua: Its development was unplanned; it is in many places ramshackle; very cheap food and accommodation are available everywhere. There are touts on every hand, and at the south end of the beach barely five minutes pass without someone approaching you to sell you a T-shirt or give you a massage. To some people this is an intolerable intrusion, but you do not have to walk far in the direction of Legian to avoid most or all of this attention.

The fact remains that, in addition to its supremely magnificent beach, Kuta teems with irrepressible liveliness. The beach scene at the southern airport end resembles nothing so much as a circus, but it's the circus of democratic life in the late twentieth century and is something not to be missed. It's doubtful that there's anywhere else in the world quite like it.

Australian grannies, who no doubt live modestly back home in Adelaide, can be seen surrounded by a veritable court of hair

Kuta— "The circus of democratic life in the late twentieth century." ABOVE LEFT: Heard melodies. ABOVE RIGHT: Hair beaders at work. OPPOSITE LEFT: The clothes market on Jalan Bakungsari. OPPOSITE RIGHT: Hats and mats for sale.

The key to it all is that while Kuta remains an extraordinarily cheap and "exotic" holiday destination for the huge numbers of Australians, Japanese, Germans, French, British and many others who flock there, this same conglomeration is an unparalleled magnet to Balinese for whom tourism represents an opportunity to make profits unheard of in other departments of the island's life. Everyone thinks he has a bargain at Kuta, and the result is a fairground of happy buying and enthusiastic sellers, all under the glorious sun on one of Asia's most fabulous beaches.

The essential difference between Kuta and the exclusive resorts to the east is that at Kuta the tourists and the local population interact by and large as individuals. This is not to say that the one group is not more advantaged than the other. But whereas elsewhere most of the Balinese you will encounter will be employees of hotel syndicates and acting out the roles of servants, in Kuta some at least will be in business on their own behalf.

This applies too and indeed particularly, to the accommodation scene. Because Kuta grew without official planning, many of the businesses in the area remain in local hands. Thus the profusion of small, budget priced *losmen* is no coincidence: They exist because Kuta grew from travelers in the Sixties arriving at what was then only a medium-sized village and asking to be provided with food and a place to stay. First-class hotels have, of course, moved in since that time, and today there is a huge amount of top-price accom-

modation in Kuta, too. But this only contributes to the democracy of the place: All tastes and all bank balances are catered for. All the world comes to Kuta Beach, and almost all Bali, it sometimes seems, is waiting there to greet them.

A DAY IN THE SUN

The day on the beach follows a regular cycle. The Surf Rescue take up their positions at

6 AM, and even then there are the early morning joggers and swimmers out before breakfast. By nine the beach is filling up and many of the suntan zealots are already in place. Soon the colorful scene is at the first of its two daily heights. The beach traders are all at work: Boys with a single woodcarving wrapped in its cloth and constantly being polished, children offering to bring you cold drinks for a very small commission, one elderly lady bearing ancient *lontar* (strips of palm leaf inscribed with sacred texts) and the inevitable and welcome sellers of hats and beach mats.

Midday sees a dramatic diminution, most of the Balinese retreating from the sun's ferocious glare and only clutches of sun drunk Northerners remaining to play Frisbee relentlessly before collapsing in one of the beach bars for protracted lunches of seafood, beer and grainy Indonesian coffee to the sound of dated Australian and American pop hits.

If the afternoon seems slow to take off, it's no doubt because the morning went on so long, and sunset here in the tropics is anyway very early. This, you quickly realize, is why the Indonesians get up at 5 AM — in this land of eternal summer, light is gone by 6:45 PM.

THE SUNSET EVENT

Kuta's sunsets were renowned even in K'tut Tantri's day (see RECOMMENDED READING) and nowadays, as the coaches pull up from Nusa Dua's five-star hotels, all of Kuta, from its tattooed Japanese surfers to its Jakarta businessmen down for a week by the sea, set up their cameras where they will best catch the reflection on the wet sand and wait.

The event itself is very like a prima donna's operatic performance — maybe the

A MEETING OF CULTURES

On Sundays the Balinese themselves come down to savor some of the relaxing activities enjoyed by the foreigners. They set up goal posts on the sands or wade into the ocean wearing, in many cases, knee-length dresses. Or they simply gaze from above the high-water mark, in their polished Sunday shoes, at the splendor and luxury before them.

Inland, Kuta resembles a Hollywood set for a cut price Western. A couple of paces

miracle will happen, maybe it won't. Sometimes Great Nature has a cough and, despite cloudless skies, the sun sinks with no more attendant glory than a fifty-cent piece dropped into a puddle. But sometimes, ah, sometimes… then the beams shoot up like chiseled shafts, the colors deepen through apricot to salmon to a final consummating crimson, the great Indian Ocean surf laps as if entranced, and the planes drift in to land stage right like windblown stars. All at once it's night. The moon has established her quiet sovereignty above the palms, the motorbikes — mere spots of light — putter across the sand, plying their night trade, and the audience disperses to supper and other pleasures and diversions.

behind the single-story façade of boutiques and restaurants is another world, one of pastoral *losmen*, coconut groves, tethered cattle and free-ranging poultry. Take your choice of which is stranger — the magical world of the immemorial pastoral round or the tacked together world of Kuta's main streets, part fashion shops, part potholes.

Stand at night at **Bemo Corner**, with your back to the beach, and the two faces of urban Kuta lie on either hand. To the right is the **Night Market**, pure Indonesia. It is a world of interiors illuminated by kerosene lamps, hemmed in by the black and humid night. The small restaurants have adapted themselves to tourists needs, but otherwise you could be anywhere in the archipelago.

A few hundred meters in the other direction is the flashing world of discotheques and bars, each attempting to outdo the other with amplified noise. Entrance is usually free for tourists, but for Indonesians only if they can be seen to be bringing in a tourist. A tourist, it is assumed, can be guaranteed to pay for entrance with drinks bought at the bar.

LETHAL RIPS

There is only one setback to Kuta Beach, but it's one that could prove serious. Hundreds to misjudge the force of these strong "rips" on particular days.

The greatest danger lies in novices leaving the safe areas and trying their hand unsupervised in the surfing areas. (I did just that on my first day in Bali and was swept out well beyond the area in which the waves break. I owe my life to the prompt intervention of the Surf Rescue, who noticed me, even though I was far from the flagged area.)

A book containing the names of those rescued can be inspected at the Badung Tourist Office in Denpasar.

of thousands of people swim safely at Kuta every year, but the fact remains that at certain points along the beach currents pull out seawards from the shore. Their strength varies according to the size of the surf and the phases of the moon. These danger areas are well known to the Kuta Surf Rescue teams, and every day safe bathing areas are marked and watched all along the beach.

The problem is that the best surfing areas are exactly those areas where the currents are dangerous. Indeed, surfing is not permitted inside the designated safe bathing areas. Experienced surfers are likely to be aware of the problem, and be able to deal with it should they begin to be pulled away from shore. But even they have been known

The **Kuta Surf Rescue** service is run by the Badung Government Tourist Office in Denpasar. It maintains four stations along the beach, at Kuta, Half Legian, Legian and at the Kuta Palace Hotel. In addition, the Bali Oberoi pays for a private service. Officially known as the Badung Surf Life Saving Bali, the service was set up in 1972 in response to the increased use of Kuta Beach for surfing and the number of lives being lost there.

The men employed by the service are on duty every day of the year, with the one exception of the Balinese New Year, Nyepi,

Sunset on Kuta Beach — OPPOSITE: "...the great Indian Ocean surf laps as if entranced." An international crowd ABOVE waits for the sunset on a December evening.

KUTA: YELLOW SANDS AND TECHNICOLOR SUNSETS

KUTA'S HISTORY

when no one is allowed on the beach anyway. Their hours are 6 AM to 6 PM. The service operates with additional help from their counterparts at Cottesloe Beach, Perth, Western Australia from whom advice and materials have come over the years.

Remember—if you are in danger, try not to panic. Raise one hand high above your head. This is the international distress signal and is what the Surf Rescue are looking for. If you do feel strong enough to swim, paddle sideways and horizontal to the beach, out of the current, not against it.

KUTA'S HISTORY

It was probably here that Gajah Mada invaded from Java in the fourteenth century with his Majapahit forces. In 1580 the Englishman Sir Francis Drake may have called in for provisions. In 1597 a small Dutch expedition of three ships under Cornelius de Houtman dropped anchor off Kuta, and a party was landed. Later, the ships sailed round to the better anchorage off Padangbai, with the added purpose of being near the court of the Dewa Agung, the most powerful of Bali's chiefs, and his court at Gelgel, near Klungkung.

In the succeeding centuries Bali became a source of slaves, sold to Java but also as far afield as Mauritius. Kuta (encompassing also the anchorages nearby on the east coast) was the center for that trade.

In the 1960s Kuta Beach became a major staging post on the international hippie trail. What is now the splendid Oberoi Hotel was then a semi-derelict drug city of international standing where life was free and magic mushrooms were consumed under the palm trees and among the grazing cattle.

Kuta had always been to some extent disreputable, an area where vagabonds congregated and foreigners were allowed to settle. Parallels with its modern character need not be emphasized.

A LEAP IN THE DARK

No description of Kuta would be complete without some mention of its bungee jumps (see also BRAVE A BUNGEE in TOP SPOTS, page 13). At **Adrenalin Park**, for instance, not only can

you leap from the traditional 15-m (50-ft)-high tower but you can also be shot upwards in a capsule attached to elasticized ropes, spun round on swivels and have your reactions recorded by a video camera inches from your face. That the camera continues to work in these circumstances is one of the few reassurances you have on this, the Slingshot.

A J Hackett's, on the other hand, is part of the Double Six Restaurant and Disco complex. Here you can leap away, on Saturday at least, to your heart's content, just a few feet away from the dance floor, until four in the morning.

WHERE TO STAY

There is so much accommodation in Kuta and Legian it is only possible to mention some of the more expensive places that intending visitors might want to contact to make advance reservations. The many small and inexpensive *losmen*, which can still be found there, can only be selected after inspection on the grounds.

Beginning in the south, in the area nearest to the airport known as Tuban, there is the **Holiday Inn Bali Hai** (0361-753035 FAX 0361-754548 (200 rooms; average and above), comfortable yet with a Balinese ambiance, and the large **Kartika Plaza** (0361-751067 FAX 0361-752475 (386 rooms; average and above). Both are on the sea, though ten minute's walk from the best part of the beach.

Soon you are in the heart of Kuta, the center of the beast. The giant new department store, Matahari, dominates a most un-Balinese shopping mall called Kuta Square that pavement cafés and struggling palm trees do little to domesticate. But the beach nearby is good, and the spectacular **Sol Elite Paradiso** (0361-761414 FAX 0361-756944 (243 rooms; average and above) which opened its doors in 1997 is guaranteed to raise anyone's spirits.

Once you arrive at Jalan Bakungsari, running at right angles to the sea and joining the beach at a large cheap clothes market, you are in the thick of things. Good value here is the **Kuta Village Inn** (0361-751095 FAX 0361-753051 (moderate), tucked away down a narrow lane, or *gang*, a little further along the road on the same side. The welcome is friendly, there is a choice of rooms, some air conditioned, some with ceiling fan, and prices vary accordingly.

On the next road north, Jalan Pantai Kuta, stands the **Natour Kuta Beach** (0361-751361 FAX 0361-751362 (137 rooms; average and above) 200 m south of the site of the hotel with the same name that was Kuta's first hostelry back in the Thirties. There's a Garuda office in the lobby and Japanese food in the restaurant. Off the same street is the very reasonable **Ida Beach Inn Bungalows** (0361-751205 FAX 0361-751934 (64 rooms; moderate). With an attractive garden, a pool and air-conditioned rooms; this is good value for money.

Tucked away along Poppies Lane and just past the restaurant are the cottages of the same name, **Poppies Cottages** (0361-751059 FAX 0361-752364 (20 rooms; average and above). This famous and popular place has thatched bungalow rooms in a garden setting on the standard Kuta, indeed Balinese, pattern. Self-catering facilities and babysitters can be made available.

Also facing the beach in this area is the **Hotel Kuta Segara Ceria** (0361-751961 FAX 0361-751962, formerly Kuta Seaview Cottages (79 rooms; average and above).

In Legian proper, and right on the best part of the beach, is the **Legian Beach Hotel** (0361-751711 FAX 0361-752651 (190 rooms; average and above). It stands at the end of the road known as Jalan Melasti. With a large and beautiful garden, a swimming pool and access directly onto the sand, this four-star hotel with three-star prices will be many people's first choice in Legian. Hawkers are prohibited from the areas around the sun chairs immediately in front of the hotel, and it is generally a friendly, welcoming place. The hotel has some rooms that have been specially adapted for the handicapped.

Parallel to this, and the next lane north, is Jalan Padma, where the **Bali Mandira Cottages** (0361-751381 FAX 0361-752377 (118 rooms; average and above) are located.

North again and right on the beach is the large **Bali Padma Hotel** (0361-752111 FAX 0361-752140 (400 rooms; expensive). Slightly further on, along Jalan Double Six, a quiet street at right angles to the beach, is

the **Taman Legian Hotel** (0361-730876 FAX 0361-730405 (25 rooms; average and above).

Six kilometers (four miles) north of the airport in the area called Seminyak is the **Bali Oberoi** (0361-730361 FAX 0361-730954 (75 rooms; expensive), built as an executive haven and one of the truly special places to stay in Bali — private, intimate and well-managed. All rooms are villas standing in a lush garden.

Further on still, beyond Seminyak in **Canggu**, stands the **Hotel Tugu Bali** (0361-

731701 FAX 0361-731704 (34 rooms; expensive). The beach here is quiet, though you should be careful of strong currents when swimming.

Kuta is famous for its inexpensive accommodation, and it truly is possible to stay within minutes of this incomparably fine beach for around US$4 a day. The best *losmen* consist of the simplest possible rooms set around a lush Balinese garden, probably with a shrine in the middle. Inspecting them is half the pleasure, though it's always hard telling the owner that you've decided to stay somewhere else. Nevertheless, you'll need somewhere to stay that first day while you look around, so opt for the friendly and clean **Senen Beach Inn** (0361-755470 (23 rooms; inexpensive) down a narrow lane off Jalan Malasti. As at most *losmen*, breakfast is included in the low price.

The best eating in Kuta combines quality with informality, amiability with economy, and all under a traditional Balinese roof. The variety of cuisines is enormous, and the relaxed joviality of many establishments is a joy.

WHERE TO EAT

The restaurants in Kuta are as varied as the accommodation. Prices, however, tend to be comparable. The variety in Kuta's eateries lies not in their prices but in their cuisines.

You can eat Japanese, Mexican, German, Chinese — the only problem posed might be finding Balinese food, but even that is possible.

Made's Warung (0361-755397, on Jalan Pantai is an historic site, the first place,

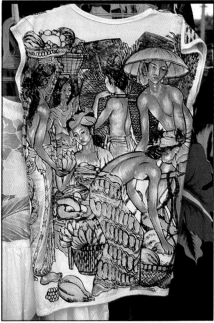

25 years ago, to offer high-quality Western dishes in Kuta. Today it remains a good place to eat — the range of food is vast, from strawberries to roast beef and encompassing Indonesian and Chinese specialties on the way. The menu overflows onto the very walls, and the atmosphere is half Paris and half Amsterdam, both shabby and chic. A couple of glasses of *arak madu* (palm spirit with lemon juice and honey) have seen many a lunch extended into the mid-afternoon, with the patrons finally managing to stumble the short distance along the road and collapse on the beach just in time for the sunset.

Today, **Made's Warung II** (0361-732130, at the center of a fashionable shopping square in Seminyak gets more attention and a more chic set of diners than its parent in nowadays raucous Kuta.

A few yards down the narrow lane immediately to the left of the Jalan Pantai Made's lies a fine establishment, **Un's** (0361-752607, named after the Swiss owner's wife. Set in a beautiful courtyard with flowering trees, it is deservedly popular at dinnertime.

Poppies (0361-751059, on Poppies Lane, is an old favorite now become trendy; the food remains excellent, and the restaurant is so popular that tourists come from Sanur and Nusa Dua; it is advisable to book in advance.

TJ's (0361-751093, close to Poppies serves excellent Mexican food.

Many establishments go in for a vigorous ambiance — **Glory** (0361-751091, on Jalan Legian not far from Goa 2001 club, for example, serves hearty food of all kinds, while back in the heart of Kuta **Dayu II** (0361-752262, specializes in duck Balinese style.

Northerners who long for potatoes and homemade sausages will find the land of their heart's desire at the **Swiss Restaurant** (0361-751735, on Jalan Pura Bagus Taruna. Bratwurst, wiener *kartoffelsalat* and *apfelstrudel* rub shoulders with *fondue bourguignonne*. The owner is the Swiss Consul.

For French food at a very reasonable price try **The French Restaurant** at **Topi Kopi** (0361-754243, a few yards along from the Swiss Restaurant. French food can also be eaten at **Le Bistro** (0361-730973, on Jalan Legian. Far and away the classiest place for dining French style is the **Kafe Warisan** (0361-731175, overlooking rice paddies not far from the Oberoi hotel. This place has re-opened recently and to much acclaim. Food and wine are of a very high standard.

Italian food is big business in Legian and Seminyak. Top prices can be paid at the ultra-fashionable **La Lucciola** (0361-730838 right on the Seminyak Beach, and booking is essential for tables from sundown onwards. Many enthusiasts believe the food is even better at the **Café Luna** (0361-730805 opposite Goa 2001. Fresh pasta is made every day on the premises. It's an elegant establishment that mounts fashion shows in a large and beautiful hall behind the main restaurant space at 11 PM every Friday. It's as much a cult place as La Lucciola and particularly popular with the nightlife set.

A good, attractively-housed coffeeshop is **Warung Kopi** (0361-753602, in Legian and on Jalan Legian. It serves homemade ice cream containing only natural ingredients and serves meals, too, including an Indian buffet on Wednesday. There's another branch on Jalan Padma Utara.

Good Thai food is served at the **Kin Khao Thai Restaurant** (0361-732153, with a second location in the heart of Kuta on Jalan Kartika Plaza. Should you hanker for Jakarta style

NIGHTLIFE

Kuta's nightlife is both raucous and extensive. In Kuta itself there are a string of places — **Peanuts, Casablanca, Hard Rock Café, Studebaker's**. All these are open nightly and cater for a partying, rock-and-roll clientele. Also catering for the younger set is **001** (formerly the Pink Panther), situated in front of Aromas Café, famous for its vegetarian food.

Legian caters for a slightly different set. There, **Goa 2001** offers old musical favorites

food there's **Warung Batavia** (0361-243769, on Jalan Raya Kerobokan in Seminyak.

If you want to eat overlooking the surf, then head for the **Surya Café** (0361-757381 at the end of Jalan Padma. The food is average but the location excellent. In addition, many of the tiny outlets with pointed roofs actually on the beach serve simple meals; the one known as **Tivoli**, close to the part of the beach just before the Oberoi known as Blue Ocean, is good and fastidiously clean.

Lastly, for cheap but often excellent food, try **Depot Kuta** (0361-51155, in Kuta's Night Market. There are several very inexpensive restaurants and food stalls in this area, but this one, specializing in Chinese food, is among the best.

together with Japanese sushi and lemon meringue pie under a high Balinese roof, from 10 PM until 2 PM. After that hour the crowd goes on to a prescribed dance venue depending on the day of the week. On Sunday, Tuesday and Wednesday it's **Gado Gado**, on the beach at Seminyak (though Wednesday is also the night for the **Taj Mahal**); on Friday it's **Warung Tapas** further up the road (though Gado Gado is also open); and on Monday, Thursday and Saturday it's **Double Six**, also on the beach and the finest disco in town. It's right next to the A.J. Hackett bungee

Every Balinese is an artist, or so the early visitors to the island claimed. Perhaps the truth is that all people everywhere are. OPPOSITE: A handpainted T-shirt. ABOVE: Work is displayed and admired in a fashionable boutique in Kuta.

jump, and patrons have been known to dance, take a bungee jump and return to the dance floor exhilarated and refreshed.

In addition, there are drag shows at 10:30 PM every Wednesday, Friday and—the big one—Sunday at **Hulu Café (** 0361-756848 on Jalan Menuh in Legian.

One note of importance — the **SC** (Sari Club) on Jalan Legian in Kuta, at the time of writing, systematically excludes all Indonesians. Perhaps a reason for right-thinking people to give it a miss.

SHOPPING

Kuta is an excellent place for shopping, combining, in the best places, quality and value for money. There is a huge choice in Kuta in general and in particular for clothes and leather goods. Visitors staying in upmarket hotels in Nusa Dua and Sanur invariably come to Kuta on shopping sprees, and shops selling good quality goods are plentiful, mixed in with those offering tourist souvenirs.

The trade in cheap cassettes is not what it was before Indonesia agreed to comply with international copyright. Even so, at under US$6 a foreign tape (those by Indonesian artists are cheaper) and US$15 per CD, there is still a savings over prices in Australia and Europe, and there are a dozen shops in Kuta selling nothing else.

There are several bookshops specializing in vacation reading. Particularly recommended, both for the range and quality of its stock, is the **Kertai Bookshop** on Jalan Pantai, on the left as you walk toward the beach. New and secondhand books are available and can be traded in at half the price paid for them.

The further you go up Jalan Legian towards Seminyak the classier things become, and eventually it's all boutiques where a tiny number of exquisite objects are sold in grand and resplendent surroundings.

Good buys can be found everywhere. You'll find designer sunglasses at **Sol (** 0361-755072 on Kuta Square, Australian sportswear at less than Australian prices at **Dreamland (** 0361-755159, also on Kuta Square and surfing accessories at **Aloha Surf Station (** 0361-758286 at the Kuta end of Jalan Legian.

Fabrics with crazy designs, fabulous for wall-hangings, can be seen at **Irie Collection** FAX 0361-754732, and bizarre candlesticks are a specialty at **Titien Collection (**/FAX 0361-730448 in Seminyak. Custom-made picture frames are the specialty of **Toko Kaca Taman Sari (** 0361-730424, while **Ulu Watu (** 0361-753428 (Jalan Bakungsari branch) specialize in Balinese lace. They have locations in all of most popular tourist areas in Bali.

A road to visit if you're looking for sarongs is Jalan Double Six where there are many shops specializing in fabrics.

Back on the main road, **Nona (** 0361-755919 has bits of everything — furniture, ceramics, mirrors — while **Tidore (** 0361-730934 sells antiques and collectibles. Gems and jewelry can be seen in many places —

one is **Miko Opals** (0361-761231 on Jalan
Pura Bagus Taruna. Fine silver is sold at the
shops of **Suarti Designer Collection** (0361-
754252.

Furniture can be found in many places,
too — try **Setya Budi Art** (730560 on Jalan
Tunjung Mekar. More furniture and *objets
d'art* are on sale in Seminyak at **Warisan**
(0361-730710, and both clothes and furniture are sold by **E. Ekstra** (0811-398685 in
the same area.

Back in Kuta, the island's biggest department store is **Matahari** on Kuta Square (not
to be confused with the smaller Matahari
building containing Kuta's cinemas on Jalan
Legian). A new Kuta shopping complex fo-
cusing on the arts is **Bali Plaza**, close to
Waterbom.

SOUTH BALI: TANAH LOT TO UBUD

South Bali in many ways embodies the
island's essence. Here is the intense rice cultivation on the banks of the fast-flowing rivers
that rush down from the mountains, cutting
themselves earthy gorges as they do and providing for the irrigation that has always been
the basis of the island's prosperity. This abun-
dant water supply and the immensely fertile volcanic soils that it feeds, is the key to
Bali's ceaseless rice production, which continues regardless of season, so that the rainy

Tanah Lot — The coach loads of tourists arriving to
photograph the temple outlined against the sunset
have rendered this particular image one of modern
Asia's archetypes.

season is as much an inconvenience as a blessing. The great lakes in the volcanic calderas ensure an endless water supply, and this in turn guarantees food production.

Famine, so common elsewhere in Asia, is in Bali only the product of political upheaval or volcanic eruption. Thanks to the relatively new "miracle" rice, producing three crops a year is now the status quo, and all stages of growth can often be seen in adjacent fields, providing the varying tones of yellow and green that have so delighted painters.

It is this agricultural abundance that has allowed Bali to develop its arts. Leisure time has never been in short supply, and with carving, painting and metalwork all originally dedicated to a religion that looked to the hills from which came the abundance, it can seem as if the whole formed a self-contained, beautiful and life enhancing system. It was thus that many of the island's first visitors regarded Bali.

Ubud is at the heart of it all. East Bali is lush too, but the plains are less extensive, there are many subsidiary ridges of hills, and the region is subject to earthquakes, albeit rare ones. North Bali is a mere coastal strip. The area of Bali which lies south of Denpasar, now so prosperous on account of tourism, was not so long ago seen as a more or less arid waste. West Bali has always been considered a rocky, waterless and infertile wilderness.

For the purposes of this guide, the central southern area will be considered as running from Tanah Lot in the west to Bangli in the east, with Ubud as its center.

TANAH LOT

The celebrated Tanah Lot, overrated in the first place, has now been all but destroyed by the attentions of the tourist industry.

Originally it consisted of a small temple perched on a rocky islet one hundred meters out from the coast. Today it hosts the unwelcome addition of a host of kiosks selling T-shirts and sarongs, two small hotels, a shop selling Polo Ralph Lauren fashions and the vast Le Meridien Hotel with its 18-hole golf course.

Except at high tide you can walk over the rocks to the site of the temple, but you will not be allowed into the temple itself — it's locked except at festival times. Most people have little desire to go there; what they want to do is photograph it from the shore, preferably against the backdrop of a sunset.

There are essentially three places from which this picturesque if slightly twee ensemble can be captured on film: from down in the cove itself, from along the low cliff, and from the headland on the right. From this last position a natural arch in the rocks to the north can also be taken in, with Mount Batur in the background.

Tanah Lot has little to keep you for more than a brief visit. You can, however, while down in the cove, see the "holy snake" or guardian of the temple, which lies conveniently coiled on a ledge in a small cave. Boys will illuminate it for you with a small flashlight and collect a donation for the service.

The temple itself has five small thatched shrines and is thought to date from the sixteenth century when the priest Danghyang Nirartha is believed by the devout to have crossed over to Bali from Java floating on a leaf. He instructed several temples to be built, Tanah Lot among them, as was the far more spectacular temple at Ulu Watu.

Entrance to the beach area adjacent to the temple is Rp1,100, half-price for children. You will be asked to pay an additional donation but there's no need to do so.

If you are keen on spending the night at Tanah Lot, the small hotels are the **Dewi Sinta** (0361-812933 FAX 0361-813956 (27 rooms; moderate) and the **Mutiara Tanah Lot Bungalows** (0361-225457 FAX 0361-222672 (10 rooms; average and above). There are also the large, new **Le Meridien Bali** (0361-243691 and **Bali Nirvana Resort** (0361-815900 FAX 0361-815901, also a golf course, (both expensive).

Tanah Lot is 12 km (seven and a half miles) from Kediri on the main road from Denpasar to Tabanan. Kediri is five kilometers (three miles) beyond **Kapal**, the village where carved architectural details are produced, seemingly for the whole of Bali.

It's easy to get as far as Kediri by *bemo*, but from there you will probably have to find

Taman Ayun, Mengwi — The temple is particularly spacious and, surrounded as it is by a wide moat, the peaceful ambiance is remarkable. Note one of the temple's multitiered black *meru* in the background.

someone to take you down the road to Tanah Lot by motorbike. Most people, however, arrive on organized tours.

KEDATON'S FRUIT BATS

There was a time when Sangeh was the only place in Bali to claim a "monkey forest." In fact, it still is the only such place. But at **Kedaton**, a ten-minute drive from Kediri up a pleasant side road, a site has now opened that offers a few monkeys and some trees, but in addition something far more spectacular—hundreds of gigantic tropical fruit bats.

These bats hang from the treetops surrounding a small temple, leaving only to flap to another tree and display their russet-tinted wings as they're caught in the sun's rays. It's an extraordinary sight, comparable only to the massed bats at Goa Lawah (see page 208). But at Goa Lawah the bats, though much more numerous, are far smaller. Here the huge creatures have a wingspan of perhaps a meter. They're among the wonders of Bali and shouldn't be missed. Admission is around US$.50, half-price for children.

MENGWI

Taman Ayun, the Water Temple at Mengwi, was once an attractive, peaceful place, but now, like so many other celebrated sites on the island, it has been all but taken over by vendors selling T-shirts and trinkets.

Built on rising grass slopes and partly surrounded by a wide moat, Taman Ayun is one of the great Balinese temples, spacious and almost trim in a way that is uncharacteristic of most of the others. As if to establish this garden-like quality, there is a pool with a fountain in it on the left as you enter the first compound.

In the second compound, in the bottom left-hand corner, is a small tower that can be climbed; the top provides a good viewpoint of the temple and its watery surrounds. Immediately below, gnarled frangipani trees exhibit their fabulous blossoms.

Women returning from the fields near Ubud. The central area of Bali is the island's heartland, a rich alluvial rice growing region where the many ancient monuments testify to a long history of human settlement and cultural sophistication.

The last, or inner, court contains ten fine *meru*, the tall tiered towers thatched in black *ijuk*, a fiber derived from the sago palm. The number of tiers is always uneven, as with the tiers on cremation towers. Here the tallest have eleven.

The inner court also contains a fine stone *padmasana*, in effect a giant and highly ornate chair on which it is hoped the unseen supreme god will deign to sit on days of high festival. The back of the chair is oriented toward Mount Agung. Also notable, on the left, is an ornate brick and stone shrine with

a thatched roof. At the corner of each base is a carving of Garuda attacking Naga. The inner court is surrounded by a miniature walled moat that echoes the great moat that nearly encircles the temple.

To the left of the upper part of Taman Ayun is a lush, overgrown area, abandoned to nature and silent except for the chirping of insects.

Food and drink are available on the far side of the outer moat overlooking the temple.

SANGEH

An exceptionally pleasant winding country road links Mengwi and the Monkey Forest at Sangeh, 9 km (six miles) away. Take the road on which the Water Temple stands, turning left as you leave the precinct. Turn left after approximately 5 km (three miles), then left again after a further 2 km (one and a quarter miles). The forest is then on your left, opposite a car park.

Sangeh consists of some 10 hectares (24 acres) of *pala* trees in the middle of which

is a temple. It is in fact a sacred wood. About a thousand monkeys are said to inhabit the area, and they too are believed to be sacred.

There are stories of coach loads of tourists overwhelming Sangeh from morning till night, a horror only exceeded by the bands of thieving monkeys that leap on you at the least rustle of a packet of peanuts. A visit at about 4 PM, however, makes it possible to appreciate the beauty of the place.

The trees are tall and symmetrical, some reaching to a height of 50 m (164 ft) with no side branches. The place is scented by the five-petaled flowers of the trees which lie scattered underfoot. The shady cool and the silence induce an air of sanctity, and the temple is simple and potent. It is dedicated to Wisnu and much visited by farmers.

Monkey Kings

Here at Sangeh there are around 1,000 monkeys, organized in two groups, east and west, each with its king. No monkey will cross into the other group's territory. At sunset, they retreat to the tops of the trees to sleep. Locals will tell you the biggest monkeys are the kings (thereby providing an insight into Indonesian attitudes to politics). They also insist that no dead body of an old monkey (as opposed to younger ones killed accidentally) has ever been found.

Entrance to Sangeh is by donation. Young men will attach themselves to you and chat as you walk along, but by the time you are ready to leave you will realize you have in fact made use of the services of a guide, and a payment will be in order.

The statue at the entrance is of Hanuman, the white monkey god of the *Ramayana* and the *kecak* dance.

TAMAN BURUNG BALI BIRD PARK

Taman Burung Bali Bird Park (0361-299352 FAX 0361-299614 is well worth seeing and can be conveniently visited on the way to Ubud. It is situated on Jalan Serma Cok Ngurah Gambir in Singapadu, the village just after Celuk on the road from Denpasar to Gianyar.

The park contains 250 kinds of Indonesian birds spread over two hectares, and there is a walk-in rainforest aviary. Several of the park's species are endangered; a permit is required for the park to hold these and an extensive breeding program is being undertaken.

Most popular of the park's inhabitants is the king bird of paradise, little bigger than a canary but with a long and spectacular tail. This tail was nearly the cause of the bird's extinction as it was much prized in ladies' hats in the nineteenth century — at the height of their popularity some 50,000 bird of paradise pelts were exported annually to Europe and the United States. The bird can be difficult to spot as it tends to sit high up in trees.

The park is open from 9 AM to 6 PM.

UBUD

Fifty years ago Ubud was the inland village of choice for painters and other artists wanting to settle down on the island, live the quiet life and imbibe the unique atmosphere of rural Bali. Today it's an upmarket resort resplendent with New Age specialties, such as courses in spiritual healing, aroma therapy, reflexology and chiropractics.

Ubud itself doesn't have the feeling of a town — more an extended village. Its long main street, running east to west, is on the main road to nowhere, and a relaxed, well-heeled ambiance pervades the place. You can begin the day with an expensive cappuccino, have your hair cut in the Italian fashion, discover your inner powers on a four- or six-day program called, "Rejuvenation, Vitality, Well-being," or simply watch the rice farmers who persist in walking down the main street bearing sickles and scythes.

People read books in Ubud, unlock their shining and stout bicycles in the morning air, still remembering the *kecak* or *legong* dances they saw the previous evening and positively shudder at the thought of Kuta and the Hard Rock Café.

Ubud is the best place in Bali to see dance dramas and to buy paintings and one of the better places to enjoy the relaxing effects of watching other people at work in the countryside. It's the cultural side of Bali, and if it inevitably is no longer the unspoiled rural retreat it once was — just as Seminyak is no longer the unspoiled beachside village — the approximation is close enough to suit all but the most fastidious of tastes.

General Information

Bemos from Denpasar to Ubud leave from the Kereneng terminus. Ubud has a market every third day, from 5 AM to 3 PM. There is a **Tourist Information Office** on the main street, not far from the Lotus Café. Full details of dance and drama performances are available here.

There are a couple of places where you can send and receive faxes and e-mail messages. One, on Jalan Bisma, is the **Roda Tourist Service** (/FAX 0361-9765582 E-MAIL rodanet@denpasar.wasantara.net.id.

Another, on the main drag, is the **Pt. Kartika Chandra Telecommunication Center** (0361-96136 FAX 0361-976478 E-MAIL kartika @dps.mega.net.id.

What to See and Do
DANCE

Traditions are carried out in style at Ubud. One knows from the first strike on the gong that the performance culminating in the *legong* dance (every Monday at 7:30 PM at the Puri, or Palace) is authentic. The concentration of the *gamelan* as they play their introductory overture, their costumes and the beautifully painted mounts for their instruments, the setting itself — all are perfect. It's an introduction, and you settle down for the extended pleasure of what will follow, confident that nothing is going to be stinted. The relish with which, later in the week, the narrator begins his story in the

Ubud — OPPOSITE: The lotuses that give their name to the village's most delectable eating place. ABOVE: Deer-like Balinese cattle being taken for a walk.

wayang kulit puppet theater is just as reassuring.

All these accomplished performers are in the daytime workers in restaurants, shops or in the fields. These Ubud performances are genuine folk dramas, like the European medieval morality plays. You see the Monkey King or Shiva, but he's really the local butcher or candlestick-maker.

ART MUSEUMS AND GALLERIES

There are three important museums exhibiting Balinese paintings in Ubud. Newly opened, the **Agung Rai Museum of Art** (ARMA) has a magnificent collection of work by artists who have lived and painted in Ubud. The exhibit here formed part of the private collection of the art dealer Agung Rai, until he mounted this museum complex. There is a fine restaurant and a hotel under the same management. If, after seeing this interesting collection, you want to buy something of quality, visit Agung Rai's Art Gallery in nearby Peliatan where there are paintings for all pockets.

The older (1982) **Museum Neka** has 13 rooms and orders its material into styles. This, therefore, is the place to go if Balinese art seems to you either uniform or a confusion of contrasting tendencies. The museum is about one kilometer (just over a half mile) beyond the bridge by Murni's Warung; carry straight on up the road on the other side of the river, and it's on your right. Hours are 8 AM to 4 PM; entrance fee: approximately US$1.25.

Puri Lukisan Museum, the oldest (founded in 1954), is in the center of the village and contains 10 rooms — seven in the main building and three in a separate gallery on the left as you arrive. All styles of Balinese art are on show, though less neatly categorized than at the Neka. Nevertheless, many paintings crucial to the history of Balinese art and the changes brought about by the arrival of artists from Europe between the wars can be seen here. Times and fee as for the Neka.

More useful still is the display in a separate building, a short walk across a paddy field (follow a sign labeled "exhibition" pointing right as you come out of the main museum). There are a large number of pictures

for sale here. As they are by a wide variety of artists, and as they have fixed prices marked on the back of their labels, a wander around can give you a fair idea of the going rate for Balinese art and the prices you might consider reasonable should you want to negotiate with the local painters themselves in their private galleries elsewhere in the district.

Be warned that these days the museum is in bad shape. Mildew and damp have affected it badly, and there's a current appeal for funds (it receives no government support). If you'd like to contribute, contact Rosemary Oei (0361-975136 FAX 0361-975137, the museum's curator.

AN ARTIST'S HOUSE

If museums tend to make you cross-eyed with their bewildering variety, you'll enjoy visiting a place which is all of a piece — a work of art in its own right, Antonio Blanco's House. Erotic illuminated poems hang beside fantasy portraits of the painter's Balinese wife. You are unlikely to get to meet the venerable Filipino artist himself, but you can certainly look around his studio and gain a real sense of what Ubud and Bali once were, both for him and for the other expatriate artists who made it their home. A photograph of Blanco talking to Michael Jackson hangs in the reception area where you will pay the entrance fee of around US$1.25. The house is open daily from 9 AM to 5 PM.

Where to Stay

Not surprisingly, there are many ultra-luxurious, high-price hotels in Ubud. Bali as a whole is booming, and the top end of the market, for better or worse, seeks the quiet and the sense of exclusivity it provides. Ubud's hotels some of the most luxurious anywhere in the tropics.

The most expensive are situated just outside the village. The **Amandari** (0361-975333 FAX 0361-975335 (29 suites; expensive, staring from US$460) is at Sayan, five kilometers (three miles) out of Ubud. Each suite has a walled garden and many have a private pool; yet, the ambiance is relaxed and even informal.

A kilometer away (just over half a mile), the Australian-owned **Kupu Kupu Barong** (0361-975476 FAX 0361-975079 (19 villas;

expensive, starting from US$335) is another ultra-luxurious hideaway organized on the same principles as the Amandari, with a stunning view down to the river far below, and a particularly fine restaurant.

To the northeast of town, the **Banyan Tree Kamandalu (** 0361-975825 FAX 975851 (58 villas; expensive) has a flowery ambiance and four-poster beds. It used to be known as the Puri Kamandalu. A short drive to the north of Ubud, there's the larger **Chedi (** 0361-975963 FAX 0361-975968 (60 rooms; expensive) with beautiful rooms in two-story

river. A path zigzags down and there are bungalows dotted around at various levels. It has a tennis court and swimming pool. The artist Walter Spies once lived there. It aims to be somewhat exclusive, but these days finds itself outclassed in the frantic Ubud scramble towards super-exclusivity.

In the center of Ubud, close to the *puri* and the intersection with the Monkey Forest Road, are two mid-priced places offering good value for money. One is **Han Snel Siti Bungalows (** 0361-975699 FAX 0361-975643 (eight rooms; moderate). A short way

blocks, plus top-ranking suites with baths surrounded by carp pools.

Closer to the center of Ubud are the **Pita Maha Tjampuhan (** 974330 FAX 974329 (24 villas; expensive) built to resemble a Balinese village and with views (if you're lucky) of Mount Agung. Also close to the center is **Ibah (** 0361-974466 FAX 0361-975567 (10 rooms; expensive), a smaller place with, again, beautiful gardens.

For mid-range-priced accommodation in Ubud itself, beginning from the Campuhan end, the area down by the two bridges and Murni's Warung, there is the **Hotel Tjamphuan (** 0361-95871 (64 rooms; average and above). This long-established bungalow hotel sits on the steep sloping bank of the

down a lane, this is a pleasant place with an adjacent restaurant and cocktail bar of the same name. Back on the road, the **Puri Saraswati (** / FAX 0361-975164 (18 rooms; moderate) offers standard bungalow rooms around a courtyard.

Budget accommodation can still be found in Ubud, though the gap between these and the more expensive places speedily increases. To locate these dwindling options, head down the Monkey Forest Road. **Tjanderi's** (or Candri's) is a long-established staging post for overlanders that now has the feel of

Painting from life is not typical of Balinese practice. Bali, however, is increasingly coming under the influence of foreign customs, and the Balinese are showing themselves remarkably adaptable while remaining true to their cultural roots.

having known better times. Down a narrow *gang* is **Anom** with just four rooms, while **Suarsena** has 10 rooms; both places offer simple fan-cooled rooms with mosquito nets.

Some people still come to Ubud, get to know artists, find places to stay far from the tourist trails and live on for months virtually as part of the family.

Where to Eat
Many of the most expensive restaurants so characteristic of Ubud share the same features — homemade cakes, European style bread, tiled floors, antique wooden doors, a view of a lotus pond or a river gorge, original paintings on the walls — and an assumption of superiority over all the others.

The first upmarket eatery in Ubud was the **Café Lotus** (0361-975660. It is almost opposite the tourist office, and both food and ambiance are superb. Pink lilies stretch their necks like flamingos in the pond, and music chosen with discretion (no Vivaldi's "Four Seasons" here) plays unobtrusively. The menu still offers (among many other delights) wheat bread, salads with olive oil dressing, freshly made pasta with mushrooms and strawberry tart. The restaurant can seat 200 people. Every stomach now and again insists on something it knows and preferably loves, and the Lotus Café unashamedly provides for these moments. The pleasure of eating delicacies you long for, but never expect to meet in this part of the world, is compounded by paying somewhat less than what you would pay for them in Paris, Frankfurt or Los Angeles (though much more than you would have paid in the place's early days ten or more years ago). The Café Lotus is open from 8 AM to 11 PM.

Other places serving choice food in the center of Ubud are: **Casa Luna** (0361-96283 FAX 0361-96282, open from 9 PM to 11 PM and serving Italian food in elegant surroundings; **Mumbul's** (0361-975364, a slightly cheaper place, though still with excellent food, and with a wonderful ice cream parlor next to it; and **Ary's Warung** (0361-975063, on the same side of the road as Casa Luna.

Too chic now for its former clientele, like so many places in Ubud, **Murni's Warung** (0361-975233, down by the old suspension

and modern road bridges over the river, occupies four levels. It too specializes in Western food — look for unexpected items such as vichyssoise and gazpacho, as well as "Upper Elk Valley authentic hamburgers." Murni's also stocks souvenirs and books on Bali. It's open 9 AM to 11 PM.

The **Nomad Wine Bar and Restaurant** (moderate), further down the main street in the direction of Denpasar, is a pleasant place, open from 8 AM to 10 PM. There's live music at night and a relaxed ambiance prevails. The owner also offers a guide service with car.

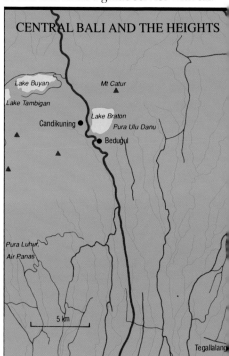

Eating cheaply is no problem in Ubud. Many of the *losmen* down along the Monkey Forest Road have small restaurants attached to them where you can eat well for under US$3.

Shopping
There are many upmarket shops in the center of Ubud. Notable among them are **Ary's Bookshop** (0361-975162, next to the restaurant of the same name, and **Lotus Studios** (0361-975363, which houses a boutique as well as a gallery. If you are interested in buying paintings the best tactic to follow is to ask for advice at the Puri

Lukisan Museum first, or visit Agung Rai's Art Gallery a couple of kilometers away in Peliatan (see ART MUSEUMS AND GALLERIES, above).

AROUND CENTRAL BALI

The area east of Ubud is rich in archaeologic and historic sites. The following takes in the most interesting of these sites in a round-trip tour. Note that to do justice to all of these places in a single day would be, in the Balinese climate, a near impossibility.

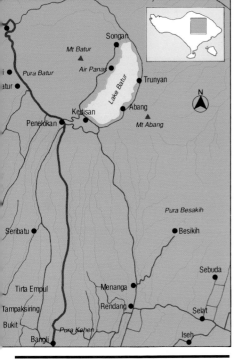

TEGALALANG, PUJUNG AND SEBATU

Leaving the center of Ubud on the road that leads eastwards (in the direction of Denpasar) keep a lookout for a sign to Pujung (15 km or just over nine miles) away. This is an attractive road, scenic in a typically Balinese way and brimming with artists' workplaces and sales stalls.

On the way to Pujung, you pass through **Tegalalang**, a small center for the production of painted, softwood carved statues, usually depicting fruit or plants. As you drive up the road you will pass small shops, each specializing in one particular form or style. At **Pujung**, the main occupation of the populace is the manufacture of the banana tree carvings to be seen at tourist centers all over the island, and increasingly in many places elsewhere in Asia as well.

Turn right at Pujung and descend to the bottom of the valley where, at **Sebatu**, there are some attractive public baths. From there the road climbs again — past many shops offering painted softwood carvings of various kinds — to the junction where you bear left, after one kilometer (just over half a mile), for Tampaksiring.

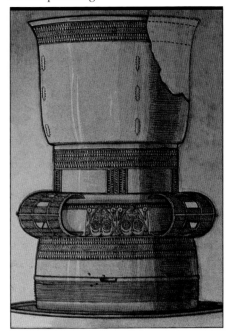

TIRTA EMPUL

The **Sukarno Palace** at **Tampaksiring** is reached after climbing a good number of steps. The palace — a fifties-era pile with Western style carpets, Western style windows and international-level security — is built in two sections connected by a footbridge over a small valley.

At the foot of the steps is the important **Tirta Empul**, consisting of holy springs, public baths and a temple. The water emerges from the rock into a large basin and from there into the bathing pool. The water is considered both sacred and magic, so bathing in it

An early twentieth century drawing of the great drum of Pejeng.

is a popular pursuit. The temple itself is one of the six most important in Bali, and the sight of it creates a particularly vivid impression. Entrance is about US$.50, which includes the rental of a sarong. An additional few cents is charged for any visible camera and around half a dollar for a video camera. The site is open to visitors from 8 AM to 5 PM.

GUNUNG KAWI

Take the road south from Tampaksiring in the direction of Gianyar and you will shortly

and without ornament. There are four on your left before you cross the bridge, five ahead of you on the other side and a last one further down the valley. There are also passages cut into the rock, reminiscent of modern wartime pillboxes.

Taken together, the site has a feeling that is almost Egyptian in its formality. The monuments are thought to date from the eleventh century and to be the resting place for the remains of King Anak Wungsu, who reigned over Bali from 1049 to 1077 AD, and the remains of his wives and sons.

arrive at the King's Tombs, or **Gunung Kawi**, on the left side of the road.

A few meters from the car park, steps descend the side of the steep valley. If you arrive at the end of a long day or, worse still, in the heat of the early afternoon, you might be content to view the site from above — if so, there is a convenient viewing point a few dozen steps from the car park. If you opt to inspect the site at close quarters, descend until the path crosses the River Pakrisan by a bridge, where far below, young boys have set up a lucrative business diving for coins thrown from the parapet above.

The ruins consist of large mausoleums, formal rectangular shapes cut into the rock

The charge for entrance is around US$.50, and the site is open from 8 AM until 6 PM.

THE MOON OF PEJENG

Continuing further south, after another 11 km (around seven miles) you reach Pejeng and, on the left side of the road, **Pura Panataram Sasih**.

This temple, another of the Balinese top six, is above all famous for its gigantic bronze drum, known as the Moon Face. It is more

OPPOSITE: The great rock tombs at Gunung Kawi are mysterious in origin. Situated on the valley floor of the Pakrisan River, they are probably 1,000 years old and thus testify to a formal culture on the island long before the Majapahit invasion. ABOVE: One of the stone fountains in Goa Gajah, or Elephant Cave.

than two meters (six feet) high, its striking end 160 cm (5 ft) in diameter, and it is 1,000 years old, dating from the ninth century. Unfortunately, it is kept high up under a roof, and is not clearly visible.

A kilometer further on, to your right, is the **Pura Kebo Edan**, or Crazy Buffalo Temple, best known for its statue of the dancing Bhima, strongman from the epic poem the *Mahabharata*, with its multiple penises.

Only a short distance further, on the other side of the road, is the **Archaeological Museum** (Museum Arkeologi) containing a variety of historical objects and fossils.

YEH PULU

Shortly after this, the road divides, turning right for Ubud and left for Gianyar. There is, however, a third, untarred road that leads off from this junction — follow this for two kilometers (one and a quarter miles) and, after passing through a village, you will arrive at Yeh Pulu.

A short walk between rice fields at the point where the road ends takes you to the site of a frieze, of about 40 m (120 ft) in length, carved in the rock on one side of the path. Depicting men on horses in a hunting scene, the frieze is strangely dynamic and forceful; there is an energy and a simplicity here that vanishes from later Balinese work where the emphasis is on poise and the sublime. These carvings at Yeh Pulu are more reminiscent of the rough but vigorous archaic Greek sculpture, brave, heroic and independent of the requirements of a later orthodoxy. The frieze is thought to date from the fourteenth century.

GOA GAJAH: THE ELEPHANT CAVE

Back at the crossroads, take the road toward Ubud and after about a kilometer (just over half a mile) you will arrive at the popular **Goa Gajah** or Elephant Cave.

Visitors to the cave might be excused for thinking the place had received an excess of

Washing cattle in Lake Batur. K'tut Tantri's book *Revolt in Paradise* contains a description of cattle being drowned as ritual sacrifices in this lake. The upland central area of the island is much cooler than the coastal region; it's frequently in cloud and experiences heavy rainfall.

publicity. Coach loads of sightseers unload every day to stumble through a small cave, knock their heads against the roof in the inadequate light and stare at a single small sculpture of Ganesa (elephant-headed son of Siwa) illuminated by an oil lamp. Yet the usual *warung* and souvenir stalls are assembled, and a fee of about US$.50 is charged as if this were one of Bali's great splendors.

Even so, the man-made cave does date back to the eighth century, and the carving around the cave's rectangular entrance is indeed marvelous, a typically bug-eyed

From Goa Gajah, it is five kilometers (three miles) back to Ubud, turning right at Teges where you meet the road coming up from Denpasar.

BANGLI

Bangli is a small town (though referred to in Penelokan as a "city") on the border of the central and eastern regions, 14 km (nine miles) from Gianyar.

The small hotel–restaurant, the **Artha Sastra Inn** (0366-91179 (14 rooms; inexpen-

monster appearing to prize open the rock with his fingertips. The statue to the left of the cave entrance is of Durga, destructive mother and consort of Siwa. In front of the cave are some large baths, with six standing figures holding bowls from which water pours. They are a testimony to past splendor and are basically in good condition; they could easily be restored.

Some 50 steps lead down from the temple compound that contains the cave and baths to a pleasant natural amphitheater where ponds and a small altar to Buddha enhance the natural serenity of the area. As neither Buddha nor elephants have ever been native to Bali, the site is something of an historical mystery.

sive) is actually the old palace of the former king of Bangli. A photograph of the young rajah, with two attendants, hangs on the walls of the verandah where lunch is served. It was apparently taken as recently as 1950. Together with the painted doorways and faded gilt mirrors, it provides a key to the atmosphere of a former world. Lewis Carroll's Alice could have slipped through a time warp and been there in a trice, you feel. One of the attendants told me a figure sweeping the steps was the former king's daughter. A glimpse into the once great rooms reveals camping furniture and a table with shampoo and a toothbrush.

Bangli's main temple is **Pura Kehen**. Carvings of trumpeting elephants welcome you to the flight of 38 steps leading up to a highly ornate gateway. The temple is built in tiers up a steep slope, and its obligatory banyan tree is vast. Otherwise there is little of interest, but it is austerely imposing for all that. It was the state temple of the old kingdom of Bangli.

Bangli is also the site of Bali's major psychiatric hospital (something romantic attitudes to the island would have you believe shouldn't exist). Laid out in large grounds with ornate gardens, it looks from the outside to be a fine model of progressive thought. It's not the kind of place one visits though, and prying visitors are the last thing anyone connected with this establishment needs.

THE HEIGHTS

PENELOKAN

The mountain area is most dramatically first seen if you arrive there at **Penelokan**. The main road up to this superb vantage point is through Bangli, and nothing is seen of the country you are approaching as you ascend until you pass through a ceremonial gateway and everything is suddenly laid out before you.

Turn right here, where the road swings left having finally achieved the crater rim, and admire the serenely beautiful spectacle.

What you are looking at is a vast caldera, 11 km (seven miles) across, the hollowed-out remains of a gigantic volcano that in prehistoric times exploded, blowing away its cone and leaving only the bony, saucer-shaped rim on which you're sitting. It's as if you are in the back row of a circus that's in the process of being dismantled; you are looking down at the ring unaware of the giant big-top tent that once stretched from just behind your seat to a point high above you.

Mount Batur, whose broken crest rises 1,717 m (5,633 ft) above sea level, is central to the view. Its slopes are scarred with lava flows, and all around is a scene of lonely splendor and dramatic desolation. Magnificent though the mountain is, it is the product of several more recent and smaller eruptions and its summit is actually only 328 m (1,066 ft) higher than the outer crater rim at Penelokan.

The volcano is not to be underestimated, however. Its last major eruption in 1926 completely destroyed the village of Batur, situated at that time on the western shore of the lake. It was never rebuilt, but its important temple was relocated on the outer crater rim, between Penelokan and Kintamani; this site is what is meant nowadays when Batur Village is spoken of.

To your right lies **Lake Batur**, 492 m (1,600 ft) below. It is eight kilometers (five miles) long and three kilometers (two miles) wide and fills almost a third of the area of

the caldera. The cliffs that fall abruptly down to the lake's eastern edge rise to their maximum height in the summit of Mount Abang, 3,153 m (10,250 ft) and in a direct line between Batur and Agung.

The right-hand (eastern) shore of the lake appears to press right up against these cliffs, but long ago some Bali Aga remnants, retreating in the face of invaders, found a flat piece of land and established the village of Trunyan, where few would be interested in following them. The village is clearly visible, a

OPPOSITE: Mount Batur from the crater rim. The volcano erupted in 1917 and then again in 1926, on the second occasion destroying the ancient village of Batur on the shore of the lake. ABOVE: Lake Batur lies within the crater of the volcanic Mount Batur. On the distant skyline is the crater rim.

prominent patch of red in an otherwise pastel landscape played over by the changing shadows of the clouds.

At your feet the road zigzags down from Penelokan, branching right to Kedisan on the lake's edge immediately below you and continuing across the lava flows to the hot springs of Air Panas, about halfway along the left-hand shore.

Accommodation at Penelokan is available at the **Lakeview** (0366-31394 FAX 0366-51464 (eight rooms; moderate). The hotel has recently been renovated and upgraded, and the view is wonderful. The hotel organizes treks to see the sunrise from the crater of Mount Batur, departing at 3 PM and returning to the hotel at 10 PM. Penelokan is only a fifteen-minute drive from Air Panas, and the latter is the logical place to stay if you plan to climb Batur. But it doesn't have Penelokan's marvelous view.

AIR PANAS: HOT SPRINGS

The road to Air Panas is bad, frequently subject to floods and consequent erosion. The springs themselves consist merely of a communal bathing pool where the hot water runs into the lake. You can sit in the water at sunset in the company of fifty-odd villagers, some of them scrubbing their washing on the side. It's nicer, though, to swim in the lake itself which the waters of the spring make warm at this point.

A charge of around US$.50 is levied for entrance into the village, plus an additional US$.50 for a vehicle.

The big new hotel here is the **Hotel Puri Bening** (0366-51234 FAX 0366-51248 (38 rooms; average and above). Few people were staying there when we visited and it is possible the place will become something of a white elephant. At present, anyway, Air Panas is mostly visited by backpackers keen to hike in the cool upland air, and the place many of them choose to stay is the friendly **Under the Volcano Homestay** (0366-51166 (inexpensive). You are most likely to arrive at the upper of the place's two sites (10 rooms and a restaurant) close to the road; there are an additional 14 rooms down by the lakeside.

There are several other *losmen* here, all inexpensive. If you want somewhere a little

more comfortable, but less expensive than the Puri Bening, you could try the **Puri Wisata Pualam** (six rooms; moderate).

The road continues beyond Air Panas to **Songan** where there is an attractively situated temple up a track to your left in the center of the village.

THE ASCENT OF MOUNT BATUR

There's no need for a guide in order to climb Mount Batur, unless you plan to set off in the early morning to see the sun rise; in this case you will need to start at 3:30 AM and can easily find a guide by asking around at Air Panas.

A small *warung* has been established right on the crater rim, manned whenever there are likely to be walkers arriving in urgent need of refreshment.

Even for those who are not going up to watch the sunrise, an early start is advisable, not because of the distance but because of the heat later in the day. From Air Panas, take the lane that leads toward the mountain from the center of the village. Anyone will point it out to you if you say, "Batur — jalan jalan" (meaning "Mount Batur on foot"). It curves gently round to the left until, after about a kilometer (1,100 yards), you reach a temple. Pass the temple, continuing on the clear track, and follow it as it winds across the now cindery scrub land around the base of the mountain. After crossing the second of two (usually dry) river beds, the path turns upwards, heading directly for the peak.

Next comes a steep, dusty bit where the assistance of handholds is provided by some small pine trees. At the top is an orange refuse bin that marks the junction of the track with another coming up from the left. From here the path crosses a level stretch and then diverges into several subsidiaries, all making for the ridge on the right. Once you have achieved this, the path becomes unified again and runs clearly ahead of you toward the summit. Views back over the lake are superb.

As you climb, Agung begins to appear behind you above the rim of the outer crater to the east.

Around the Crater Rim

After a time, the path divides, one branch carrying on straight ahead, the other leading off to the left. Take the left-hand branch for the gentler ascent. This will lead you to a low point on Batur's crater rim, and with any luck you will encounter local boys offering cold drinks. Considering the distance they have come and the weight they have had to carry, it's only charitable to buy one, and for only a little less than the price they ask.

From here, the around-the-crater path rises steeply to the right. The ground is sandy and loose and in fact most comfortably negotiated barefoot. The wind sings in the tough grass. Make for two small pines.

An Eerie Silence

The crater itself is an awesome place, with steam rising silently from several clefts and giving rise to lush vegetation on the cliffs immediately above. As water is not a constituent element of the inner earth, and this is steam not smoke, the hot vapor must be caused by water percolating down from the surface and boiling on contact with the molten lava below. Eerily, the steam rises without sound, and the silence is broken only by the twittering of birds and the occasional ominous sound of a falling stone. At its cen-

Finally you arrive at the high point of the volcano's crater rim, the pinnacle that has been ahead of you throughout most of the ascent; and here there are two orange refuse bins to prove it.

You are here standing on the top of the high crest that rises so impressively on the right of the volcano when viewed from Penelokan.

The around-the-crater route is narrow but well trodden. It is not, however, for the fainthearted. At least at one point the track crosses a narrow ridge with steep cliffs on either side and steam issuing out of the rocks just below. Anyone with a fear of heights will not need to be told to keep away.

ter the crater is extraordinarily deep and sheer. The steam rises not only from a vent near the bottom, but also from high up, close to the crater rim.

The descent on the route toward Kedisan begins a little way further around to the left from where you first attained the crater coming up from the springs, at the next refuse bin, in fact. The path descends steeply and unpleasantly in a continuous incline to the plain. This is a common ascent route but inferior to the one from Air Panas because its steepness is unrelieved. You are rewarded on arrival at level ground by a small *warung*

A road leads down into the crater at Mt. Batur and here you can walk on the solidified lava, in parts still devoid of life, from previous eruptions.

where you can buy soft drinks and small cakes; sometimes the *warung* is unmanned and you are invited to leave the money due in a box. (Beware: The owner is said to be a trained *leyak*, or witch, and well aware when his dues have not been paid, and by whom!)

ACROSS LAKE BATUR

The boats leave across the lake for the Bali Aga village of Trunyan from **Kedisan**. Accommodation and meals are available here at **Hotel Surya** (0366-51139 (28 rooms; inexpensive) and **Hotel Segara** (0366-51136 FAX 0366-51212 (40 rooms; inexpensive). The latter is situated one mile along the road to Air Panas.

Arranging your crossing to Trunyan on one of the colorful wooden boats, like so much else in Bali, involves negotiation. There are official rates, advertised at an official booking office, but the ferries depart when they are full. Consequently passengers must either charter a boat (and this means in practice negotiating a price with the skipper) or wait for a group planning to charter a boat to come along and then make arrangements to join them.

Up in Penelokan, you will hear preposterous prices quoted for chartering a boat; at the lakeside prices are reasonable — if you negotiate with determination and if you're prepared to wait. The official rates are about US$20 per boat, or US$3.50 per individual. This fee should include both a visit to the cemetery at Kuban (a short distance from Trunyan, but accessible only by boat). Check whether or not a visit to the hot springs at Air Panas is included in the price.

TRUNYAN

The trip across the lake takes approximately half an hour. The donations that are the theme of any visit to the Bali Aga village of Trunyan begin at the quay. As you pull up at the little beach serving the cemetery, a reception committee of two solicits the first donation and presents you with a register for signature.

The place of the dead is on the right. In Trunyan, the custom is neither to cremate nor bury the dead but to lay them out to decay in the open air and be picked clean by the

elements of nature. Consequently visitors often enter the designated territory with some trepidation. It's not clear exactly what horrors the tourist might be allowed to see in periods shortly following a death. When I was there, there were merely seven or eight wicker tents containing, in some cases, a skull, more often simply bones and scraps of clothing, plus some funeral gifts such as a Sprite bottle or a few hundred rupiah coins.

A small group of skulls placed on a ledge near the entrance marks the spot where a further donation is requested. In the same way that the donation register you sign on the beach — like almost all such registers in Bali — shows only previous donations of several thousands of rupiahs, so, any small notes you donate as you enter the cemetery itself have been removed (for setting a bad example) by the time you leave.

Back to Kedisan

It used to be claimed that boatmen on the lake were in the habit of stopping in the middle and demanding an increase in the fare. The existence now of an official ticketing office seems to have curbed this custom for the most part, and simple requests for more as you approach the landing stage back at Kedisan should be treated on their merits. The appeals may sound slightly threatening; but it is very unlikely they are not meant to sound that way. The only relevant English phrase the boatmen may know is likely to be a blunt-sounding, "More money." Don't be taken aback. He's only requesting a tip.

CLIMBING MOUNT ABANG

Back up at Penelokan and again facing the view, you have the alternative of either going around the rim left in the direction of Kintamani and Penulisan, or right and attempting the ascent of Mount Abang.

If you decide on the latter, follow the road down (as if you were going back to Bangli), and take the second turning on the left immediately after the road begins to drop down from the ridge (the first left leads to a restaurant). It's only a few meters down, and there's a shop on the corner, but no sign. This road quickly leads back onto the outer crater rim, but this time running east. After four kilometers (two and a half miles), the main section of the road peels off to the right and descends, eventually to Besakih. The road along the rim continues for another kilometer or so, passes a couple of *warung*, skirts to the right of a small temple, descends a hill, then turns right. There is a house nearby. From this point on you have to walk. The path is well defined but slippery, and it's about two hours to the summit, which is marked by a temple. (There is another temple about halfway up the ascent).

struction. Its situation is magnificent, and to watch the gorgeously clad celebrants processing round the outside of its walls on its festival days, the wild country of mountain and lake contrastingly pale in the background, is to see something both wonderful and sad — humans struggling to placate the insensibility of Nature — and very much of the essence of Bali.

The best place to stay in the region of Kintamani is the **Lakeview** (0366-31394 FAX 0366-51464 (eight rooms; moderate) at Penelokan.

BATUR AND KINTAMANI

Going west along the rim of the caldera from Penelokan, you pass several restaurants: the **Puri Selera**, the **Suling Bali**, the **Puri Dewata** (all moderate), and the smartest of them, **Restaurant Gunawan** (0366-51050 FAX 0366-751050 (average and above). Since these restaurants conclude their entire business serving tourists visiting the crater rim during the day, they are only open at lunch time.

The **Temple of Ulu Danu** at Batur dates from 1926 when its predecessor down on the shore of the lake was destroyed. Like all temples in Bali, it faces the mountains, in this case the one that was responsible for its de-

PENULISAN

After Kintamani the road continues to Penulisan. This is one of the loveliest routes in the island, temperate in vegetation now on account of the altitude, and luxuriant on account of the heavy rainfall. It's like an English country road in summer, but forever in leaf.

The temple at Penulisan, **Pura Tegeh Koripan**, is the tallest in Bali. Three hundred and thirty-three steps lead from the road up to this easily achieved viewpoint. Few people visit the temple, and there is no commercialization whatsoever. The atmosphere at the

A meditating figure along the wayside.

top is secluded and quiet, as mossy and crumbling as a Victorian churchyard. The air is scented from the various bushes that sprout on all sides and obscure the view — which is spectacular to the north, with the coast and the blue sea lying far below you almost at your feet and extensive but less well defined to the south. The air is fresh, and this is a wonderful place to sit and think. It's almost certain no one will disturb you.

For all Kintamani's scruffy ambiance, and Penelokan's deserved reputation for excessive hustling, these crater rim villages

ending in Penulisan are remarkable places, perched on a narrow volcanic ridge with barely room for more than the one main street. They haunt the imagination when many a more pretentious settlement has long been forgotten.

BESAKIH

The road from Penelokan to Besakih begins along the route to Mount Abang (see CLIMBING MOUNT ABANG, above). This first section has magnificent views down to the left through the trees to the lake and volcano below. After the turnoff to the right it becomes steeper and potholed. The road has been tarred at some time in the past but has

deteriorated and is now broken in several places. It poses no problems, though it is not a route for fast drivers.

The road descends along a giant spur, affording wonderful views, in good weather, of Mount Agung to the left. At **Menanga**, turn left for Besakih (six kilometers or four miles). After a descent of about a kilometer (just over half a mile), the road traverses a wooden bridge over the River Yehunda; the bridge replaced one that was destroyed by the 1963 eruption of Agung. On the right of the road just before the bridge is the **Arca Valley Inn** (inexpensive), a modern restaurant but no longer offering accommodation.

From here on, the road ascends steadily toward Besakih. As you approach, a slip road leads off uphill to the left. If you take this road you will arrive nearer the central area of the temple than if you go straight on to the official entrance, though the latter approach is the more spectacular, being a processional avenue along the temple's major alignment. Taking the left-hand route, you arrive at a car park on your left (where you must leave your car) followed by a mass of food and souvenir stalls as wall as permanent shops. Beyond these is the temple.

The Mother Temple of Besakih is the oldest and the largest in Bali. (There are precincts for all the sects of Hinduism and for all of the old Balinese kingdoms.) Thousands of pilgrims visit Besakih every day of the year, and in former times the old kings made annual pilgrimages with their courts to the temple.

The temple is constructed over a mass of terraces that ascend what are in fact the lower slopes of Mount Agung. This is, of course, the Mother Temple because Mount Agung is Bali's highest mountain. The various courtyards and enclosures are connected by flights of steps, and it is these, together with the tall, multistory *meru* that, with Agung rising steeply immediately behind the central enclosures, make the prospect of Besakih so impressive.

The day-to-day business of the temple is run by the *pemangku*, easily identifiable by their white clothes. They receive the offerings, sprinkle the pilgrims three times with holy water as they offer up flowers, also three times, and place clusters of wet rice grains on each temple and on the brow in such a way that they remain there for some time. The Brahmanic *pedanda*, or high priests, only appear for the great ceremonies, though they can regularly be seen at cremations sitting in their high lofts chanting their mantras and wafting incense to the gods.

The main temple complex, or Pura Panataran, at Besakih (there are other, subsidiary ones, especially away to the right) consists of six walled courts, each higher up the mountain than the last. Before you

Under the Volcano

The Mother Temple was, not surprisingly, badly damaged at the time of Agung's 1963 eruption, but has been entirely rebuilt. The eruption occurred just as the most extensive and important of all Bali's many rituals, the once-in-a-hundred-years Dasa Rudra, was about to be performed. Details of the events at that traumatic time in Balinese history can be found in Anna Mathews' *The Night of Purnama* (1965).

The countryside around the temple is especially lovely. Mandarin oranges grow

reach the first of these there is a small walled shrine containing a seven-tiered *meru* on your right — this is the original shrine of the temple.

The wide central staircase, flanked on each side by seven rising stone platforms each carrying six carved figures, leads to the first large court. It contains the usual pavilions for offerings, for *gamelan* orchestras and the like. The second court is similar but contains three ceremonial chairs situated on a high stone platform known as a *padmasana*, or world shrine, intended for the three major manifestations of God — Siwa, Wisnu and Brahma. The other courts follow on up fewer steps and contain many of the thatched *meru* that are so characteristic of the temple.

everywhere, and there is a sense of relaxed peacefulness in this cooler, wooded area overlooking the coastal plains.

As is so often the case in Asia, the presence of items from modern life — cigarettes, radios broadcasting advertisements for hair conditioner — act as authenticating devices for religious observances. There is no trace of the idea, common in the West, that antiquity and sanctity go hand in hand, no trace of the idea that the modern is faintly vulgar.

OPPOSITE: Trunyan cemetery, where the village dead are laid out on the surface of the earth to decompose. These skulls have been placed at the cemetery entrance to elicit donations from tourists.
ABOVE: The Mother Temple at Besakih, the island's premier place of worship, situated on the lower slopes of Mount Agung, Bali's highest summit.

There is nothing antiquarian about the religion of the Balinese.

THE ASCENT OF MOUNT AGUNG

Besakih is a popular place from which to begin the attempt on Mount Agung. Note that "attempt" is the operative word — the ascent is not easy. Though some have claimed that the climb there and back can be done in a single day if a very early start is made, it is far wiser to go prepared to spend a night on the volcano.

steps and then turning right and going up the broad lane between the central complex and the large one immediately to its right.

After initial meandering (not apparent until you see it in daylight) the path begins to climb. It rises, virtually straight now, along the crest of a long spur, through lush temperate forest. It's earthy underfoot, and on the steeper sections it can be slippery. Handholds are often needed, and some well placed branches have become worn smooth by frequent use; at other times there are only thorny briars, which you should do your best

A guide is essential as the early part of the route winds through fields, but more importantly because, if an accident were to occur, it is vital to have someone capable of going back quickly and organizing help. It is fairly easy to find a guide in Besakih — Wayan Pasak, Dalam Puri, Besakih, took me up and can be recommended. He is the owner of a *warung* at a car park on the left of the upper (left-hand) road leading to Besakih, about a kilometer (just over half a mile) before the temple. A reasonable fee is Rp50,000.

For the climb you will need a flashlight and adequate food and water; also required are stout boots and a hat.

The trail climbs right through the center of the Mother Temple itself, ascending 34

to avoid. For predawn ascents the temperature is moderate, and there is little problem with insects, but you should choose a date when there is a full, or three-quarter moon.

First light comes shortly before 5 AM and is marked by the instantaneous eruption of bird song. This wonderful moment is followed half hour later by sunlight appearing on the plains behind you, with the triangular shadow of the mountain lying dramatically across the landscape. This shadow shortens as the early morning advances and, soon after, the trail itself is sunlit.

The wooded ravines falling away precipitously on either side of you, only dimly discernible in moonlight, are now brilliantly and breathtakingly illuminated.

The spot where the ridge of the trail joins onto the central stock of the volcano is called the **Door of Agung**. At the point of contact there is a steep area of loose black ash where progress is difficult, but it doesn't last long. Another short ridge takes you to the Door, on the right.

At the Door of Agung, large slabs of rock overlook some broad ledges where it is possible to camp (though there is no water), and indeed various useful items such as cooking pans are often left there. There are also shrines and the remains of offerings. The rock faces

makes going down, grasping for dear life at trees while your feet shoot away from under you, both tiring and agony for the toes. You'll not want to linger long on the summit if you hope to be back in Besakih before dark (5:45 PM).

From Sebudi

If your aim is to see into the crater of Agung, it is far better to make the ascent from Sebudi, rather than Besakih. Take the road to Selat, east of Rendang, and ask from there. Again, hiring a guide is advised as the path is not

themselves have been painted with the names of innumerable visitors, many of whom attempted the ascent no further than this spectacular point. The view over southern and western Bali is extensive, though the lack of any other mountains close by makes it less than spectacular. Clouds frequently drift by beneath you.

From here to the summit is another two to three hours' climb across terrain that is partly firm, partly ash. The peak you reach is actually the highest point on the mountain, but you cannot see the crater itself from there as it lies across unstable and dangerous terrain further to the east.

The descent is hardly easier than the ascent. The unrelievedly steep and earthy track

well marked. Sebudi is a small village, so it might be more practical to engage a guide in advance of your visit.

RENDANG TO KLUNGKUNG

From Rendang, south of Besakih, a most attractive road runs east then south through Selat and Sidemen to Klungkung.

Not far out of Rendang, on the right side of the road, there is a high, tapering barnlike building used for drying tobacco.

Iseh has had its share of resident artists and writers, but is itself of little interest. The

---

Mount Agung — OPPOSITE: The first rays of dawn strike the mountain. ABOVE: A hiker above treeline in the grayness of first light.

attraction of this area of Bali is the country-side itself, rice terraces with forest above them and Mount Agung on the skyline. This steeply hilly countryside is reminiscent of the Massif Central of France, or mid-Wales.

At **Sidemen** there is a modern dam across the river, several new out-of-town houses, children who ask for money and the feeling that the idyll has come to an end. But the road continues down via **Sukat** through pleasant country, until the gradient lessens and you find yourself entering the ancient provincial capital of Klungkung (see EAST BALI, below).

BEDUGUL

Fifteen kilometers (nearly 10 miles) west of Kintamani and 51 km (32 miles) north of Denpasar, Bedugul is a lakeside mountain resort that provides welcome relief from the heat, and especially the humidity, of the coast.

Lakes Bratan, Buyan and **Tambingan** fill another huge caldera, comparable to Batur's. Here, however, the crater's northern walls have slipped seawards, and it is consequently neither as distinctive nor as impressive.

Ulu Danu

At Candikuning on the edge of the lake (35 m or 115 ft deep) stands the **temple of Ulu Danu**, set in delightful gardens. Temple buildings occupy two minute offshore islets, and these, with their three- and eleven-tier *meru*, are much photographed. The temple is dedicated to the spirits that control the irrigation systems that derive their waters from the lake; there are also Buddhist and Islamic temples close by.

It is possible to be taken by row boat on a 45-minute lake trip to see a cave and visit the **Bedugul Hotel and Restaurant** (moderate), where water skiing and parasailing are on offer. Accommodation and meals can also be had at the **Bali Handara Kosaido Country Club** (0362-23048 or 0361-22646 (average and above), which has an 18-hole golf course.

There is a trail encircling the lake, and the walk takes about three hours.

Botanical Gardens

Half a kilometer (550 yards) from the lake (along the road back towards Denpasar) by a flower and vegetable market, a road runs off to the right to the Botanical Gardens.

The gardens consist of a large wooded parkland. Pathways have been established, and the clearly labeled trees on this south facing upland slope are fine. Flowers bloom in what look like natural conditions.

It's a place for quiet, extensive walks among glades, with views up to the wooded hills, and, on a weekday at least, a place for almost total solitude. On an island where a huge variety of tropical and subtropical plants, both native and introduced, flourish

with ease, the variety here is immense. The gardens are open daily 8 AM until 4:30 PM.

EAST BALI

KLUNGKUNG

Thirty-nine kilometers (24 miles) east of Denpasar lies the former royal capital of Klungkung. You can transfer here for a *bemos* to Besakih in the north and for Padangbai, Candi Dasa and Amlapura to the east. The bus fare from Denpasar is around US$.50 by large bus and US$.75 on a small one.

The town is quiet and tidy. There is a market, some shops, one passable hotel (see below), and a famous monument, **Kertha Gosa**, the courthouse of the old kingdom of Klungkung. It consists of two buildings, an elegant little "floating palace"—a raised and

Klungkung — ABOVE: Handpainted movie posters. OPPOSITE: Part of the "floating palace", Kertha Gosa. Klungkung has the charm of an Indonesian country town little touched by the tourist influx that has inundated nearby locations.

much-decorated pavilion set in the middle of a wide moat and originally used as a retreat for the judges — and the actual court, raised high on your right as you enter.

The dreadful punishments said to be reserved for sinners in another life are vividly illustrated on the roof of the little court — mothers who refused to suckle their young being forced to give the breast to a poisonous fish, confirmed bachelors being savaged by a wild boar, and so on. These pictures are not in fact very old but are 40-year-old copies, made on asbestos, of the originals.

Where to Stay

The only hotel in Klungkung that is remotely satisfactory is the **Logi Ramayana (** 21044 at Jalan Diponegoro N°152 (nine rooms; inexpensive). The owner, Nyoman Gede, speaks excellent English, and there is a large temple attached, reached down a few steps from the restaurant.

Shopping

The **market** has recently been relocated one kilometer (just over half a mile) out of town and is over by early afternoon.

Everything is very delicate, not least the worn red-brick floor, and the only pity is that the compact complex, so restful in design, is situated so very close to Klungkung's main intersection. This was, however, the intention of is builders: The open-sided court was not only raised up high but set at the very center of the town, open, public and for all to see. A quieter place among the water lilies was set aside for the judges — high priests (*pedanda*) from the Brahmana caste — to consider their judgments.

Both buildings are intricately carved; the stone animals supporting the pillars in the courthouse are particularly noteworthy. Entrance is about US$1; children pay half. The monument is open daily, 6 AM to 6 PM.

Klungkung itself is a combination of a quiet country town and an Oriental market. Marigolds piled by their thousands on blue tarpaulins, groups of girls skinning tiny mauve-colored onions, *bemos* arriving from all parts, patented scorpion medicines being sold at the curbside, the harsh glare of kerosene lamps as corn cobs are toasted and yesterday's hits from Jakarta jangle out from a mobile juke box, a post-cremation *angklung* (processional *gamelan*) in the intensely hot afternoon. Klungkung may

ABOVE and OPPOSITE: The terrors that await evildoers in the afterlife, and the glee with which their tormentors go about their work, are vividly depicted on the walls of the Kertha Gosa (the ancient courthouse) in Klungkung.

have only the one monument, but it is attractive in a way Denpasar no longer is, its atmosphere little diluted by the impulse to cater to the foreign needs and tastes of tourists.

GELGEL AND KAMASAN

Directly to the south of Klungkung, leaving the town by Jalan Puputan, are the villages of Gelgel and Kamasan. Gelgel is the old, pre-eighteenth century capital of the area and, though it was ravaged by lava in 1963, the old **Royal Temple** still stands. Pottery making can also be seen here. Kamasan is the center for a traditional style of painting (see under ART AND CRAFTS in BALINESE CULTURE, page 133).

THE COAST ROAD

From Klungkung, the main road east to Amlapura (almost universally known by the Balinese as Karangasem) runs down to the coast. You leave town along Jalan Diponegoro, passing the Logi Ramayana Hotel on your right, then crossing the River Unda by way of a high bridge.

During the eruption of Mount Agung in 1963, a former bridge was destroyed by the lava coming down the river valley, and a few kilometers out of Klungkung extensive lava fields can be seen to the right of the road. The lava flowed seawards in two arms, this one to the west and another, following the valleys of the rivers Buhu, Banka and Njuling, to the east. Both Amlapura, which stands on the banks of the Njuling, and Klungkung were thus lucky to escape serious damage.

After seven kilometers (four miles), the road runs through **Kusamba**'s main street. This is the small market and fishing village from which boats leave for Nusa Penida and Nusa Lembongan. To reach the sea, turn right in the middle of the village. A lane runs straight to the beach past a mosque. Ask at the last *warung* on the right about boats to the islands. Don't, however, expect to be able to leave any later than early afternoon: Waves tend to build up in the Badung Strait during the day and by mid-afternoon landing on the beach at

Kusamba — there is no jetty — becomes dangerous. The one way fare in a wooden motorized *prahu* is about US$2.50, and the trip takes an hour. As usual you will have to wait for enough passengers to turn up to justify the crossing. If you want to go on your own and at once it will cost you in the region of US$75. Boats will also take you to Nusa Lembongan (see under NUSA PENIDA in OFF THE BEATEN TRACK, page 221, for information on the speedboat ferry there from Padangbai).

Bat Cave

A couple of kilometers east of Kusamba is the extraordinary **Goa Lawah**. It's only a relatively small opening in the limestone cliff, but it is the home of what appear to be hundreds of thousands of semi-nocturnal bats. A temple has been built immediately in front of the caves entrance, and it's necessary to pay a donation of about US$.50, in return for the loan of a scarf.

It isn't possible to enter the cave as the low roof is completely covered in bats and the floor coated in a thick layer of guano. Several shrines stand just inside the cave, also guano-crowned. But there's no need to go in to see the bats at close quarters — they crowd together over large areas of the outside walls, and it is easy to get within half a meter of them. Hanging upside down in full daylight, they twist their necks and peer at onlookers as they approach, preparing themselves no doubt for flight. With the massed creatures, they're squeaking, the crowds of kneeling devotees, the incense, the priests' prayers and the flashing of tourists' cameras — it's at one and the same time grotesque, comic and wonderful.

The cave is situated directly on the main road and no one should drive past without sparing a few minutes for a look, however pressed they are for time, or however anxious to get on to the comforts and consolations of Candi Dasa.

Salt from the Sea

Directly over the road from the bat temple, on the black sand beach, is a primitive salt factory, where salt is procured from sea water. Under a thatched roof water drips down bamboo pipes and a solitary worker displays a bowl of gleaming salt crystals for your admiration. Nusa Penida shimmers along the horizon.

The saltmaking process is as follows: Wet sand is spread out on the beach and when partly dry is placed in a container inside one of the huts. Eventually a salty liquid begins to drip out, and this is transferred to long wooden troughs where the last of the water evaporates. It's an interesting process to observe, and like the bats of Goa Lawah, at once wholly natural and surprising.

moderate). It has both air-conditioned rooms priced in United States dollars and cheaper fan-cooled rooms priced in rupiah. It is well-kept and has a clean, cheerful restaurant under separate management that serves just about every kind of food, including Indonesian, Chinese and Western. For a change, the **Pandan Restaurant**, a few yards away from the Puri Rai, can be recommended.

There are many *losmen* nearby offering ultra-cheap rooms, and for inexpensive but good food there is the **Depot Segara**.

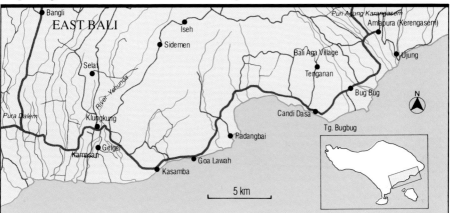

PADANGBAI

Eighteen kilometers (11 miles) from Klungkung is Padangbai, the terminal for the ferries to Lombok. The village is no more than a single street running inland from the harbor, and tourist accommodation plus some simple fishermen's huts on the left.

Padangbai has the attraction of being a fishing village away from the main tourist centers. The sandy beach is home to many colorful *prahu*, and the sale of the night's catch in the early morning alongside the boats is a colorful spectacle. Also, many of Padangbai's inhabitants are Moslems, and to stand on a hillside above the bay at sunset and hear the muezzin's song from the mosque — as a bird orchestra circles the valley as if in harmony with the words of the Prophet — is to experience something of the Old East preserved almost intact.

Where to Stay

The best place to stay in Padangbai is the biggest, the **Puri Rai** (0363-41385 (31 rooms;

Diving is catered for by **Equator Dive Travel** (0363-41505. For flight reconfirmation, tours and accommodation in Lombok there is a **Tourist Information Office** (0363-41502 FAX 0363-4178, facing the harbor.

Padangbai is small — all of the places listed are within 200 m of each other.

Ferries for Lombok leave Padangbai every two hours, 24 hours a day. Fares are approximately US$2.75 economy and US$5.50 first class. The fee for automobiles is about US$30.

A Hidden Cove

There is an attractive little cove just round the headland on your right when you're looking out to sea. Turn right as you approach the wharf and then, after about 200 m, turn left at the sign for **Biastugel Beach**, a white sand beach; it's a 10-minute walk from the village and a classic secluded location.

TENGANAN

Immediately before you arrive in Candi Dasa from the west, a road leads off to the left

running four kilometers (two and a half miles) to Tenganan. Motorbikes wait to take those with no other means of transport.

Tenganan is Bali's foremost example of the social organization of the Bali Aga (see from JAVA MAN TO GOLKAR in VOLCANOES IN THE SEA, page 76). It is as tidy and prosperous as Trunyan (the Bali Aga village on Lake Batur; see page 198) is grubby and impoverished. Fortunately the village is not yet spoiled by rows of stalls selling cheap mass-produced clothes to tourists.

The prime feature of Tenganan life is that everything is held communally; membership in the community is as a result strictly controlled. As the village is a major landowner in the area, its privileged three hundred or so inhabitants do little menial work and are free to devote their time to weaving, writing on *lontar leaves*, or simply admiring one another's fighting cocks, some of which are dyed pink. Styles and forms of dance (the *rejang*), ritual fighting (*pandan*), instrumental music (*gamelan selunding*) and ikat cloth (*gringsing*) are found here that occur nowhere else in Bali. Full details can be found in Madi Kertonegoro's *The Spirit Journey to Bali Aga, Tenganan Pegringsingan*, a whimsical and informative book that depicts well the genial spirit of the village.

The village looks utterly unlike any other in Bali. The family compounds are arranged in long lines on either side of the north–south concourses which rise in successive terraces as they move uphill. Because the compounds each have a pavilion with an overhanging roof immediately inside the external wall, the appearance is of a street of houses with thatched roofs in, perhaps, the west of England. At the far end is a communal meeting place, the *bale paruman desa*, while the village temple is near the entrance from the road, surrounded by frangipani trees.

The section of the village away to the right (east) is reserved for villagers who have in some way forfeited full membership of the community. It is known as **Banjar Pande**. Here small windmills (*pinengan*, meaning wings) can be seen above the houses, serving no practical purpose but constructed just for pleasure. Up the hill behind Banjar Pande is the cemetery; the Bali Aga here do not expose their dead like their cousins in

Trunyan but bury them in the ground in accordance with the practice of the Indra sect of Hinduism.

Lontar

At first sight it looks as if Tenganan is mostly tourist shops. All the sales activity, however, is concentrated in the first street you come to; in the parallel street to the right there is none at all. All the shops are part of people's houses. In the **Indra Art Shop**, for example, you can take a coffee while the owner, I. Wayan Gelgel, inscribes a motto for you on a *lontar*. First he cuts in the words with a pointed knife, then rubs in a black oil from the burnt *kemiri* nut. He has a collection of old *lontar* books, leaves threaded on a string with bamboo covers. The words are inscribed on one side, illustrations on the other. The texts are old stories from the *Ramayana* (see HEROES AND VILLAINS in BALINESE CULTURE, page 113). The books are fastened closed with an old Chinese coin, Bali's first money, used now only for ceremonial purposes. The *lontar* leaves have been first boiled in salty rice water to strengthen and preserve them.

The craft shop of I. Nyoman K. Nurati is in the house where the Swiss writer Urs Ramseyer stayed while writing his *Art and Culture of Bali* — he now runs a hotel in Sidemen.

CANDI DASA

Candi Dasa (pronounced "chandi dasa") is a compact resort 13 km (eight miles) south-west of Amlapura. It is the only stretch of this coast that has experienced any degree of tourist development. The name probably means Ten Tombs and refers to some ancient monuments near the village of **Bug Bug** (pronounced "boog boog") two kilometers (one and a quarter miles) to the east.

Candi Dasa's tragedy is that unlike 10 years ago, it today has no beach. Following the construction of a sea wall in the 1980s what beach there had been was swept away by ocean currents. Concrete groins have been

Goa Lawah — Because this home of bats is considered sacred, a temple has been built there and throughout the day a stream of devotees arrives, many bearing offerings. The temple is as interesting as the bats, and the juxtaposition of the two is astonishing.

constructed to prevent further erosion, and their rectangular patterns now dominate what's left of the shore. There is still good swimming over a sandy bed at Candi Dasa, but along much of the shoreline there is now effectively no beach.

Even so, there is considerable peace and quiet, and at a lower cost than that at Sanur, for example. Candi Dasa originated in the rage to find a quieter alternative to Kuta in the lower price bracket, and though the unspoiled ambiance of the early eighties is now gone, the place does remain relatively tran-

double suite) is perched on a hillside with an extraordinarily spectacular seaview across to Nusa Penida and Lombok. Each room is a self-contained villa and a road winds down to what is essentially a private beach.

In Candi Dasa proper the **Puri Bagus Beach Hotel** (0363-41131 FAX 0363-41290 (50 rooms; average and above) is situated at the end of a drive at the far eastern end of the beach, and though there is no beach as such, both the site and the swimming are good.

Candi Dasa has some smart new accommodation offering luxurious villas in garden

quil, and with luck you can perfect your suntan in the hotel garden or along the sea wall with the minimum of interruptions.

Where to Stay

The only hotel in Candi Dasa with a beach is the **Candi Beach Cottage** (0363-41234 FAX 0363-41111 (64 rooms; average and above) situated half a mile before you reach the village center when coming from Klungkung. It has a swimming pool and a lush garden, together with an excellent restaurant.

The most exclusive place to stay in the area is not in Candi Dasa but situated a few minutes' drive to the west. **Amankila** (71267 FAX 71266 (34 suites; expensive, starting from US$460 for a regular suite up to $1,300 for a

settings. The two to consider first are the **Kubu Bali** (0363-41532 FAX 0363-41531 (20 villas; average and above) and the slightly more expensive **Hotel Taman Air** — also known as **The Watergarden** (0363-41540 FAX 0363-41164 (12 villas, five with air conditioning; average and above). Both of these are a few meters up the hill on the left of the main road when arriving from the Klungkung.

For simple accommodation try the **Puri Pandan** (/FAX 0363-41541 (inexpensive). It has a pleasant restaurant overlooking the sea

ABOVE LEFT: As in this example from Amlapura, erotic dalliance is in no way alien to Hindu art, while at Candi Dasa ABOVE RIGHT a different aesthetic is enforced. OPPOSITE: The beach at Candi Dasa is lined with small hotels along all but this unusually solitary stretch.

— it's under separate management but with the same phone/fax number. Another option is the nearby **Pondok Bambu Seaside Cottages** (0363-41534 FAX 0363-41818 (13 rooms with fan; moderate).

The **Candidasa Beach Bungalows Two,** also known as **The Candidasa Hotel** (0363-41126 FAX 0363-41537 (63 rooms; average and above but "negotiable") feels slightly impersonal on account of its large size, but it has pleasantly fitted-out rooms, all with air conditioning. Note, however, that the Candidasa is building a disco-

Other good dining spots are the restaurant belonging to the **Kupu Bali**, on the main road and below the hotel itself, and **TJ's**, up against the Hotel Taman Air and sharing the same phone number. The latter serves good Western meals.

Don't change your money in Candi Dasa if you can help it — rates are better almost everywhere else. If you must change here, the best rate is likely to be at the **Pandawa Travel** (0363-41101 on the main road in the center of town. Or try the **Bank Danamon** next door, Candi Dasa's only bank.

theque in the hotel courtyard, which might make sleep difficult on nights when it's in operation.

A large place, out on the road a little way towards Klungkung, is the **Hotel Rama Candidasa** (0363-41974 FAX 0363-41975 (72 rooms, expensive), a resort hotel on the Sanur pattern.

Also at this end of town are some *losmen* offering very inexpensive accommodation. Of these, the **Pelangi Homestay** (0363-41270 (nine rooms) is clean and friendly and can be recommended.

As for food, a superior place to eat in Candi Dasa is the **Lotus Seaview** (0363-41257, an offshoot of the famous Café Lotus in Ubud. It's expensive, but they serve only first class fare.

There are places to shop, too, all near the sea front; **Lenia**, for instance, sells handicrafts.

AMLAPURA (KARANGASEM)

The Balinese usually refer to their main towns by the name of the districts, or *kabupaten*. Denpasar is Badung; Singaraja, Buleleng; and Amlapura, Karangasem. This last substitution is so common that occasionally, even when the name Amlapura is being used, it is listed in alphabetical indexes under the letter "k." The name Amlapura was only officially adopted in 1963, and Karangasem is still the name on the lips of every *bemo* conductor in the streets of Klungkung touting for passengers heading east.

There are two *bemo* stations in Amlapura, a small one for Ujung and a big one for all other destinations.

The Palace

There is only one site deserving of a visit in the town: the palace (entrance: about US$.50). Its setting, however, is the real draw, and shouldn't be missed.

The various *puri* are part of one and the same complex and together originally constituted the living quarters of the family of the rajah of Karangasem. Some — the Mad-

hura, for instance — are now virtually taken over by humbler residences that continue, however, to have the air of being within the domain of a palace.

The Puri Amsterdam, with its "floating" pavilion (i.e., a pavilion set in the middle of a lake), is still largely intact. Unfortunately you cannot go inside the main building. Karangasem was one of the old Balinese kingdoms that made an accommodation with the Dutch, and as a result the rajah's family was allowed to retain its former status, at least outwardly. The portraits and other items that can be seen on the verandah of the main

ABOVE: The palace gate at Amlapura (Kerangasem). OPPOSITE: A section of the ruins of the water palace at Ujung.

building suggest, in their combination of Dutch and Balinese styles, that the interior must have been a stately place indeed. Now cocks crow in their cages, and only the click of the rare tourist's camera and the rustle of the wind in the trees break the silence.

From here you can go down through the triple-tiered, red brick gateway and across the road to inspect more royal outhouses. In this area the problem of knowing whether or not you are in someone's house or an ancient monument becomes acute. The problem is easily solved by engaging some of the children who will gather around you as guides; wherever they take you, consider yourself invited. The area is extensive, on both sides of the road, and exceptionally delightful because it is quiet, lived in and — with its trees and muted elegance — human and touching.

Where to Stay

The **Homestay Balakiran** (inexpensive) is part of the Puri Madhura. It is recently reported to be open for visitors whenever the owner happens to be there. It's very pretty, the reception dignified yet friendly, and with the owner a guide too, it's an attractive place to spend a night in this little-visited town.

The owner of the Balakiran can probably be persuaded to show you a local bird orchestra. The doves sit preening themselves in their red and blue cages in a garden overlooking the Moslem village of Nyuling. Bells and flutes of different sizes are fitted on collars under the birds' ruffs so that the instruments stand out on their chests. They seem perfectly attuned to Amlapura's general ambiance of sedate tranquillity.

WATER PALACES

One of Amlapura's twentieth-century rajahs constructed two water palaces, one north and the other south of the town. **Tirtagangga** (Ganges Water), five kilometers (three miles) to the north, is the more frequently visited because it is still in working order, though damaged in the 1963 eruption. It's a charming place, little known to tourists. Fountains play and lotus flowers beam with transcendental serenity. You can swim in one of the two pools, eat in a café

and even stay the night in rooms at **Restaurant Tirta Ayu** (0363-21697 (six rooms; inexpensive). Around US$.50 is charged to go in, with an additional US$1 if you want to swim; children pay half.

It's three kilometers (two miles) from Amlapura to **Ujung**. *Bemos* charge a mere US$.25, and a motorbike rider will charge you around US$.75 each way, with perhaps another US$.50 if they wait for you before bringing you back.

The site is almost wholly in ruins, but the concept is so magnificent, and the crumbling

remains now given over to agriculture so picturesque, that the complex leaves an indelible impression on the mind.

Ujung was built with Dutch aid in 1921 but severely damaged by volcanic activity in 1963. It was in the process of being restored (by two Australians who began work in 1974) when it was finally destroyed by an earthquake in 1979. The present descendants of the rajah have agreed with the government on a restoration program, and work has begun on a small scale. It is expected to be finished by the end of the century.

A member of the rajah's family living on the site might offer to act as your guide and also show you a tattered photograph of the area taken a year before the earthquake.

It's quite evocative in its present ruined condition.

Frangipani (*kamboja*) and palms sprout from among the fallen pillars and make artlessly elegant compositions with the grazing cattle and the one remaining dome. Above the white masonry and its flowering vegetation rise tier after tier of terraces, once gardens, topped at the skyline with further ornamental structures. A walk up steps and then away to the right will lead you to a magnificent carved head from which gushes water, against the background of the foothills of Mount Agung.

That dereliction can have its own distinctive beauty is nowhere in Bali more evident than in the ruined water palace at Ujung.

AMED

Amed consists a series of small beaches in the extreme northeastern corner of the island, which have been recently developed to take advantage of the fine diving nearby.

As the road to Singaraja approaches the sea 16 km (10 miles) north of Amlapura, turn right at a village called **Culik**. (Currently there is no sign for Amed itself, but that may change soon.) The road reaches the sea at a beach with well over a hundred *prahu* drawn up on the black sand. There is a fish market every morning beginning at around 8 AM and lasting a couple of hours.

To get to the diving locations and associated accommodation, turn right immediately before you get to this beach. The numerous wooden structures you see on your left are for saltmaking.

Amed Beach appears after a couple of kilometers (just over a mile). This is where the most serious diving takes place, and many minibuses are drawn up here, having come from Candi Dasa and further afield.

The road continues on over a headland and then down to **Jemeluk Beach** at **Bunutan**. Then comes the village of **Lipah** and the **Hidden Paradise Cottages** (DENPASAR 0361-431273 FAX 0363-21044 (16 rooms; average and above). Further on and under the same management are the **Coral View Villas** (0361-31273 (19 rooms; moderate). Another 500 meters (third of a mile) brings you to the **Vienna Beach Bungalows** (12 rooms; moderate). After another one and a half kilometers (one mile) you reach **Good Karma** (10 rooms; moderate). The rooms are quite pleasant here, though without fans. Sea breezes suffice, I was told. Electricity, from a generator, comes on only at night and then only for lights.

All of these places are situated right on the sea, facing small sandy coves with excellent snorkeling, and diving by arrangement.

At Amed Beach, the diving operator most in evidence is the **Nusantara Bahari Explorer Diving Club (** 0361-431273 FAX 0363-21044 (the coastline past Bunutan is under serious

War II ship sunk by the Japanese. It's 150 m (500 ft) long and has attracted such a wealth of tropical fish and other marine life that it is today one of Bali's premier diving sites. (For details on this wreck, see under SPORTING SPREE in YOUR CHOICE, page 32.)

At Tulamben you can either stay at the large **Emerald Tulamben Beach Hotel (** 0363-22490 WEBSITE http://www.iijnet.or.jp/inc/bali/ (26 rooms; expensive and "subject to change without notice"), or head for one of the small beach hotels — the best of which is **Paradise Palm Beach**

threat from quarrying work to supply rock for the controversial mega-development on Pulau Serangan). From Amed it's a 15-minute drive to the other important diving location in northeast Bali, Tulamben.

TULAMBEN

From the road, Tulamben appears dramatic yet uninviting — dramatic, if you look left and see the flank of Agung descending in one long sweep from the volcano's summit into the sea — uninviting, because the coast is stony and treeless. But no matter, the great attraction of Tulamben is under water.

Five hundred meters (550 yards) from the shore lies the wreck of an American World

Bungalows, also known as the **Bali Sorga Bungalow (** 0363-41052 (24 rooms; moderate). Four of their rooms offer air conditioning, though at a higher price. In addition to being a comfortable and deservedly popular place, it has the advantage of housing **Dive Paradise Tulamben (** 0363-41052. Its Japanese manager is Emiko Shibuya, and she lives on the premises.

OPPOSITE: Frangipani, often found in cemeteries, perfume the air with their strong fragrance. ABOVE: More arid than the southern regions of the island, the eastern strip of lowland, behind Candi Dasa, is also devoted to rice cultivation.

Off the Beaten Track

NUSA PENIDA AND NUSA LEMBONGAN

NUSA PENIDA LIES long and gaunt along the coastal horizon of East Bali, and from Sanur and Benoa its southern cliffs present a magnificently etched spectacle in the late afternoon light. Few tourists, though, make the trip over.

By contrast, the smaller Nusa Lembongan, a short boat trip from Penida, has recently become a popular spot for surfers and divers. Together the two islands constitute a fine round-trip tour, one arduous, the other restoring. They make a considerable change from "mainland" Bali.

Most people these days arrive at Nusa Lembongan with one of the big tour companies, on one of Bali Hai's catamarans or on the powered sailing catamaran *Wanaluka*. Alternatively, you can approach a *prahu* skipper on Sanur beach (to the left of Bali Beach Hotel) and engage him to take you across. You should leave Sanur early as the trip by these small boats takes three hours and the fishermen don't like to be out on the Badung Strait after mid-afternoon because of the increased swell.

Once on Nusa Lembongan, you can then cross over to the larger island. The inhabitants of Nusa Penida, however, and most of those from Nusa Lembongan as well, take the shorter crossing, via Kusamba or Padangbai.

Motorized *prahu* from Kusamba leave from two places on the beach about a kilometer (just over half a mile) apart (see THE COAST ROAD in THE BROAD HIGHWAY, page 208, for departure points). Crossings both ways take place in the morning as the surf at Kusamba tends to get bigger as the day progresses and can make landing and departing difficult, if not dangerous. The fare is around US$2.50 for locals, and you may be able to travel for this amount too, though it is normal to charge foreigners about 50 percent more, and it is not advisable to argue when the fare is so very low to begin with. Boats leave when they are full, so how quickly you get away is entirely a matter of chance.

As the crossing takes between two and three hours, you may prefer to take the speedboat service from Padangbai, which leaves several times during the morning, beginning at around 7 AM. There is one boat which is moored at Nusa Penida overnight; consequently, you wait on the beach at Padangbai until it arrives on its first trip of the day from the island. Wait for it immediately to the left (east) of the jetty. The crossing takes 40 minutes. Crossings later in the morning cannot be relied on to happen, so the best plan is to spend the night in Padangbai if getting there in the early morning is likely to pose difficulties.

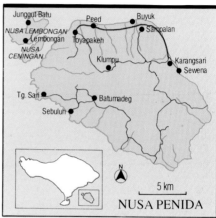

The crossing is 14 km (nine miles) from Kusamba, marginally further from Padangai.

Most of the boats from Kusamba arrive on Nusa Penida at Toyapakeh, whereas the speedboat from Padangbai arrives at Buyuk, close to Sampalan, the capital. But it makes little difference which one you arrive at as there are regular *bemo* services along the coast road, and the trip from Toyapakeh to Sampalan will take you at most 15 minutes.

NUSA PENIDA: A LIMESTONE ISLAND

Nusa Penida is a limestone plateau, 20 km by 16 (12 miles by 10) and rising to a height of 530 m (1,735 ft). Being limestone, the relief is rocky and dry, the rainfall sinking into the ground and forming underground caverns. Because of this, the island has always been poor. In Balinese religion, the island is considered malign, and in earlier

The spectacularly precipitous south coast of Nusa Penida.

times convicts from the kingdom of Klung-kung were banished there.

Nevertheless, today it supports a population of approximately 45,000. Agriculture has improved following government assistance in building cisterns to catch the rainwater, and seaweed farming — evidence of which can be seen all along the northern coast — seems promising. A jetty recently completed at Toyapakeh should boost the economy by allowing large vessels to dock and carry away seaweed and rock (for the construction industry) which are the island's main products.

Despite the changes taking place, Nusa Penida retains an air remoteness. Foreign visitors are immediately surrounded by crowds of children — and sometimes adults — crying "Turis! Turis!" (tourist), and inland the roads are very rough. Few islanders speak even rudimentary English. Nevertheless, the cliffs on the south side of the island are worth the hard traveling, and there are a couple of other rewarding sites to visit in the north.

SAMPALAN AND EXCURSIONS

Sampalan is the main village on the island, but it has little to show the visitor other than a market. The coast road forms its main and only street worthy of the name. Nonetheless, the village is attractive. On a bright morning, its narrow, tree-lined road shades crowds of country people going about their daily round of tasks — evoking parts of eastern Indonesia more than it does mainland Bali.

The island's only accommodation for visitors is the very satisfactory **Bungalows Pemda** (inexpensive) at the east end of the village. There are five bungalows, each with two rooms.

There is no restaurant; you will have to make do with one of the several *warung* on the main street; don't count on them being open after 8 PM.

Goa Karangsari

If you take the coast road eastwards from Sampalan — your transport will probably be a truck loaded with goods as well as passengers — you will, after about 20 minutes, reach a large cave, **Goa Karangsari**. It's between Sewana and Karangsari, a couple

of hundred meters up from the road on the right. Just say "goa" (cave), and your fellow passengers will tell you when you've arrived.

It isn't strictly necessary to have a guide, but a light of some sort is essential. The odds are you'll hire the two together at the *warung* where the truck will put you down. Nusa Penida has little experience of tourism, but the word has got round that foreigners are rich. Thus the few visitors who do appear are treated as manna from heaven and prices quoted can be laughably high. You will probably spend US$2 to be shown around the cave by a guide bearing a powerful kerosene lamp. This is picturesque, but a flashlight would show you considerably more.

Entrance to the cave is through a narrow gap in the rocky hillside. Inside it's spacious, with a high roof and a level, sandy floor. It extends for some 300 m (325 yds), and at the far end you emerge on another hillside overlooking an inland valley supporting only scrub and with few signs of habitation. About halfway through the cave you pass beneath a colony of bats, and a little further on there is a place where water drips down from the roof and a small shrine has been constructed. There are various side passages, but for the most part they peter out without leading to further major features.

Peed

If you take the coast road west from Sampalan you will arrive after 10 minutes at the celebrated, or notorious, temple at Peed (pronounced "ped"). It stands on the right side of the road in the village of the same name and is the home of Bali's sourest deity, Ratu Gede Macaling. (The word "macaling" derives from a Balinese word meaning "fang".)

According to the tenets of Balinese religion, malign forces must be placated as much as benign ones worshipped, so the temple is crowded with visitors from all over Bali on its *odalan* (anniversary feast day). The place itself is large but not especially beautiful. The shrine to Ratu Gede Macaling is in an extension to the northwest of the temple.

CROSS-COUNTRY

The greatest attraction of Nusa Penida is the dramatic southern coastline. Access, however, is difficult. There is no public transport here, so it's necessary to hire someone to take you on a motorbike or possibly in a four-wheel-drive vehicle. You can also charter a *bemo*.

The road south branches off the coast road two kilometers (one and a quarter miles) west of Sampalan and rises steeply and circuitously to **Klumpu**. Thus far the road is tarred and in good condition. It's after Klumpu that the going gets difficult. The track rises and falls over rough ground, and there are frequent rocky outcrops that have to be negotiated — there are half a dozen places where a pillion rider has to get off and walk. Though generally well drained, there are patches that are slippery after rain.

Bear right at **Batumadeg**, avoiding the road left which leads via Batukandik to the east of the island. The road now is even rougher than before. On both sides are terraces of manioc, corn and occasionally tobacco, wherever the terrain allows cultivation. The high hills that form the island's center rise to the left. The entire drive, from Sampalan to Sebuluh, takes an hour and a half.

From Sebuluh, a village of thatched houses set in a hollow, it is necessary to walk. A child — who will be surprised to receive payment — can easily be found to take you. Something in the region of US$.25 should be offered. You descend into a dry valley, and then up again to the cliff edge, a walk of twenty minutes. Monkeys play in the trees en route.

A Cliff Stairway

The path arrives at the cliff via a most spectacular and terrifying path. The highest point on this coast, 228 m (750 ft) above sea level, is in this area, and this extraordinary aerial stairway descends almost the entire distance, running diagonally down across the cliff face. It is constructed of bamboo and wood, and though it makes use here and there of natural ledges in the cliff it is elsewhere supported only on trees growing out from the cliff face.

The purpose of this exposed stairway (which no one with the slightest vertigo should consider negotiating) is give the villagers of nearby Sebuluh access to a place where fresh water gushes out in great profusion a few meters above sea level. In earlier times this was an invaluable source of drinking water during periods of drought. The women would ascend the horrendous route carrying giant buckets of water on their heads, while the men carried two containers apiece slung on either end of a pole. The villagers still go down every 210 days for the *odalan* of the temple below on the rocks at the sea's edge.

The best place to see the whole structure lies 15 minutes' walk to the west. You follow the track down over some terraces to where a left-hand turn-off leads along a deep and grand valley, heavily wooded on the far side, and onto a spur jutting out into the sea and culminating in a small temple. From here you can see the extent of the stairway, the water pouring out over a large rock, and the impressive coast to the east.

There are three other such stairways on the south coast of Nusa Penida, known as **Seganing**, **Anceng** and **Swean**. But the one at Sebuluh is the longest.

It is a peculiar feature of the island that its supply of fresh water, otherwise in such short supply, is situated here at the inaccessible south coast rather than in the north where most of the population lives. The resulting cliff routes are immensely dramatic and one of the most impressive and extraordinary things to be seen anywhere in Bali — yet they are almost wholly unknown to travelers.

NUSA LEMBONGAN

Almost everyone gets to Nusa Lembongan on tours from Benoa Harbor. But there are other ways. *Prahu* leave Nusa Penida for Nusa Lembongan from Toyapakeh in the mornings. It is important you establish the fare on his route before leaving. They go either around Lembongan to Jungutbatu on the far side, or the shorter distance to the village known simply as **Lembongan**. The trip takes under an hour. From Lembongan it's a 20-minute walk to Jungutbatu, and another 10 minutes to the beach north of the village where most of the accommodation catering to tourists is to be found.

OVERLEAF: Balinese *prahu* on the beach at Sanur, where crossings are launched to Jungutbatu on Nusa Lembongan.

The brighter, more cheerful aspect of this smaller island is apparent even as you make the crossing. The colorful wooden *prahu* are remarkably stable, and the channel separating the islands is anyway very shallow. Fish dart over the coral and schoolchildren wave as you leave the clouded heights of Nusa Penida behind you.

The southern end of the island manages to attain a few meters in height. From then on it descends to the long sandy spit where accommodation, in the form of hotels and *losmen*, are situated.

Essentially, Lembongan's tourist facilities are divided between two beaches, Jungutbatu and Mushroom Beach (not a psychedelic haven, but named after some mushroom-shaped rocks nearby). Jungutbatu is rough and ready, Mushroom Beach cleaner and more exclusive.

JUNGUBATU

The beach at Jungutbatu is sandy and faces a reef offering snorkeling and SCUBA diving. Beyond the reef there is surfing as well. A wreck to the right, its prow rising from the water like a giant shark's fin, is a prominent feature of the seascape.

The only completely satisfactory place to stay at Jungutbatu is the **Puri Nusa** (/FAX 298613 (10 rooms; moderate) at the far end of the beach — even this is relatively simple. Young divers and surfers perfect their suntans on the terrace and strum guitars in the evening. If you're looking for the quiet life and are content with early nights, Puri Nusa might be the place for you.

The other places are very inexpensive and look as if they cater for backpackers who don't have many rupiahs left in their pockets. The most popular of them are the brightly-painted **Agung's** (15 rooms, some with fan) and **Mainski** MOBILE (0811-94426 (30 rooms). The others, **Tarci Bungalows** (20 rooms), **Ketut Losmen** (six rooms), **Nusa Indah** (seven rooms), **Bunga Lombongan** (eight rooms) and, in the village itself, **Bungalow N°7** (nine rooms) have little to recommend them but the low price.

Mushroom Beach

The daily Bali Hai day-cruise ships from Benoa bring their passengers for lunch to Mushroom Beach, and they maintain a restaurant, small pool and two rows of beachside chairs here for their use.

In addition, there are two hotels. The smart one is the **Waka Nusa Resort** (0361-261130 or 723629 FAX 0361-722077 (10 bungalows; expensive) with swimming pool, restaurant and facilities for sailing, snorkeling and picnics. On the low cliff at the other end of the short beach stands the **Mushroom Beach Bungalows** (inexpensive) with 10 fan-cooled rooms.

WEST BALI

WEST BALI NATIONAL PARK

Owing to its low rainfall and distance from any other water supply, West Bali has always been thinly populated. Virtually the only significant settlements are around the coast, and the hilly, scrub-covered interior for the most part comes within the boundaries of the **West Bali National Park**. Its establishment in 1983 expanded an earlier but much smaller nature reserve set aside by the Dutch.

Trails link the major features of the mainland section of the West Bali Park. The few who use them are for the most part amateur naturalists on the lookout for the rare species thought to be present in the area, for example, the white starling, the cattle-like *banteng* and the Balinese tiger. It is now so long since a sighting of the last was reported that it is thought to be, tragically, extinct.

In order to enter the national park it's necessary to have a permit. This can be obtained at any of the offices of the Directorate General of Forest Protection and Nature Conservation. Their headquarters is at the Directorate General of Forest Protection and Nature Conservation (PPHA) in **Cekik**, three kilometers (two miles) south of Gilimanuk, the terminal for the ferries from Java. The PPHA has another office south of Denpasar at Jalan Suwung N°40 (P.O. Box 320). There is also an office at Labuhanlalang, 12 km (seven and a half miles) east of Cekik.

coming from Tabanan, there is an attractively situated clifftop temple with frangipani trees at **Rambutsiwi** (turn left down a short side road). On the northern section, between Gilimanuk and Pura Pulaki (see NORTH BALI in THE BROAD HIGHWAY, page 149), there are hot springs at **Banyuwedang**, seven kilometers (four miles) east of Labuhanlalang.

BUFFALO RACES

Most visitors come to West Bali in September for the water buffalo races at **Negara**. Two

Labuhanlalang is the site of the jetty for boats to **Menjangan Island**, within the national park, as is much of the coastal water in the area. The aim of this arrangement is to protect the coral reefs around the island, the best remaining off Bali.

Menjangan Island is the main attraction in West Bali. Both snorkeling and SCUBA diving are possible here, but the traveling time from Denpasar (three hours in each direction) makes the day-trips advertised by agents in southern Bali a poor option.

ALONG THE COAST

The long coast road offers little interest. Some eight kilometers (five miles) before Negara,

carts compete at a time, each pulled by two buffaloes. Because the 11.5-km (seven-mile) track isn't wide enough for passing, there are separate start and finishing lines for each competitor, and the one that crosses its own finishing line first stands a good chance of being declared the winner. Nothing is certain, however, as "style" as well as speed is taken into account by the judges.

The date of the races varies from year to year, so consult the **Badung Government Tourist Office (** 23399 or 23602 in Denpasar if you are in Bali in September.

OPPOSITE: Dive boat for Menjangan Island, Labuhanlalang. ABOVE: The coast of West Bali is almost entirely devoid of foreign travelers. In the absence of a tourist trade, Balinese toil away to make a living from the sea.

The Earthly Paradise

THE FIRST WESTERN ARTISTS arrived in Bali the Thirties, bumping over the rough roads in their early-model Mercedes, easels piled in the back. There they sat exchanging glances of wild surprise on discovering a people who worshipped volcanoes, cremated their dead and performed dance dramas that originated in northern India; they declared Bali a paradise. What exactly did they mean? Can the culture that so excited the minds of those early visitors survive now that the island has become a tourist mecca?

What constitutes a "paradise" depends largely on who's looking at it, and more especially what he's looking for. The artists of the Thirties were a mixed bunch, but they all to some extent felt themselves to be fugitives from the materialism of the Western industrialized world. They were looking for a place that had none of the vices of the West, and displayed all the virtues that the West lacked. Here in Bali, they believed they'd finally found it.

INFINITY EVERYWHERE

Bali came to represent for a generation of Westerners not only an idyll where the sun shone forever along palm-lined beaches, but a place where men related to each other and to the universe in ideal ways. Their relations were not commercial but brotherly, their sexual life was unrepressed and guiltless, they practiced art naturally and without thought of gain, and their religion harmonized with nature and strove to reconcile the contradictions of good and evil. Above all, they lived their daily lives surrounded by a sense of the infinite in all things.

When these Westerners saw the Balinese at festival time dancing in their flower-laden temples under the full moon, they saw a people who possessed all the virtues their own societies lacked — a people who were (they believed) unaggressive, unexploitative and were serenely and simply occupying their place in the natural order of things. By contrast, the people back home were aggressive, neurotic, obsessed with money, and practiced a religion that justified their violent colonialism and condemned them to lives of sexual unhappiness and industrial and commercial slavery.

The proof of it lay in the Balinese attitude to art. In the West, the artist was considered a rare talented individual set aside from his fellows, nice to have about the place but, nevertheless, slightly odd. The arguments of the English Victorian writer, William Morris, that all men were artists before industrialism forced the artist into the margin, went largely unheeded. But here in Bali was the very situation William Morris had described. Everyone painted or carved, danced or played the *gamelan*. Here was paradise indeed!

There was another, however, an entirely different tradition about the nature of these islands. The archipelago as a whole was seen by some not as a paradise but as positively malign. Along the banks of the rivers the trees rotted into the water in a seasonless torpor. Disease was everywhere. The climate was enervating and oppressive, and here the white man's virtue seemed to wither and die, leaving him a callous and exploitative brute. As for the locals, they might smile, but they were both superstitious and treacherous, and when stung, quick to violence. It's a vision of the islands presented in Szekely's *Tropic Fever* and hinted at in the despairing last chapter of Brian May's *Indonesian Tragedy* (see RECOMMENDED READING, page 250). Bali, in contrast to the archipelago as a whole, invariably received a better press.

Balinese of all social classes have a poise and equanimity that bears little relation to their social standing or means of livelihood. The unaltering round of life — OPPOSITE: fishing for shellfish near Singaraja; ABOVE: women bearing offerings, on the beach near Goa Lawah.

THE HIPPY TRAIL

The tradition of Bali as a paradise was revived in the Sixties for exactly the same reasons that it had been created in the Thirties. The criticism of conventional Western society offered by the hippies was identical to that of their more select band of predecessors, and when they voted with their feet to condemn the industrial and commercial societies of the West, many of them ended up on Kuta Beach admiring the sunset, usu-

ally with the aid of the local psychedelic mushrooms. It was a mass movement, and their analysis may not always have been well framed, but in its essential points it coincided with that of their predecessors entirely.

THE FUTURE

The pre-World War II generation only began to establish a rudimentary beach culture, and the Sixties travelers were the first to place Kuta on the international tourist map. Today surf, sun, sand and sea undoubtedly occupy first place among Bali's tourist attractions. How does this bode for the future of an island whose unique art and religious life — whether or not it is still what its first Western

admirers took it to be — unquestionably places it among the great cultural treasure houses of the world?

Bali's modern story is comparable to what happened in the south of France at the beginning of the twentieth century. Onto a traditionally esteemed local culture has been grafted an international, pleasure-loving one. As in Provence, the local culture has survived, but at the cost of retreating to the uplands for its purest expression.

To date, Bali's culture has survived remarkably. It may well be that this is not because it has been treated with discretion by tactful, highly educated visitors, but the reverse. Paradoxically, it may have survived because by so many people it has simply been ignored.

When they have met in Bali, the spiritual has often found little difficulty cohabiting with the hedonistic. The surfer who rides the great waves at Ulu Watu for 12 hours a day, drunk on Foster's and salt spume, is in a sense as single-minded and loyal to his gods as the girl who carries her offerings on her head at sunset to the village temple.

Sometimes the meeting of the two cultures is more than fortuitous. After I was snatched from the rip current by the Surf Rescue on Kuta Beach, the head of the rescue team asked me if I'd like to attend the anniversary festival of his village temple which happened to be taking place that same evening. Of course, I accepted. I knew the Balinese offered up gifts of fruit, cakes and flowers on such occasions, so I asked him what I should bring.

He stood there on the warm sand of the great bay looking out to sea, the long line of volcanoes rising smoothly in the distance. Then he turned to me and smiled.

"The gods have need of nothing," he said quietly.

ABOVE: The sight of Tanah Lot at sunset is one which epitomizes the beauty and force of Bali, an arresting image which remains in the minds of travelers long after they have returned home. OPPOSITE: At the house of Filipino artist Antonio Blanco, Ubud. There is hardly a corner of Balinese life where some indication of hope, some sign of joy can't be found.

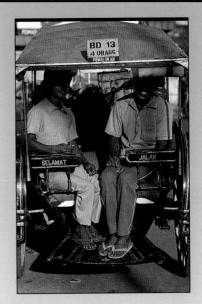

Travelers'
Tips

GETTING THERE

Most people arrive in Bali by air. The island is well-served by flights from most points in Asia, Australia and Western Europe. There are also direct flights from the west coast of the United States.

The airport receives a large volume of flights from other Indonesian cities and smaller towns in the Indonesian archipelago.

For the adventurous—and for those who have the time — there are plenty of long distance buses which travel between Java and Bali. Indeed there are some travel companies (see BEYOND BALI, below) who run special bus trips for tourists, starting or finishing in the north of Sumatra and running through the vast islands of Sumatra and Java, before arriving in Bali — or vice versa.

Other visitors arrive by boat. PELNI, one of the national shipping lines, has regular services between Java and Bali, Sulawesi and Bali and Bali and the Moluccas. There are plenty of small boats, ferries and other marine transport to and from Lombok. Any visitor coming from Lombok (or even Sumbawa) will find a range of options to suit even the most modest of budgets.

At the luxury end of the scale, a number of cruise ships now visit Bali as part of their regular schedules. But the time allotted to visitors, in these cases, is minimal.

FROM THE AIRPORT

Ngurah Rai is the official name for Denpasar airport, after the hero who led a resistance group against the Dutch in 1946. There's a statue of him at the junction at the end of the airport road, where you turn left for Sanur or right for Nusa Dua. The airport is often just referred to as Tuban, after the village nearby. The airport is very close to all the major resorts in southern Bali.

At the point where arriving travelers emerge from the airport onto the forecourt, taxis are available. The rates are somewhat inflated but fixed, so at least travelers are spared the difficulties of bargaining during the first hour or so of their stay.

Those on their way to Kuta who want to economize can catch a *bemo* (daylight hours

only) by leaving the international terminal through the car park, passing the domestic terminal on the right and continuing on until a road leads in from the left. It's about 400 m. Stand at the junction and the *bemos* (blue transit vans) coming out of the side road will find you. The fare to Kuta is around US$.25.

TRAVEL DOCUMENTS

Passports must be valid for six months from date of entry into Indonesia.

You do not need to acquire a visa in advance if you are a passport holder of one of the following countries: Argentina, Australia, Austria, Belgium, Brazil, Brunei, Canada, Chile, Denmark, Egypt, Finland, France, Germany, Greece, Iceland, Ireland, Italy, Japan, Kuwait, Luxembourg, Malaysia, Malta, Morocco, Mexico, the Netherlands, New Zealand, Norway, the Philippines, Singapore, South Korea, Spain, Sweden, Switzerland, Saudi Arabia, Taiwan, Thailand, Turkey, the United Kingdom, the United States, the United Arab Emirates and Venezuela.

OPPOSITE: Along the north coast, near Lovina, there are some refreshing hot springs. ABOVE: The charm of Bali is the charm of its people.

For all of the above, passports will be stamped allowing a stay of 60 days on arrival in Indonesia. These visas cannot be renewed. You must be in possession of a ticket out of the country (though "purchase of a ticket is also accepted"), and entry must be through one of the following by air: Jakarta, Medan, Manado, Ambon, Bali, Biak, Surabaya and Batam or the following by sea: Semarang, Jakarta, Bali, Pontianiac, Balikpapan, Tanjung Pinang and Kupang. For entry or exit through other places a special visa is required.

Nationals of all other countries must obtain their visas in advance. Because of the situation in East Timor, holders of Portuguese passports are, at the time of writing, likely to experience difficulties if they apply for an Indonesian visa.

It is common practice for foreigners living in Bali to fly from Bali to Singapore and then back again on the same day, in order to obtain another 60-day stamp in their passport.

If you do hold a renewable visa and need to renew it in Bali, the **Immigration Office (Kantor Imigrasi)** (0361-227828 is at Renon Complex, Niti Mandala in Denpasar, with another on your right immediately before you pass under the ceremonial arch going into the airport (0361-751038, Jalan Ngurah Rai, Kuta. They are open Monday to Thursday from 7 AM to 1 PM, Friday from 7 AM to 11 PM and Saturday from 7 AM to noon; closed Sunday.

CUSTOMS ALLOWANCES

Indonesian customs allows a maximum of two liters of alcoholic beverages, 200 cigarettes or 50 cigars or 100 grams (three and a half ounces) of tobacco, and a "reasonable" amount of perfume per adult. Photographic equipment, cars, typewriters and tape-recorders must be declared on arrival and must be taken out again with you. Radios, television sets, radios, narcotics, arms and ammunition, printed matter in Chinese characters and Chinese medicines are prohibited.

Advance approval must be acquired for carrying transceivers, and all movie films and video cassettes must be controlled by the Film Censor Board. Fresh fruit, plants and animals must have quarantine permits.

DRUGS

Don't be tempted to import or use drugs in Bali. Under the Indonesian Narcotic Drugs Law of 1976, it is an offense for anyone to have knowledge of drug use and not pass it on to the police. As for actual possession, amounts are irrelevant, and it is in no way the case that having a small amount constitutes only a minor offense.

Maximum penalties are as follows: For possessing cannabis or cocaine: six years' imprisonment, with a fine of Rp10 million; for possessing "other narcotic drugs:" 10 years and Rp15 million. Selling or importing drugs is punishable by a 21-year sentence, or life, while the death penalty is given for the second category of substances (though to date this has not been imposed in a drugs case anywhere in Indonesia).

The prison for southern Bali is at Kerobokan, just north of Kuta, and there are at all times foreigners incarcerated there serving sentences there for drugs offenses.

There was a time when Bali was considered a paradise for psychedelic experiences. It is emphatically not so now. Visitors should neither import nor use any narcotic substances there — you may never know who told on you as informers are protected by Indonesian law from identification in court. Be warned.

HEALTH

There are no obligatory vaccinations for entry into Indonesia, other than for yellow fever if you have been in an infected area during the previous six days. It's prudent, though, to consult your doctor and perhaps have an anti-tetanus vaccination before leaving home.

Malaria exists all over Indonesia, though the risk in Bali is negligible. The medical authorities no longer recommend taking anti-malaria pills for vacationers visiting the island. Many doctors believe that long trousers and long-sleeved shirts provide more protection than medical prophylactics. You should therefore play it safe and cover up as evening approaches and mosquitoes become active. Put on repellent and light anti-mosquito coils where appropriate. Taking vitamin B complex is reputed to help repel mosquitoes, too.

Dengue fever is more common than malaria, but even so not very common. Still, identified cases of dengue fever have been found in the tourist areas as well as elsewhere on the island. Protecting yourself from mosquito bites is again the best precaution — and note that the mosquitoes that cause dengue fever bite at all times of the day. But the risk, as we say, is small. The main symptom of dengue fever is dizziness, with aching bones, headache and fever as secondary symptoms.

The uplands around Kintamani and Lake Batur are too cool at night for mosquitoes of the dangerous kinds to flourish.

Because of the risk of hepatitis, beware of food sold from roadside stalls or carts, and drink only bottled water and soft drinks, or water that has been properly boiled.

Your main enemy is probably the sun. Get into the habit of wearing a hat, avoid sunbathing in the middle of the day, and only lie on the beach for short periods during your first few days. Suntan lotions with a high protection factor will help. Take care to find your own tolerance levels, and don't expect to look like a sunkissed surfer after your first afternoon.

If you get ill, there are local health clinics known as *puskesmas*, but tourists are not expected to use them and you could find yourself being charged distinctly non-local rates for very elementary treatment. It's better to go to one of the Western doctors — associated with the **Hyatt, Bali Beach, Club Meditérrannée** or **Nusa Dua hotels** — who will usually see patients, even if they're not guests of the hotel or resort.

Alternatively, you can ring the **Nusa Dua Emergency Clinic** (0361-771118. There's a hospital in Denpasar, the **Sanglah Hospital** (0361-227911-5 HOT-LINE 0361-226363 on Jalan Nias. In addition, **Doctor Andre Dipa** (HOME 0361-222866 (OFFICE 0361-226363 (PAGER 13099 (24-HOURS 0361-83720 can be recommended.

Contact **AEA (worldwide medical assistance)** at (231443 FAX 0361-231442.

For dental treatment you can contact the **Emergency Dental Clinic** at the same number as the Nusa Dua Emergency Clinic above, or contact **Dr. Ritje** (0361-772241, Jalan Pratama N°81, Nusa Dua.

In case of **serious illness or injury**, it is best to leave Bali as soon as possible for treatment in Singapore or Australia. Local hospitals and clinics are not well equipped.

Mosquito bites do tend to become septic, almost as a matter of course. It's wise to carry some antiseptic ointment for use on these and more serious cuts and abrasions.

CURRENCY AND BANKING

You can bring unlimited amounts of foreign currency into Indonesia but only up to

Rp50,000 in Indonesian money, and this latter must be declared on entry.

There's very little reason for acquiring rupiahs before you arrive in Bali. The exchange kiosk at the airport stays open until after the last flight of the day has arrived, and rates are virtually identical to those offered by the banks and the moneychangers in Kuta, Sanur, etc. In addition, exchange rates for the rupiah are often not particularly advantageous outside Indonesia.

Rupiahs come in 25-, 50-, 100-, 500- and 1,000-rupiah coins and 100-, 500-, 1,000-, 5,000-, 10,000-, 20,000- and 50,000-rupiah notes. Small denomination coins are very rarely seen nowadays. (At the time of writing 2,000 rupiahs bought a mere US$1. There isn't much you can buy for that, even in Indonesia. For more on money matters, exchange rates and pricing, see PRICES AND RATE OF EXCHANGE, below.) In the supermarkets you will often be given candy instead of small change.

Renting a motorbike is easy in Bali — but you do need a license.

Moneychanging facilities are found everywhere in the tourist areas of southern Bali, but many charge a commission or offer a poor rate of exchange. Two places in Legian that offer a good rate and take no commission are PT. Central Kuta, opposite Goa 2001 (it's also a bookshop) and the Kodak Film outlet directly opposite the entrance to the Legian Beach Hotel on Jalan Malasti in Legian.

ATM machines have now begun to appear in the Kuta and Legian areas — look for the signs BCA and PLUS. There's one, for instance, on Jalan Seminyak, almost opposite the Khao Thai Restaurant.

When receiving money transfers from abroad, it's a good idea to have the sender send you a copy of the transfer notice to an address other than the bank, just to be sure.

When traveling to villages upcountry, make sure you have plenty of small change as vendors away from the tourist areas may not have change for large notes.

PRICES AND RATE OF EXCHANGE

At the time of writing the exchange rate was Rp2,000 to US$1. Since that time, Indonesian currency has plummeted, and at press time was valued at approximately Rp8,000 to US$1. Entrance fees and other charges have therefore been provided in United States dollar approximations in order to give travelers an idea of relative costs.

GETTING AWAY

It is worth noting that Bali is a source for inexpensive air tickets. A number of outlets in Kuta (in particular) offer attractive fares to destinations worldwide. For the tourist who might be interested in either cut-price Business Class and First Class air tickets, or a multi-leg vacation, this can prove a great saving.

DEPARTURE TAX

There is a tax of US$12.50 on international flights and US$5.50 on domestic flights.

AIRLINE OFFICES

The main branch in Bali of **Garuda Indonesia** (0361-227825 or (0361-22028 FAX 0361-

226298 is at Jalan Melati N°61, Denpasar. They also maintain the following branch offices :

Natour Kuta Beach Hotel (0361-751179 in Kuta; **Hotel Grand Bali Beach** (0361-288511 in Sanur; **Sanur Beach Hotel** (0361-288011 in Sanur; **Nusa Indah Hotel** (0361-771906 in Nusa Dua.

Telephone numbers for the other airlines are as follows:

International
Air France (0361-287734
Air New Zealand (0361-756170
Ansett Australia (0361-289637
Cathay Pacific (0361-286001
Continental (0361-287774
Eva Air (0361-751011
Japan Airlines (0361-287576
KLM (0361-756124
Korean Air (0361-289402
LTU International Airways (0361-753778
Lufthansa (0361-287069
Malaysian Airlines (0361-285071
Qantas (0361-751472
Singapore Airlines (0361-261666
Thai Airways (0361-288141

Domestic
Bouraq (0361-223564
Merpati Nusantara (0361-228842
Sempati Air (0361-754218

BEYOND BALI

Numerous bus companies operate on the Denpasar–Surabaya route, usually traveling overnight. Any place offering bookings for the shuttle bus can book you onto one. The fare includes the short ferry crossing from Gilimanuk to Banyuwangi, and a free meal at one of the stops. The air-conditioned buses are much more comfortable than the non air-conditioned variety. Videos are screened on these buses during the first part of the journey.

There is no railway on Bali, but from Banyuwangi on the tip of Java, a fast and modern service runs to Jakarta. The best Indonesian trains are luxurious and a pleasure to travel on, and the express train to Jakarta is sometimes one of these. Local trains are a different matter, however, though extraordinarily cheap. Information about connections to Surabaya and Yogjakarta, as well as the special train to Jakarta, can be obtained locally at the railway's office at Jalan Diponegoro №172, in Denpasar.

To go to Lombok, the Mabua company-run jet-powered sea shuttles depart from Benoa Harbour (not to be confused with Tanjung Benoa), and you can even go there for the day. Spice Island Cruises offer three-and four-night excursions by sea to Sumbawa (Badas); Komodo Lombok is included on the four-night trip. For trips to Sulawesi, contact the **Ujung Tourist Office** (0411-320616.

GETTING AROUND

CAR RENTAL

A rental a car is one way of getting around Bali, and the Suzuki Jimny, handy for the rougher roads, is a particularly popular option. These and other vehicles can be rented in the Kuta–Legian area from the following: **Toyota Rent-a-Car** (0361-751282, 701747 or 753744; **Chit Chat** (0361-752192; **Jaya Mertha** (0361-751233; or **Bali Van Car Rental** (0361-228271.

You must be in possession of an up-to-date international drivers' license.

BEMO CULTURE

Although there are a number of taxis, operating mainly between large hotels and the airport, many travelers prefer to use *bemos* — a way of life and one of the easiest ways of seeing something of the life of the Balinese people. It's a common occurrence to ride in these small, open-backed vans in the company of sacks of rice, chickens and even a couple of pigs.

Fares are fixed, and everyone except the tourist knows them. It isn't a bargaining situation. Nevertheless (as it seems eminently reasonable to take from a foreigner money he seems to want to throw away), larger amounts than necessary are usually accepted if you don't keep your wits about you. The best plan, if you don't know the correct fare, is to watch what the locals hand over, and to keep a stock of small coins so that you can offer the exact fare, or what you judge might well be the right fare. This avoids leaving it

up to the conductor to decide whether or not to give you any change. There are no tickets.

Nor are there timetables. The *bemo* drivers hire their vehicles on a day-to-day basis and consequently have to do their best to recouperate the hire charge and make what profit they can. *Bemos* leave when they're full, rarely before. They can't be relied on to run after dark. Except on the Denpasar to Kuta route in some places, such as the mountain villages of Penelokan and Kintamani, or in the country around Ubud, the last *bemos* of the day tend to leave well before five. Inquire on your outward journey, so as not to take a chance on getting stranded.

You can sit in the front alongside the driver if you like; there's no extra charge (i.e., it isn't "first class"). You pay the conductor (*kernet*) for the distance you've traveled when you get off. There are no fixed stops, other than at each end of the route. When you want to get out, shout "Stopa!" or "Stop!" To get on, wave one down — you won't have any trouble as they're on permanent lookout for customers, with the *kernet* calling out the *bemo*'s destination to pedestrians as the vehicle passes. If you aren't sure if the *bemo* you are about to hail is going where you want to go, just ask. No one will mind if it turns out you stopped the *bemo* for nothing — they're as hungry for travelers as bees for nectar. Crowd in wherever you can: No *bemo* is ever too full to refuse taking on another passenger.

You won't have been using *bemos* long before a driver suggests you charter one. This means you decide where the vehicle goes, just as if it were a taxi; the driver is an independent operator and is under no obligation to ply any particular route. It's a good way to get off the beaten track fast, but it won't especially cheap, and the driver will hope you're not going to mind if he picks up extra passengers in the normal way as well. But the system has all the charm and convenience of earlier times in more "developed" countries, when travel, like buying and selling, was a simple matter of an arrangement between those who needed and those willing to fulfill the need. The existence of the need made certain that someone would move in to satisfy it. *Bemos* are undoubtedly bumpy and hot, but riding in one often conveys something unavailable in air-conditioned coaches — the romance of travel.

MOTORBIKES

Thousands of visitors a year rent motorbikes while on Bali. It's an excellent way to see the island, and especially good for getting away from the main tourist trail. Take extra care on the main roads, however, where the traffic in recent years has become very heavy.

Most people rent from **Bakor Motor**, an agency that is in effect a collective of motorbike owners. Register with them, tell them the kind of machine you require, and a bike plus its owner will quickly appear at your address, ready to negotiate a deal. The deal is then registered by Bakor, and you take out an insurance policy, also through the agency. Any subsequent dispute with the owner can be settled through Bakor.

If you don't have an international driver's license validated for motorcycle use, you will have to get a special permit to ride a motorbike in Bali. For this, you'll go to the Denpasar Police Office (Bakor will take you) and undergo a written test. (The unconfirmed leg-

end is that someone always makes sure you put down the right answers.)

Bakor's main office is in Kuta, with branches in Ubud and Sanur.

ACCOMMODATION

There is every possible type of accommodation available in Bali, but the range of choices drops dramatically once you leave the southeast.

All of the international-standard hotels are in Nusa Dua, Sanur or Kuta. There is no accommodation other than in five-star hotels in Nusa Dua; a reasonable range, but nothing cheap, in Sanur; and everything from the most expensive beach hotels to rooms for US$4 a night in Kuta, Legian and Seminyak.

Like everything else in Indonesia, accommodation is excellent value when you're bringing in major foreign currencies, though the now usual habit of quoting rates in US dollars in the more expensive hotels fails to disguise a major rate hike there in recent years.

At the other end of the scale, a cheap room in a *losmen* or homestay will almost invariably be clean, have an overhead fan and look out onto a central garden. It will have a cold water shower and breakfast (tea or coffee with toast and fruit) will be included in the price.

Once you leave the tourist belt, however, it is unlikely that you will have much choice in lodging.

There are *losmen* almost everywhere, and even where there are none the friendly local people will be only too eager to adjust the family arrangements in order to provide you with a room for the night and themselves with some additional income.

There are, of course, subsidiary tourist enclaves, such as at Lovina in the north and Candi Dasa in the east, where there are better quality small hotels. In Denpasar there is one reasonable hotel and others that are far from prepossessing. At Ubud there is again a very wide range to choose from, many very expensive, though less expensive ones can be found.

The **rates** in the body of the text are based on the price of the average double room. Equivalents are — **inexpensive**: under US$12; **moderate**: US$12 to 30; **average and above**: US$30 to 80; **expensive**: over US$80.

Note that Bali's high seasons are July to August and from 20 December to approximately 20 January. Higher prices can be expected at these times.

EATING OUT

In the Kuta–Sanur area, Indonesian food approaches rarity; it's sometimes easier to get a Mexican, Italian or German meal than a Balinese one. You certainly never need eat non-Western food if you don't want to. In Nusa Dua, all the hotels have several restaurants offering food that could well have been prepared in New York, Paris or Rome.

Elsewhere on the island you'll have to put up with what you find. In all the places tourists frequent, attempts will be made to offer Western style food, but these will not differ greatly from the local fare. There are eating places here and there, however, that are delights to discover.

Note that prices for alcoholic beverages are generally at Western levels or above, and a couple more drinks can quickly double the price of any meal.

It is important to keep in mind that prices at the budget end of the scale can be extremely affordable. It is entirely possible to have a simple meal for around US$1 and to find a room in a *losmen* for US$5 almost anywhere in Bali, even along the southern tourist belt.

THE PRESS AND RADIO

There are two English-language papers published in Jakarta, *The Indonesia Times* and *The Jakarta Post*. They are normally on sale in

southern Bali from about mid-morning on the day of issue.

The Indonesia Times advertises a price "in Jakarta" of US$.50, but expect to pay twice this amount in Bali. This increase represents airfreight expenses, plus the extra palms the newspaper has had to pass through on its journey to the newsstand. Remember, too, that the vendor who will probably sell you the paper depends on the difference between what you give him and what he must hand over to his employer for his only income.

OPPOSITE: Creating its own Balinese paradise, the Grand Hyatt Hotel. ABOVE: Fishing *prahu* on the beach at Sanur. They will even take you across the Badung Strait to Jungutbatu on Nusa Lembongan — a trip that seems frighteningly far for such simple craft.

In any case, don't begrudge him the odd US$.20 extra.

Bali has an abundance of free publications paid for by the often useful advertisements they carry. The best of them is *Bali Plus*, published monthly. It's pocket-sized and there isn't room for many articles, but its "What's on in Bali" has no equal.

Then there's the full-color broadsheet *Bali Kini*, the similar *Bali Now*, the government tourist office's *Tourist Indonesia*, and lastly the *Bali Advertiser*, "advertising for the expatriate community". All can be found waiting for you in hotel lobbies, cafés and business centers such as Krakatoa in Legian.

COMMUNICATIONS

TELEPHONE

Telephone service used be one of Bali's weaknesses. Subscribers told stories of "secret sharers" who occupied their line and pushed up their bill even when they were temporarily disconnected for nonpayment, and you would as a matter of course have to try 20 or 30 times before getting a line.

The situation is much better now. There are phones taking phone cards from which you can make **international calls**. Much cheaper, however, are the now numerous Wartel offices; they're virtually everywhere, and foreign residents without private phones use them for all their international calls.

You will soon realize that there are two different **access codes for international calls**: 001 and 008. The first is for calls via the official telecommunications organization, the second via a private company. Charges are the same, but 008 is generally considered the more efficient, with a shorter waiting time.

You'll often see the word "hunting" after a phone number. This means there are several lines to the one number.

The **area code** for South Bali, including Kuta, Sanur, Nusa Dua, Ubud and Denpasar, is 0361. For North Bali it's 0362, 0363 for Candi Dasa and the northeastern beaches at Tulamben and Amed, and for the central heights — Kintamani, Penelokan, Kedesan and Air Panas — 0366. The full numbers (including area code) are shown throughout this book.

When dialing within area codes omit the first four numbers.

The following numbers may be useful:
Operator (100
Fire (113
Police (110
Ambulance (118 or (26305
International operator (102
Time (103
International inquiries (106
Directory inquiries (108
Complaints (117
Search and Rescue (111

MAIL

To find the post office, ask for "kantor pos". In **Kuta** the main office is located near the Night Market, with a very efficient branch in Jalan Bakungsari, close to the junction with the main Denpasar to Tuban road. In **Sanur**, it's on Jalan Segara. The **Denpasar** post office is inconveniently located on the road to Sanur, away from the town center.

As in many Asian countries, it is advisable to make certain the mail clerk cancels your stamps. Relative money values are such that the postage on a heavy letter overseas can equal a day's pay for an Indonesian worker; consequently, the temptation to remove your stamps might occasionally be irresistible. (I have never heard of this happening in Bali, however.)

Many postal agents will sell stamps, accept your mail and post it for you; they are generally quite reliable.

Express mail is quite inexpensive and should save a couple of days.

Register any important or valuable mail.

Postal rates are approximately as follows: For sending an **airmail postcard** to Australia and Asia US$.50, to Europe US$.75, to the United States US$.75; for **airmail letters** (to Australia and Asia US$.50, to Europe US$.75 to the United States US$.75; for **aerograms** to all destinations US$.40; for **parcels** rates vary depending on the country of destination. Sample rates for parcels up to half a kilogram (1.1 lb) are: Australia US$16.60, Canada US$17.95, France US$21.65, Germany US$18.75, Italy US$21.70, the Netherlands US$17.60, Spain US$17.65, Switzerland US$15.55, the United States US$16.85.

TIME

Bali is one hour ahead of Java, seven hours ahead of Greenich Mean Time and three hours behind Australian Eastern Standard Time. It is 13 hours ahead of New York and 16 hours ahead of California.

WHAT TO WEAR

The Indonesian government used to issue a poster detailing undesirable and preferred

For women, modesty is the keynote. Remember that it's going to be hot, sometimes very hot, and that loose-fitting clothes are much cooler than close-fitting ones. Cotton is also cooler than synthetic fabrics.

To enter a Balinese temple, one must wear a sarong and a sash. Most temples will rent these for a small fee, but it is simpler to buy them for a few thousand rupiah and carry them with you.

A moment's thought is worth pages of advice. You would never dream of turning up at a funeral at home in beachwear, but it's

modes of dress. Its essential message was that tourists should remember that this is someone else's country and local conventions should be adhered to. The beach and adjacent streets are one thing, but the rest of the island is very much another.

It's particularly important to wear reasonably formal dress when visiting government offices; this may differ from what's considered formal back home. Observe the better-off Indonesians to get an idea of expectations. Short sleeves, for instance, are perfectly acceptable for men, and ties are rare. But long trousers, shoes as opposed to sandals or thongs, and above all a neat, pressed, generally tidy appearance are essential ingredients in such situations.

astonishing how many tourists turn up in shorts and a T-shirt to a Balinese cremation.

BARGAINING

Be prepared to bargain for most things in Bali. It's the most natural, and surely the most ancient, system in the world. Think of it this way: If you want to buy, and he wants to sell, why should anything as rigid as a fixed price come between you?

You can even bargain for your hotel room, along the lines of "What price will you give me if I stay a week?" or "What's the discount,

ABOVE: The enjoyment is evident as these girls proceed to a purification ceremony on Kuta Beach.

seeing as it is low season?" It may turn out to be inappropriate, but it's necessary to understand the Balinese will never be surprised — to them, it is fixed prices that are unnatural, the foreign importation.

The secret of successful bargaining is to get your offer in first. Once the vendor has named a price, it would involve loss of face to accept anything much less than 60 percent of it. Nevertheless, for you to make the first offer, and then go on to describe it immediately as your last price, is to go against the spirit of the business, and is guaranteed to remove the smile off any Indonesian face. You've simply broken the rules, and been very rude in the bargain because you've left him no room to maneuver.

There are places where you don't bargain — restaurants and the larger shops, for instance. The Balinese don't bargain over *bemo* fares, though you might find yourself having to if you haven't managed to find out the correct fare in advance. But wherever you're dealing with someone who's master of his own business, whether it's a girl hawking T-shirts on the beach or a boy offering to drive you around on the back of his motorbike, bargaining is the accepted, and expected, way to go about things.

In Bali sellers frequently approach tourists with their wares. This often annoys visitors, on Kuta Beach for example, but remember that any answer, even "No thanks," or simply making eye contact, can be taken as an indication of some degree of interest. A silent shake of the head — and a smile — will normally see you aren't disturbed any longer.

TIPPING

Tipping isn't customary on Bali, but this shouldn't prevent you from rewarding someone who has provided you with a useful service. You might, for example, tip your room boy after an extended stay. There's no need to tip in restaurants.

WATER SPORTS

Surfing is a world all of its own. It's a quasi-religious cult with its own language and sacred locations.

Bali is considered one of the world's ideal surfing venues because of the consistency of its waves, which break in exactly the same way for hours on end. It's also popular because when conditions make the ocean on one beach flat, there are other beaches only a short drive away where the surfing is likely to be stupendous.

The classic place for surfing is Ulu Watu. Here the waves are world class — surf movies have been filmed here and international competitions have been held. Close by is Padang Padang. Neither is for the beginner. Both are well off the usual tourist routes and ideal for watching the masters of the art at play.

At Kuta the waves are smaller (though they can still be too dangerous to surf). Here, the classic locations are Half Legian, Kuta Reef and Canggu and, further north up the beach, Medowi.

In addition, some surfers make the trip out to Nusa Lembongan, and, in the rainy season, surf off the reef at Sanur.

Sailing and **windsurfing** are available on the sheltered eastern side of the island during the dry season. Inquire at any of the larger hotels at Nusa Dua or Sanur. For more reasonable rates, ask along Sanur Beach or at the Rai Restaurant at Benoa. Sailing is on local outriggers or Hobie Cat catamarans.

There's superb **diving** on the remote northwest island of Menjangan, at Amed and at Tulamben. The Lovina beaches in North Bali have good snorkeling, and there's diving offshore at Tepokong (but beware of the very strong currents). Both **snorkeling** and diving are available on Nusa Lembongan. For more information on diving see under SPORTING SPREE in YOUR CHOICE, page 32.

In recent years, **rafting** has become quite popular in Bali. The following outfits can set you afloat: Ayung River Rafting (0361-238759 FAX 0361-224236, Bali International Rafting (0361-757052 FAX 0361-752956 or Sobek (0361-287059 FAX 0361-289448. For more on rafting in Bali, see RAFT THE WHITE WATER in TOP SPOTS, page 20.

WATER SAFETY

Lives are lost every year on Bali's beaches — as recently as 1992 there were 29 people drowned there. See the section under KUTA , page 173, for information on the Surf Rescue teams.

Remember: Never go more than waist deep unless you are a very strong swimmer. If a current is pulling you out to sea, don't try to swim against it, but rather paddle sideways out of the current. If in distress of any kind, raise a hand above your head — it's the international signal for help and doing it represents your best chance of being rescued.

CHURCH SERVICES

Visitors who want to attend church services have the following options:

Catholic: St. Franciscus Xavarius Church, Jalan Kartika Plaza, Kuta. There's a Mass in English every Saturday evening at 7:30 PM.

Protestant: Bali Protestant Church, Gang Menuh (off Jalan Legian), Kuta. A service is held every Sunday morning at 10 AM.

ETIQUETTE

The Balinese are a polite people and visitors should try to follow suit. A few simple points will see you a long way toward fitting in with the local environment.

- Give and take everything with the right hand; the left is considered unclean.
- Never touch anyone on the head, even a child.
- Don't photograph people bathing in rivers, and in other circumstances ask first, if only with a smile and a gesture.
- Don't beckon someone toward you with your index finger as it's very rude.
- Wear a sash around your waist whenever you go into a temple, and at a ceremony such as a cremation don't wear shorts, thongs and a skimpy T-shirt. No one will be the slightest bit amused if you wear a sarong; they will be delighted, and many people will compliment you on your taste.
- Pointing at people, standing with your arms folded or with your hands on your hips are widely considered vulgar.

The Balinese, incidentally, rarely say "thank you" in the normal run of things on receipt of a gift. If they do so, it will be because they have been trained to do it by the hotel where they work. Similarly, it's impolite to call someone simply by his first name, but hotel workers have been trained to accept this slight along with other imported barbarisms.

SEX

Inevitably, male visitors will be offered prostitutes in Bali, especially in Kuta. Men are sure to hear the whispered words, "Balinese girl, very young," on some dark night. The prostitutes, incidentally, will almost certainly be from one of the other islands.

There's an **AIDS Center** (0361-239191, dealing with all aspects of the illness on Jalan Sudirman, Denpasar.

LANGUAGE

The language known as Bahasa Indonesia ("the Indonesian language") is actually Malay. The language of Bali is Balinese, a difficult tongue with different forms for addressing the various social classes. All Balinese now learn Bahasa Indonesia in school, and as it is very easy and can be used throughout Indonesia as well as in Malaysia, it's the one you should try to master at least a few phrases of. There are no articles, no plurals, and no tenses, and the verb "to be" isn't used (e.g., *Bali bagus* = Bali is beautiful).

Pronunciation is easy and straightforward: The important point is that Indonesian is easy to *hear*. Most Westerners can pick up the sounds and general intonation almost at once. In this, Indonesian contrasts strongly with most other Asian languages which, with their complex systems of tones, are complex and very difficult for the Westerner.

Because the language is so easy, it's immense fun to try. It's also very poetic. Start off with some of the following:

Good Morning. *Selamat pagi.* ("May your action be blessed this morning.")

How are you? *Apa khabar?* ("What's the news?")

I'm fine. *Khabar baik.* ("The news is good.")

Thank you. *Terima kasih.*

It's a pleasure. *Kembali.*

Goodbye (when *you are* leaving) *Permisi.* (The reply to this is *Mari.*)

What is your name? *Siapa namamu?*

My name is… *Nama saya…*
Please speak slowly. *Tolong bicara pelanpelan.*
I'll come back later. *Saya akan kembali nanti.*
May I come in? *Boleh saya masuk?*
This is good! *Ini bagus!*
Is it safe to swim here? *Anam berenang disini?*
How much is this? *Berapa haga ini?*
About… *Kira kira…*
1, 2, 3, 4, 5… *Satu, dua, tiga, empat, lima…*
…6, 7, 8, 9, 10… *enam, tujuh, delapan, sembilan, sepuluh.*
11, 12, 13… *sebelas, dua belas, tiga belas (belas = ten)*
20, 30… *dua puluh, tiga puluh (puluh = tens)*
100 *seratus*
200, 300… dua ratus, tiga ratus *(ratus = hundreds)*
1,000 *seribu*
2,000, 3,000… *dua ribu, tiga ribu (ribu = thousands)*
100,000 *seratus ribu*

In answer to the eternal question "Where are you going?" try *"Makan angin"* ("To eat the wind").

A helpful little booklet is John Barker's *Practical Indonesian*, available all over Bali.

CONSULATES AND EMBASSIES

Several countries maintain consulates, consular agencies, representatives or honorary consuls in Bali. They are:

Australia (also serving the United Kingdom, New Zealand, Canada and Papua New Guinea)(0361-235092 FAX 0361-231990, Jalan Prof. M. Yamin N°4, Renon, Denpasar.

France (0361-280227 FAX 0361-287303, Jalan Tambuk Sari N°5, Sanur.

Germany(0361-288535 FAX 0361-288826, Jalan Pantai Karang N°17, Sanur.

Italy(0361-288996 FAX 0361-287642, Jalan Cemara, Banjar Semawang, Sanur.

Japan (0361-227628 FAX 0361-231308, Jalan Raya Puputan, Renon, Denpasar.

Netherlands (0361-751517 FAX 0361-752777, Jalan Imam Bonjol N°599, Kuta.

Norway and Denmark (0361-235098 FAX 0361-234834, Jalan Jaya Giri VIII N°10, Renon, Denpasar.

Sweden and Finland (0361-288407 C/o Segara Village Hotel, Sanur.

Switzerland and Austria (0361-751735 FAX 0361-754457 C/o Swiss Restaurant, Jalan Pura Bagus Taruna, Legian, Kuta.

United States (0361-233605 FAX 0361-222426, Jalan Hayam Wuruk 188, Denpasar.

Other nationals may be able to get advice from one of the above, or they can contact their embassy in Jakarta.

The following are the phone numbers of the various embassies in Jakarta (the city code for Jakarta is 021).

Afghanistan (314-3169.
Algeria (525-4719.
Argentina (314-3090.
Australia (522-7111.
Austria (390-4927.
Bangladesh (314-1690.
Belgium (570-0676.
Brazil (390-4056
Brunei (571-2180.
Bulgaria (390-4049.
Canada (525-0790.
Chile (520-1131.
China (714897
Colombia (516446.
Czech Republic (390-4075.
Denmark (520-4350.
Egypt (343440.
Finland (516980.
France (314-2897.
Germany (384-9547
Great Britain (310-4229
Hungary (520-3459.
India (520-4150.
Iran (331391.
Iraq (390-4067.
Italy (337440.
Japan (324308.
Jordan (520-4400.
Malaysia (522-4947.
Mexico (337479.
Netherlands (511515
New Zealand (330680.
Nigeria (327838.
Norway (525-1990.
Pakistan (314-4011.
Papua New Guinea (725-1218.
Philippines (310-0334.
Poland (314-0509.
Romania (310-6340.
Russia (322162.

Saudi Arabia (314-5888.
Singapore (520-1489.
Slovakia (310-1068.
South Korea (520-1915.
Spain (314-2355.
Sri Lanka (315-1686.
Sweden (520-1551.
Switzerland (516061.
Syria (525-5991.
Thailand (390-4225.
Tunisia (570-3432.
Turkey (525-6250.
United States (360360.
Vatican (384-1142
Vietnam (310-0358.
Yemen (390-4074.

SELECTED INDONESIAN MISSIONS ABROAD

Australia Canberra ((06) 258600.
Belgium Brussels ((02) 7711776.
Canada Ottawa ((0613) 236-7403.
Denmark Copenhagen ((031) 624422.
France Paris ((01) 4503-0760.
Germany Bonn ((0228) 382990.
Great Britain London ((0171) 499-7661.
Greece Athens ((01) 323-0251.
Hong Kong (2890-4421.
India Delhi ((011) 602343.
Italy Rome ((06) 482-5951.
Japan Tokyo ((03) 4414201.
Malaysia Kuala Lumpur ((03) 984-2011.
Netherlands Den Haag ((070) 310-8100.
New Zealand Wellington ((04) 475-8697.
Singapore (737-7422.
South Korea Seoul ((02) 783-5675.
Spain Madrid ((01) 413-0294.
Switzerland Bern ((031) 352-0983.
Thailand Bangkok ((02) 252-3135.
United States Washington, DC ((0202) 775-5200.

Photo Credits

All photographs by Nik Wheeler with the exception of those listed below:

Alain Evrard: pages 6 (right), 44, 55, 62, 63, 232.

Rio Helmi: pages 82–83, 125, 161, 184

Leonard Lueras: pages 3, 69 right, 76–77, 78, 81, 86, 94–95, 96 left, 97 right, 108 top, 113, 115, 122–123, 132–133, 135, 144–145, 146, 147, 150–151 bottom, 187, 189 right, 199, 202, 203, 220, 227, 234, 235, 237.

Martin Westlake: pages 6 left, 10, 18-19, 21, 22–23, 25, 27, 28, 30, 31, 32, 33, 35, 36-37, 42, 45, 48, 50-51, 56, 57, 61, 64–65, 67 top and bottom, 72–73, 74–75, 98, 116 top and bottom, 138, 216, 217, 226

Bradley Winterton: pages 12, 13, 29, 38, 39, 40–41, 47 top and bottom, 58–59, 166–167, 197, 224–225, 236, 243.

Recommended Reading

BAUM, VICKI *A Tale from Bali* (1937). Reissued in paperback by OUP. Translated from German, a novel set between 1904 and 1906 when the Dutch were extending their control over the island.

COVARRUBIAS, MIGUEL *The Island of Bali* (1937). Reissued in paperback by OUP. The classic account. Essentially a systematic survey of Balinese life and culture interspersed with personal recollections from this Mexican painter who made two extended visits to the island.

DALTON BILL *Indonesia Handbook* (2nd edn 1980). Moon Publications, Chico, Ca. Though ostensibly for the backpacking budget traveler, this voluminous and outspoken account has, almost despite itself, reached classic status. Inevitably lacking detail on Bali, it has copious information on the rest of Indonesia.

EISEMAN FRED B. *Bali, Sekala and Niskala* (2 vols, 1985, 1986). The leading authority on everything Balinese, Eiseman is a retired American academic chemist who spends six months of every year on Bali. These two books, contain a vast range of information on everything from Balinese scripts (which Eiseman is computerizing) to the manufacture of concrete telephone poles on the Bukit. Breathtaking.

EISEMAN, MARGARET and FRED *Flowers of Bali* (1987). An identification aid to some of the commoner flowers of the island, with color photographs.

KERTONEGORO, MADI *The Spirit Journey to Bali Aga, Tenganan Pegringsingan* (1986). Harkat Foundation, Bali. A whimsical, eccentric but amusing account of some legends from the Candi Dasa/Tenganan area.

KOCH, C.J. *The Year of Living Dangerously* (1978). Reissued by Grafton paperbacks. An imaginative and sympathetic novel set in Jakarta at the time of the fall of Sukarno in 1965. An enormously interesting insight into Indonesian life and politics.

LEURAS, LEONARD, AND LLOYD, Ian R. *Bali, the Ultimate Island* (1987). Times Editions. The ultimate Bali picturebook, with additional photographs by Cartier Bresson and other old masters.

MABBETT, HUGH *In Praise of Kuta* (1987). January Books, Wellington. Breaking with the "cultural treasure house" tradition, this is a collection of short essays on Bali's much maligned tourist capital.

MATHEWS, ANNA *The Night of Purnama* (1965). Reissued in paperback by OUP. A low-key account of living in the village of Iseh, north of Klungkung, culminating in the eruption of nearby Agung in 1963.

MAY, BRIAN *The Indonesian Tragedy* (1978) RKP, London and Boston. An in-depth, but also personal, look at modern Indonesian politics from a journalist who worked for many years in the country. Disenchanted but passionate. A surprisingly good read.

MCPHEE, COLIN *A House in Bali* (1947). Reissued by OUP in Oxford in Asia paperback series. McPhee was an American composer who went to Bali to study the *gamelan* (which he describes as "a shining rain of silver"). The first Westerner to build a house at Kuta, his book is sensitive and intelligent.

POWELL, HICKMAN *The Last Paradise* (1930). Reissued in paperback by OUP. One of the very early books. Rather specifically American, it is by turns sardonic and lushly poetic. Describes the *gamelan* as "the muffled laughter of forgotten gods." Richly readable.

TANTRI, K'TUT *Revolt in Paradise.* Reissued in Indonesia, in English, Indonesian and Dutch, by Gramedia Paperbacks. A high-spirited account of the adventures of a young American woman who went to Bali alone in the 1930s, helped set up Kuta's first hotel, was imprisoned by the Japanese, and became famous throughout the region as "Surabaya Sue", freedom fighter with the Indonesians. Born Vannine Walker, her original pseudonym was Muriel Pearson.

VICKERS, ADRIAN *Bali a Paradise Created.* (1990) Reissued by Periplus Editions. A very informative and refreshing analysis of Bali and the Balinese and the forces that have shaped it. Republished by Periplus, the leading publisher of English-language books on Indonesia. Strongly recommended.

Limited to only five books, I'd take Vickers, Koch, Powell, May and Covarrubias, and get hold of Eiseman and Tantri when I got to Bali.

Quick Reference A–Z Guide
to Places and Topics of Interest with Listed Accommodation, Restaurants and Useful Telephone Numbers

A accommodation, general   *149, 242*
accommodation, luxury   *43–46*
accommodation, rates   *243*
Air Panas   *196*
   accommodation
      Hotel Puri Bening (0366-51234
         FAX 0366-51248   *196*
      Under the Volcano Homestay (0366-51166   *196*
airlines   *240*
   domestic reservations
      Bouraq (0361-223564   *240*
      Merpati Nusantara (0361-228842   *240*
      Sempati Air (0361-754218   *240*
   Garuda Indonesia
      main office (0361-27825 or (0361-22028
         FAX 0361-226298   *240*
      Hotel Gand Bali Beach, Sanur
         (0361-288511   *240*
      Natour Kuta Beach Hotel (0361-751179   *240*
      Nusa Indah Hotel, Nusa Dua
         (0361-771906   *240*
      Sanur Beach Hotel, Sanur (0361-288011   *240*
   International reservations
      Air France (0361-287734   *240*
      Air New Zealand (0361-756170   *240*
      Ansett Australia (0361-289637   *240*
      Cathay Pacific (0361-286001   *240*
      Continental (0361-287774   *240*
      Eva Air (0361-751011   *240*
      Japan Airlines (0361-287576   *240*
      KLM (0361-756124   *240*
      Korean Air (0361-289402   *240*
      LTU International Airways (0361-753778   *240*
      Lufthansa (0361-287069   *240*
      Malaysian Airlines (0361-285071   *240*
      Qantas (0361-751472   *240*
      Singapore Airlines (0361-261666   *240*
      Thai Airways (0361-288141   *240*
airport   *237*
Amed
   accommodation   See Lipah
   sports
      Nusantara Bahari Explorer Diving Club
         (0361-431273 FAX 0363-21044   *217*
Amlapura (Karangasem)   *213*
   accommodation
      Homestay Balakiran   *214*
   attractions
      Palace   *214*
      Puri Amsterdam   *214*
      water palaces   *214*
Anturan   *152*
art and crafts   *133–139*
   maskmaking   135
   metalwork   137
   painting   26, 133
   silverware   137
   stonecarving   137
   weaving   137
   woodcarving   24-25, 135
artists, Western   *81*
B Bali Aga   *30, 137, 195, 198, 211*
Bali Barat National Park   *See* West Bali
   National Park
Bangli   *194–195*
   attractions
      Pura Kehen (temple)   *194*
   restaurants
      Artha Sastra (0366-91179   *194*
Banjar   *153–154*
   access   153
   accommodation
      Pondok Wisata Grya Sari (0362-92903
         FAX 0362-92966   *154*
   attractions
      Buddhist Temple   *154*
      hot springs   *153*
Banyuwedang   *227*
   attractions
      hot springs   *227*
bargaining   *245–246*
Batubulan   *15*
Batur   *199*
   attractions
      Ulu Danu (temple)   *199*
Batur Village   *195*
Bedugul   *31, 205*
   accommodation
      Bali Handara Country Club (0362-23048 or
         0361-2264 FAX 0361-287358   *205*
      Bedugul Hotel and Restaurant   *205*
   attractions
      Botanical Gardens   *31, 205*
      Ulu Danu (temple)   *205*
   sports
      Bali Handara Country Club (0362-23048 or
         0361-2264 FAX 0361-287358   *205*
bemos   *241*
Benoa   *164*
Besakih   *200–202*
   attractions
      Mother Temple   *200*
bird orchestras   *132–133*
Bona   *120*
   attractions
      dance dramas   *120*
Buddhism   *79*
Bukit, The   *161–168*
   accommodation
      Hotel Bali Cliff (0361-771992
         FAX 0361-771993   *45, 167*
bungee jumping   *13–15*
   A.J. Hackett Bungee (0361-730666   13
   Adrenalin Park (0361-757845   13

Bali Bungee Co. (/FAX 0361-752658   *13*
Bungee-in-Bali (0361-758362   *13*

C calendar, Balinese   *101–105*
camel rides   *16–18*
   Bali Camel Safaris (0361-773377
   extension 210   *18*
Candi Dasa   *211–213*
   accommodation
      Amankila (0363-71267
         FAX 0363-71266   *45, 212*
      Candi Beach Cottage (0363-41234
         FAX 0363-41111   *212*
      Candidasa Hotel (0363-41126
         FAX 0363-41537   *213*
      Hotel Rama Candidasa (0363-41974
         FAX 0363-41975   *213*
      Kubu Bali (0363-41532 FAX 0363-41531   *212*
      Pelangi Homestay (0363-41270   *213*
      Pondok Bambu Seaside Cottages (0363-41534
         FAX 0363-41818   *213*
      Puri Pandan (/FAX 0363-41541   *212*
      Watergarden (0363-41540
         FAX 0363-41164   *212*
   attractions
      Bug Bug   *211*
      background   *211*
   restaurants
      Lotus Seaview (0363-41257   *213*
Candikuning   *205*
   attractions
      Ulu Danu (temple)   *205*
car rentals   *241*
caste system   *88–89, 109*
Celuk   *137*
   attractions
      silverware center   *137–139*
cigarettes *(kretek)*   *145*
Cekik   *227*
cockfighting   *130–131*
consulates and embassies   *248*
cremation   *105–110*
cricket fighting   *132*
custom allowances   *238*

D dance   *15–16, 50–52, 120–128*
deities   *101*
Denpasar   *158–161*
   access   *160*
      bemo stations   *160*
   accommodation
      Natour Bali (0361-225681
         FAX 0361-235347   *160*
   attractions
      Academy of Dance, Indonesia   *160*
      Bali Arts Festival   *160*
      Conservatory of Performing Arts   *160*
      Indonesia Jaya Reptile and Crocodile Park
         (0361-243686   *26*
      Museum Bali   *158*
      National Art Center   *160*
      Pura Jagatnatha   *160*
      Taman Burung Bali Bird Park
         (0361-299353   *26*
      Tanah Lapang Puputan Badung   *158*
   background   *158*
   general information
      Immigration Office (Kantor Imigrasi)
         (0361-227828   *158*
   restaurants   *160*

   shopping   *160*
Dewi Sri, rice goddess   *88*
diving   *32-34, 38, 66, 152, 162, 164, 217, 226, 227*
   contacts
      Bali Club Diver (/FAX 0361-462078   *34*
      Bali Diving Perdana (0361-286493   *34*
      Bali Pesona Bahari (/FAX 0361-287872   *34*
      Baruna (0361-753820   *34*
      Citra Bali Dive Center (0361-286788   *34*
      Mega Dive (0361-288192   *34*
      Dive Paradise Tulamben ᶜ/o
         (0363-41052   *219*
      Indonesian Cactus Divers (0361-462063   *34*
      Nusantara Bahari Explorer Diving Club
         (0361-4312 FAX 0363-21044   *217*
   general   *246*
dolphin watching   *18–20, 49*
drama   *117–128*
drugs   *238*
Dutch   *80–81*

E **East Bali**   *205–217*
elephant rides
   Wisatareksa Gajah Perdana (0361-286072   *18*
etiquette   *247*
Europe, trade with   *80*

F festivals   *57–60, 99, 105, 128, 166*
   information
      Badung Government Tourist Office (23399 or
         23602   *128*
flora and fauna   *73–76*
foods
   betel   *144*
   beverages   *139–141*
   coconut   *143–144*
   festive dishes   *139*
   local specialities   *139*
   tropical fruits   *143*

G **Galungan**   *57*
   gambong (orchestra)   *105, 106, 109*
   gamelan (orchestra)   *16, 115–117, 120, 128*
Gelgel   *208*
   attractions
      Royal Temple   *208*
getting around   *241–242*
Gilimanuk   *227*
   ferry terminal for Java   *227*
Goa Gajah (Elephant Cave)   *192*
Goa Lawah (Bat Cave)   *208*
golf   *34*
   contacts
      Bali Golf and Country Club (0361-771791
         FAX 0361-771797   *34*
      Bali Handara Kosaido Country Club
         (0361-22646 FAX 0361-287358   *34*
      Bali Nirvana Resort (0361-244734   *35*
      Hotel Grand Bali Beach (0361-288511
         FAX 0361-287917 28   *35*

H health   *238*
   dental   *239*
   medical treatment   *239*
      AEA (worldwide medical assistance)
         (0361-231443 FAX 0361-231442   *239*
      Sanglah Hospital (0361-227911-5
         HOT-LINE 0361-226363   *239*
herbal medicine *(jamu)*   *144*
Hinduism   *76–79, 88, 92, 96–101, 110, 115, 129–130*
history, cultural   *79*

horseback riding
Bali Jaran-Jaran Keneka (0361-751672
FAX 0361-755734   18

I Indonesia, birth of Republic of   82
Indonesia, political institutions of   82
Iseh   203
Islam   79–80

J **Jagaraja**   154
jamu (herbal medicine)   144
Java   76–79
Javanese civilizations   79
jet skiing   35, 164
Jimbaran   166–167
accommodation
Four Seasons (0361-701010
FAX 0361-701020   45, 166
Hotel Pansea Puri Bali (0361-752277
FAX 0361-752227   45, 166
Intercontinental (0361-701888
FAX 0361-701777   166
Keraton Bali Cottages (0361-701961
FAX 0361-701991   166
Ramayana (0361-702859   166
Ritz Carlton (0361-702222 FAX 0361-701555   166
restaurants   166
Jimbaran Bay   166
Jungutbatu   226

K **Kalibukbuk**   152
Karangasem   See Amlapura
Kedaton   182
attractions
fruit bats   182
Kedisan   197–198
accommodation
Hotel Segara (0366-51136
FAX 0366-51212   198
Hotel Surya (0366-51139   198
kingdoms   79
Kintamani   199
accommodation
Lakeview (0366-31394 FAX 0366-51464   199
Klumpu   223
Klungkung   205–208
accommodation
Logi Ramayana (21044   206
attractions
floating palace   205
shopping   206
Komodo dragons   24
kretek   145
Kubutambahan   154
attractions
temple   154
Kuningan   60
Kusamba   221
Kuta   168–179
access
car rental, Jaya Mertha (0361-751233   168
accommodation
Bali Mandira Cottages (0361-751381
FAX 0361-752377   175
Bali Oberoi (0361-730361
FAX 0361-730954   175
Bali Padma Hotel (0361-752111
FAX 0361-752140   175
Holiday Inn Bali Hai (0361-753035
FAX 0361-754548   174

Hotel Kuta Segara Ceria (0361-751961
FAX 0361-751962   175
Hotel Tugu Bali (0361-731701
FAX 0361-731704   175
Ida Beach Inn Bungalows (0361-751205
FAX 0361-751934   175
Kartika Plaza (0361-751067
FAX 0361-752475   174
Kuta Village Inn (0361-751095
FAX 0361-753051   174
Legian Beach Hotel (0361-751711
FAX 0361-752651   175
Natour Kuta Beach (0361-751361
FAX 0361-751362   175
Poppies Cottages (0361-751059
FAX 0361-752364   175
Senen Beach Inn (0361-755470   175
Sol Elite Paradiso (0361-761414
FAX 0361-756944   174
Taman Legian Hotel (0361-730876
FAX 0361-730405   175
background   170, 174
business facilities
Krakatoa Café and Business Center
(0361-730849 FAX 0361-73082   168
general information   168
nightlife   177–179
"001" nightclub   177
Casablanca   177
Double Six   177
Gado Gado   177
Goa 2001   177
Hard Rock Café   177
Hulu Café   178
Peanuts   177
Studebaker's   177
Taj Mahal   177
Warung Tapas   177
restaurants
Café Luna (0361-730805   176
Dayu II (0361-752262   176
Depot Kuta (0361-51155   177
French Restaurant at Topi Kopi
(0361-754243   176
Glory (0361-751091   176
Kafe Warisan (0361-731175   176
La Lucciola (0361-730838   176
Le Bistro (0361-730973   176
Made's Warung II (0361-732130   176
Made's Warung (0361-755397   176
Poppies (0361-751059   176
Surya Café (0361-757381   177
Swiss Restaurant (0361-751735   176
TJ's (0361-751093   176
Un's (0361-752607   176
Warung Batavia (0361-243769   177
Warung Kopi (0361-753602   177
safety
Surf Rescue   173
shopping   178
sports
bungee jumping   13, 174

L **Labuanhaji Falls**   154
Labuhanlalang (ferry departure point for
Menjangan Island)   227
Lake Batur   195
Lake Bratan   205
language   83, 247–248

Bahasa Indonesia 83
Balinese 83
useful phrases 247–248
Legian *See also under* Kuta
accommodation
  Bali Oberoi (0361-730361 FAX 0361-730954 43
  The Legian 43
Lembongan village 223
Lipah 216
accommodation
  Coral View Villas (03614-31273 216
  Hidden Paradise Cottages (0361-431273
  FAX 0363-21044 216
Lombok 209
access 209
Lontar 211
Lovina 150–153
access 150
accommodation
  Ansoka Hotel (0362-41841 FAX 0362-41023 152
  Bali Lovina Beach Cottages (0362-41285
  FAX 0361-233386 152
  Banyualit Beach Inn (0362-41789
  FAX 0362-41563 152
  Hotel Aneka Lovina (0362-41121
  FAX 0362-41827 152
  Padang Lovina Seaside Cottages
  (0362-41302 152
  Palestis Beach Cottages (0362-41035 152
  Palma Beach Hotel (0362-41775
  FAX 0362-41659 152
restaurants
  Sea Breeze Café (0362-41138 152
sports
  Spice Dive (0362-41305 FAX 0362-41171 152

M magic and witchcraft 15, 110, 123–124
mail 244
marriage customs 91–96
Mas (woodcarving center) 135
masks 105, 127, 135–137
making of 137
Menanga 200
Mengwi 182–184
attractions
  Water Temple 182
Menjangan Island 227
sports
  SCUBA diving 227
money 239–240
monkeys 76
motorbike rentals
  Bakor Motor Kuta, Ubud and Sanur 242
Mount Abang 195, 198–199
Mount Agung 21, 29, 195, 201–203
guides 202
Mount Batur 21, 29, 180, 195–196
mountain climbing 198, 202
musical instruments 115–117

N names 89
national park 31
Negara 227
attractions
  water buffalo races 227
North Bali 149–155
Nusa Dua 161–168
accommodation
  Amanusa (0361-772333
  FAX 0361-72335 45, 163

Bali Club Med (0361-771521
  FAX 0361-771835 162
Bali Hilton International (0361-771102
  FAX 0361-771616 162
Grand Hyatt Bali (0361-771234
  FAX 0361-772038 162
Hotel Bualu (0361-771310 FAX 0361-771313 162
Melia Bali (0361-771510 FAX 0361-771360 162
Nikko Bali (0361-773377 FAX 0361-773388 163
Nusa Dua Beach Hotel (771210
  FAX 772617 45, 162
Nusa Indah (0361-771906 FAX 0361-771908 162
Putri Bali (0361-771020 or 0361-771420
  FAX 0361-71139 162
Sheraton Lagoon (0361-771327
  FAX 0361-771326 162
background 161
restaurants
  Makuwa Pakuwa (0361-772252 163
  Matsuri (0361-772269 163
  Olé Olé (771886 62, 163
  On the Rocks 163
  Poco Loco (0361-773923 163
Nusa Lembongan 223–226
accommodation
  Puri Nusa (/FAX 298613 226
  Waka Nusa Resort (0361-261130
  FAX 0361-722077 226
Nusa Penida 161, 221–223
attractions
  cliff stairways 223
  Goa Karangsari (cave) 222
background 221–222
Nyepi (Balinese New Year's Day) 60, 105
Nyuling, Moslem village of 214

O "opera, Balinese" 120

P **Padangbai** 205, 209
access
  ferry terminal for Lombok 209
  speedboat service to Nusa Penida 221
accommodation
  Puri Rai (0363-41385 209
attractions
  Biastugel Beach 209
general information
  Tourist Information Office (0363-41502
  FAX 0363-4178 209
restaurants
  Pandan Restaurant 209
sports
  Equator Dive Travel (0363-41505 209
parasailing 35, 164, 205
Peed 222
attractions
  temple 222
Pejeng 191
attractions
  Archaeological Museum 192
  Crazy Buffalo Temple 192
  Pura Panataram Sasih temple 191
Penelokan 195–196
accommodation
  Lakeview (0366-31394
  FAX 0366-51464 196
attractions
  Lake Batur 195
  Mount Batur 195, 196
Penulisan 199–200

attractions
temple *199*
Pujung *135, 189*
attractions
woodcarving *135, 189*
Pulaki Monkey Temple *153*
Pulau Serangan (Turtle Island) *164*
puppets *128–130*
performances *128*
types *129*

R rafting *See* white water rafting
Rambutsiwi *227*
attractions
temple *227*
religious services *247*
Rendang *203*
rice, cult of *88*
rice, Dewi Sri, goddess of *88, 101*

S sailing *66, 226, 246*
Sampalan *222*
accommodation
Bungalows Pemda *222*
Sangeh *184*
attractions
Monkey Forest *184*
Sangsit *154*
Sanur *155–158*
accommodation
Bali Hyatt (0361-288271 FAX 0361-27693 *45, 156*
Hotel Tandjung Sari (0361-288441
FAX 0361-287930 *45, 156*
Natour Sindhu Beach Hotel (0361-288351
FAX 0361-289268 *156*
Radisson Bali (281781 FAX 289168 *157*
Santrian Beach Resort (0361-288009
FAX 0361-287101 *156*
Sanur Beach Hotel (288011 FAX 287566 *156*
Segara Village Hotel (0361-288407
FAX 0361-287242 *156*
attractions
hydrotherapy and massage *156*
Museum Le Mayeur *156*
background *155*
nightlife *157*
restaurants
Bali Moon (0361-288486 *157*
Café Batu Jimbar *157*
Chiku-Tei (0361-287159 *157*
Kul Kul (0361-288038 *157*
Legong Restaurant (0361-288066 *157*
Mamma Lucia (288498 *157*
Mandelo's (0361-288773 *157*
Telaga Naga (281234 extension 8080 *61, 157*
Terrazzo Martini (0361-288371 *157*
shopping *157*
sports
Bali Splat Mas (0361-289073 *63*
Sawan *154–155*
access *154*
attractions
gong making *154*
Sayan (Ubud) *45, 186*
accommodation
Amandari (0361-975333
FAX 0361-975335 *45*
Four Seasons *45*
Kupu Kupu Barong (0361-975476
FAX 0361-975079 *45*

Sebatu *189*
attractions
public baths *189*
Sebudi *203*
Sebuluh *223*
Sembiran *155*
attractions
temple *155*
sex *247*
shopping *52–55, 245–246*
bargaining *245–246*
Sidemen *205*
Singapadu *184*
attractions
Taman Burung Bali Bird Park *24, 184*
Singaraja *150*
access *150*
tourist information bureau *150*
slave trade *80*
snorkeling *31, 34–35, 66, 149, 152–153, 155, 164, 219, 226–227, 247*
Songan *196*
attractions
temple *196*
South Bali *179–189*
spice trade *80*
spirits, belief in *76*
surfing
general advice *246*
surfing and surf rescue *246–247*

T **Tabanan** *32*
attractions
Bali Butterfly Park (0361-814282
FAX 0361-814281 *32*
Taman Burung Bali Bird Park
(0361-299353 *24, 184*
Tampaksiring *189–191*
attractions
Gunung Kawi *191*
Sukarno Palace *189*
Tanah Lot *180–182*
access *180*
accommodation
Bali Nirvana Resort (0361-815900
FAX (0361-815901 *35*
Dewi Sinta (0361-812933 FAX 0361-813956 *180*
Le Meridien (021-526-1393 *45, 180*
Mutiara Tanah Lot Bungalows (0361-225457
FAX 0361-222672 *180*
background *180*
Tanjung Benoa *164*
accommodation
Grand Mirage (0361-771888
FAX 0361-772148 *164*
Novotel (0361-772239 FAX 0361-772237 *164*
tattooing *62–63*
taxis *241–242*
Tegalalang *189*
telephone service (useful numbers) *244*
temple festivals *15–16, 101–105*
Tenganan *137, 209–211*
attractions
craft shop *211*
weaving center *137*
background *211*
shopping *211*
tipping *246*

tourism, history of *81*
tourist information
  Badung Government Tourist Office (0361-23399
    or 0361-23602 *or* (0361-222387
    (/FAX 0361-226313 *158*
tours
  Bali Hai (0361-701888 FAX 0361-701777 *66*
  Island Explorer Cruises (0361-289856
    FAX 0361-289837 *66*
  Lembongan Express MOBILE (0811-393387 *66*
  Quicksilver Tours (0361-771997
    FAX 0361-771967 *66*
  Rasa Yacht Charters (0361-288756 *66*
  Satriavi Tours (0361-287074 *66*
  Sojourn (0361-287450 FAX 0361-287125 *66*
  Tunas Indonesia (0361-288581
    FAX 0361-288727 *66*
  Waka Louka (0361-484085 FAX 0361-484767 *66*
Toyapakeh *222*
transportation *160, 241*
tropical fruits *143*
Trunyan *198*
  access *198*
Tulamben *217*
  accommodation
    Emerald Tulamben Beach Hotel (0363-22490
      WEB http://www.iijnet.or.jp/inc/bali/ *217*
    Paradise Palm Beach Bungalows
      (0363-41052 *217*
  sports
    Dive Paradise Tulamben ^c/o (0363-41052 *217*
Turtle Island *See* Pulau Serangan (Turtle Island)
U **Ubud** *185–189*
  access *185*
  accommodation
    Amandari (0361-975333
      FAX 0361-975335 *186*
    Banyan Tree Kamandalu (0361-975825
      FAX 0361-975851 *187*
    Chedi (0361-975963 FAX 0361-975968 *45, 187*
    Han Snel's Siti Bungalows (0361-975699
      FAX 0361-975643 *187*
    Hotel Tjamphuan (0361-95871 *187*
    Ibah (0361-974466 FAX 0361-975567 *187*
    Kupu Kupu Barong (0361-975476
      FAX 0361-975079 *186*
    Pita Maha Tjampuhan (974330
      FAX 974329 *45, 187*
    Puri Saraswati (/FAX 0361-975164 *187*
  accomodation, budget *187*
  attractions
    Antonio Blanco's House *186*
    ARMA *186*
    Elephant Cave *192*
    Neka Museum *186*
    puppet theater *186*
    Puri Lukisan Museum *186*
    Ubud Palace, dance dramas at *120*
  background *185*
  business services
    Pt. Kartika Chandra Telecommunication
      Center (0361-96136 FAX 0361-976478
      E-MAIL kartika @dps.mega.net.id *185*
    Roda Tourist Service (/FAX 0361-9765582
      E-MAIL rodanet@denpasar
      .wasantara.net.id *185*
  general information *185*
    Tourist Information Office *185*
  restaurants
    Ary's Warung (0361-975063 *188*
    Casa Luna (0361-96283 FAX 0361-96282 *188*
    Lotus Café (0361-975660 *188*
    Mumbul's (0361-975364 *188*
    Murni's Warung (0361-975233 *188*
    Nomad Wine Bar and Restaurant *188*
  shopping *189*
Ulu Danu *199*
Ulu Watu *11, 161, 166–167*
  attractions
    Pura Luhur Ulu Watu *167*
  sports
    surfing *168*
V volcanoes *195*
W water sports *246*
West Bali *226–227*
  Menjangan Island *227*
  National Park, entry permits for *227*
West Bali National Park *31, 226*
what to wear *245*
white water rafting *21*
  contacts
    Ayung River Rafting (0361-238759 *21*
    Bakas Levi Rafting (0361-289379 *21*
    Bali International Rafting (0361-757052 *21*
    Bali Safari Rafting (0361-221315 *21*
    Raging Thunder Adventures (0361-758822 *21*
    Sobek (0361-287059 *21*
windsurfing *164, 246*
woodcarving *135, 189*
Y **Yeh Pulu** *192*
  attractions
    frieze *192*
Yeh Sanih *155*
  accommodation
    Air Sanih Seaside Cottages
      (0362-23357 *155*
    Bungalow Puri Sanih *155*